WANDERING MINSTRELS WE

The Story of Gilbert and Sullivan

SIGMUND A. LAVINE

Wandering Minstrels We

THE STORY OF GILBERT AND SULLIVAN

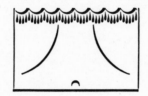

Dodd, Mead & Company · New York

1954

Library of Congress Catalog Card Number: 54-12090
Printed in the United States of America

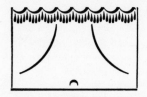

To Jerry and Maxine
and the Generations
of Children
who both precede and
follow them
through the Magic Portals of
TOPSY-TURVYDOM!

To Jerry and Maxine
and the Generations
of Children
who both precede and
follow them
through the Magic Portals of
TOPSY-TURVYLAND

"If You Give Me Your Attention
I Will Tell You Who I Am"

❍

—Princess Ida

How would you like to visit a magic land where the possible never happens and the impossible is taken for granted—and all of this set to the most engaging music?

It's a place where folk do just the opposite of what people in ordinary countries do, and act as if their way were the only correct one and any other way was wrong. Of course, these people aren't like those who live in your neighborhood —at least I don't think so—for all the inhabitants of this mysterious land are either pirates, ghosts, poets, fairies, politicians or sailors. Then, too, they have such strange customs: kings earn their keep by polishing the silver service used for state dinners, while nursemaids, who are usually either very fat or very deaf, have the annoying habit of constantly exchanging rich for poor babies in their cradles.

There's no such place, you say? How wrong you are! And tonight, as on the other nights for the past seventy years, somewhere in the world a group of people will visit this land, laugh at the antics of its residents and listen to their music. It really isn't a difficult place to visit; all that is needed for a passport is a theater ticket; for this upside-down country exists on the stage. It is the happy creation of the most famous partnership in the history of the theater —the union of the writing genius of William Schwenck Gilbert and the musical skill of Arthur Seymour Sullivan. Yet, despite the fact that this Never-Never Land can be found only behind a theater curtain, it is as real a region to thousands as any to be found in your geography book.

Those who travel in this Cuckoo-land use as guidebooks the baker's dozen of comic operas written by Gilbert and Sullivan between the years 1875 and 1896. Because this is a fantastic country, where no changes ever take place, no revised editions of their work have been necessary. Originally created to poke fun at the sober England of Queen Victoria's day, these plays, set to music, are still as full of fun and gay tunes as when a boy wore peg-leg trousers and a girl wore crinolines instead of jeans.

Just think of it, the youngest of these operettas is over fifty years old; and yet, despite all the changes in the ways of living in the last half century, they still make people laugh! Gilbert and Sullivan formed a perfect partnership: Sullivan's music giving to Gilbert's words just the setting they needed. And while they both sought fame in more serious fields, the only reason we remember them today is because of their musical plays, which perhaps ought to be, but certainly aren't, considered "corny."

Yet it is strange that these two were able to work together at all, for no two men had less in common or more different backgrounds. Gilbert prided himself on his ability to make enemies, Sullivan made friends with everyone; Gilbert was the son of a rich man, Sullivan was born in poverty; Gilbert had a quick and biting tongue, Sullivan was patience itself and never hurt anyone's feelings. If Sullivan could see the way people flock to the theater night after night to see his work, his pride would be great, for he was slightly conceited.

Gilbert would snort like an English bulldog, for he had no opinion of the public's taste. The story is told that once when Gilbert was showing a visitor over the grounds of his estate, he was asked, "Aren't you proud of having acquired all this from your own brain?" He glared at his questioner and answered tartly, "Not at all. It represents the folly of the British public!"

Folly it may be, but it is a folly that has lasted for years, and it looks as if it were going to last forever—and for more than "the British public." For Gilbert and Sullivan set fairyland to music, and their work, known as the Savoy Operas, because most of them were first produced at the Savoy Theater in London, are in their way as important in the history of the theater as Shakespeare's plays. In fact, more people enjoy performances of *The Mikado* and *Pinafore* than appreciate *Hamlet* and *Macbeth;* and if you have ever seen a performance of one of the Gilbert and Sullivan series, you are aware that everyone in the audience seems to know every word and recognize every note of the music.

What type of men were these two who fashioned musical plays back in the days of gas lamps and marble-topped furniture, and still have a hold on the theater-going public in this era of atom-smashing? This book has been written to tell you all about them, and to show you how they worked and created their own special land—Topsy-turvydom.

CONTENTS

ILLUSTRATIONS

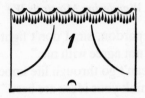

"A Promising Boy"

○

—*Pirates of Penzance*

YOU'VE been fighting again," accused the headmaster of the Great Ealing School as he motioned the boy to a chair beside his desk.

"Yes, sir, I have," acknowledged thirteen-year-old William Schwenck Gilbert as he sat down on the chair he knew so well. For quick-tempered Gilbert spent much of his time in the headmaster's office . . . not because his grades were low, but because his fists were constantly high.

"What are we going to do about it? Oh, I could give you one of the usual punishments. The difficulty is, none of them seems to bother you. In fact, Gilbert, you seem to enjoy having to translate extra pages of the Latin poets. Frankly, my boy, your verse translations of Homer, Horace, and Virgil would do credit to a university student of the classics. Nor would making you write an essay be any punishment. Writing comes too easily to you. Ever since you've been in school, you've written all your class plays. Yes, and made the scenery, acted as stage manager and played the leading roles—ah, right there is the trouble, Gilbert. You always want to be the leader. Is that why you continually fight with all your fellow students?"

1

"Begging your pardon, sir, I don't fight with all of them. Just those who do not agree with me."

"But, lad, you can't go through life knocking down everyone who doesn't think your ideas are best!"

Wisely, Gilbert held his tongue and did not say what he was thinking: that he was perfectly willing and able to try. Instead, he sat quietly and listened as the headmaster continued his lecture.

"You are a clever lad, Gilbert, and your teachers realize it; however, inclined to be lazy while your sharp tongue and superior attitude are fast making you the most unpopular boy in school. You must change your viewpoint. Now, I'll tell you what we'll do. If you give me your word, your solemn promise, that you won't fight any more, I'll forget this incident. What do you say?"

"I'll do my best, sir," promised Gilbert, and left the office absolutely determined to stay out of trouble. But these good intentions would not, unfortunately, keep him out of difficulties with those in authority, for young Gilbert simply could not control his temper.

He inherited his sharp tongue and willingness to fight all who did not agree with him. Dr. William Gilbert, his father, while a midshipman on one of the vessels of the East India Company, had refused to recognize any rules or regulations. During his three years of service in the famous trading organization which had been founded in 1500 to extend England's commercial and political power in India, the elder Gilbert did nothing but find fault with everything and everyone. Later, as an assistant surgeon in the Navy, he constantly quarreled with his superiors, whom he considered his inferiors. The chief reason for the doctor's attitude was that he claimed as an ancestor Sir Humphrey Gilbert, the famous explorer who landed in Newfoundland in 1583 and set up the first English colony in North America. Despite

Dr. Gilbert's pride, he might have stayed in the Navy, but at the age of twenty-five he inherited enough money to retire and spend much of his time traveling with his wife, three daughters, and only son, William.

On one of these trips, when young Gilbert was two years old, the family was in Italy. Dr. Gilbert told his son's nurse to take her young charge out for a walk. The good woman, anxious to see the sights of Naples, dressed the little fellow in his best and left the hotel. A simple person, she raised no objections when two men came up to her, politely tipped their hats, and in perfect English informed her that the doctor had sent them to fetch the boy. Without hesitation, she handed William over, and the pair made off to the hills with him.

Dr. Gilbert was more furious than frantic. A strong man who kept in trim by horsewhipping newspaper editors who printed articles he didn't like, the doctor roared that he was going to kill the man who had stolen his child! Mrs. Gilbert, who hardly dared open her mouth in front of her husband, suggested that they ask for assistance from the authorities.

For once, Dr. Gilbert listened to her. "Police! Call out the Army! Someone notify the British consul and have him send for Her Majesty's fleet. Kidnappers have stolen William, and I won't have it!" he shouted as he stamped his feet and pounded on the desk in the hotel lobby.

The police "force," represented by a moustached gentleman with a long, flowing plume in his hat, soon appeared. With the aid of waving arms, he assured the irate and now somewhat worried father that there was nothing to be alarmed about. Such events, he explained, were common in the Italy of 1838, and all that had to be done was wait patiently until the kidnappers sent their demand for ransom. Then one paid it, and everyone was satisfied!

Dr. Gilbert snorted, "This would never happen in England!" but agreed to wait. The note from the kidnappers was not long in coming. Soon "Bab," as the boy was known to his family, was safely returned to the hotel upon payment of twenty-five English pounds—about one hundred and twenty-five dollars in those days.

Many years later, when visiting Italy, William Gilbert claimed to remember everything about this incident. While walking in the Via Posilippo, he recalled how he had been carried away by a man on horseback, "through what seemed to be a cutting with steep banks on either side." He was, most likely, only parroting what his parents had told him, for it is extremely doubtful that even Gilbert could have remembered what happened to him at the age of two.

When Dr. Gilbert was not visiting foreign countries with his family or quarreling with editors, he was writing one of the many dozen books, plays, biographies and tracts he dashed off so easily. Most of this writing was abysmally dull and had only one purpose—to inform the world of Dr. William Gilbert's personal opinions about people, politics and religion. Some of his novels did, however, have a rather good sale. It's a strange thing, but Dr. Gilbert wrote most of his books after his son became famous. The younger man explained, "My father never had an exaggerated idea of my abilities; he thought if I could write, anybody could, and forthwith began to do so." Incidentally, even though he made fun of his father's books, William Gilbert illustrated two of the volumes.

At his home in London, Dr. Gilbert had company for dinner every evening. To his table came the leading artists, musicians and actors of the day. They sat spellbound as their host talked about his favorite subjects—insanity and murder. Few dared to argue with him, for they knew of his temper. It was common knowledge that if there were the slightest printing error in one of his books, the doctor would go into every book-shop in London, politely ask for as many copies of "that new book of Gilbert's" as were in stock, and when they were brought to him, would, in rage, tear them to waste paper before anybody could stop him!

Dr. Gilbert's pride was almost as great as his violent temper. It was pride and nothing else that made him send young William to school in Boulogne, at the age of seven. Youngsters in Queen Victoria's day were not often sent to France for an education, and for this very reason Dr. Gilbert found the idea of educating his son abroad most attractive. Doing what ordinary people did was never popular in the Gilbert family. However, when the youngster was twelve years old, he brought him back home and entered him in an English school.

Some boys could, perhaps, overcome such a background, but not William. He was in every way his father's son, so he continued to annoy his instructors and punch his dormitory mates. "I was not a popular boy, I believe," he told a friend when recalling his schooldays. Handsome, he attracted attention everywhere he went. Sir David Wilkie, the famous artist, was so impressed by his good looks that he asked permission to paint his portrait. Gilbert's schoolfellows paid little attention to his physical appearance, and laughed at his claim of descent from the Elizabethan navigator—but they had great respect for young Gilbert's ability to box. William's fighting skill got him into one difficulty after another, and it was not long before he was being blamed for all the disturbances at Great Ealing. This was too much for the family pride. At the age of fifteen Gilbert decided to run away. He did, not to the sea, which had lured his father at the same age, but to the stage.

Nothing was more natural. Gilbert had inherited a love of the drama, and his home was the London meeting place of all theatrical England. Most boys hoping for a stage ca-

reer would have tried to become a member of the company
of some country theater. But Gilbert was never content with
anything but the best. So he made his way to the London
playhouse where Charles Kean, the most famous actor of
the day, was appearing in *The Corsican Brothers*. With the
assurance that was rarely to fail him, he went backstage and
asked Kean for a place in his company.

"Well, my lad," thundered Kean in a voice trained to
bring tears or laughter to those who heard it, "I understand
you would like to go on the stage."

"Yes, indeed, Mr. Kean," came the eager reply.

"You have the advantage of me, you know my name. I
don't know yours. What is it?"

In vain, Gilbert, who in later years would be known for
his ready wit, now racked his brain for a false name. However, nothing but his own would come to his lips.

"Gilbert?" demanded Kean, "Gilbert? By any chance are
you the son of my good friend, Dr. Gilbert?"

"Y-es, I am," stammered the boy.

"The only thing I'll do for you, my lad, is to take you
home. Stage manager, kindly call up my carriage! There
will be no rehearsal today. I have to take this would-be actor
to his father."

Dr. Gilbert thanked Kean for bringing back his boy. No
sooner had the actor left the house than father and son were
on their way back to Great Ealing. Young William was to
spend three more unhappy years there before entering college. In order to make the time pass as quickly as possible,
Gilbert decided to enter all the prize contests announced on
the school bulletin board. Determined to win every one, he
studied while his schoolfellows were enjoying themselves.
As a result, by the time he had reached his sixteenth birthday he was head boy at Great Ealing. When he was gradu-
ated with honors, Gilbert entered King's College, Cam-

bridge, planning to finish his education at Oxford. He was no more popular there than he had been in prep school. Unable to get along with his fellow students, he found an outlet for his energy in writing for the campus magazine. Collegiate days fell into a regular routine of classes and literary activity—and then the Crimean War broke out.

Here was a chance to fight and win praise for doing so! Oxford was forgotten: Gilbert set to work cramming for the examination that would give him a commission in the Royal Artillery. Years later, Gilbert told how special tutors helped him prepare for the test and said, "The limit of the age was twenty, and as at the date of the examination I should be six weeks over-age, I applied for and obtained from Lord Pamure, the then Secretary of State for War, a dispensation for this excess and worked away with a will. But the war came to a rather abrupt and unexpected end, and no more officers being required, the examination was indefinitely postponed. Among the blessings of peace may be reckoned certain comedies, operas, farces and extravaganzas which, if the war had lasted another six weeks, would in all probability never have been written."

Cheated out of being a soldier and with no desire to go back to college, Gilbert did nothing for weeks. Then, thanks to another examination, he was appointed to a minor post in the Education Department of the Privy Council Office, and there, for four long and very boring years, he did routine tasks. After working hours he studied law. Gilbert's military ambitions were satisfied when, at the age of twenty-three, he received a reserve commission in a Highland regiment, eventually rising to the rank of captain. He proudly wore his kilt on every possible occasion, and dancing the Highland Fling became one of his favorite pastimes.

As a Gordon Highlander, he went on maneuvers for fourteen years, but never seemed to take his military duties too seriously. One very cold, dismal and damp night, he was called to headquarters by the colonel of his regiment. "Captain Gilbert," snapped the old soldier, "tomorrow morning, before dawn, you and your company are to take off to the hills. There you will hide yourselves. After a suitable time, the rest of the regiment will break camp and seek you and your men among the heather. Our object will be to capture you. Your task is to hide so we cannot find you. Dismissed!"

The next day, after allowing Gilbert and his company several hours to hide themselves, the colonel ordered the search to begin. The Highlanders crawled up muddy hillsides, slid down sodden banks, waded icy streams and tore their uniforms on thorny thickets. At last, wet to the skin, the colonel called off the hunt and ordered his men back to the barracks. There, reading a book, was Gilbert. He had decided it was no day for soldiering and had quietly led his company back to the comfort of dry clothing and a cheery fire!

Only a part-time soldier could have succeeded in such a ruse. A regular would have been court-martialed. There was, however, little chance to show such independence in the Education Department, and Gilbert became more and more bored. His only relief was to play practical jokes on his fellow boarders in his lodging house in the Pimlico district of London. The young ladies who usually gathered in the drawing room after dinner to gossip never knew when the curtains would be pulled aside and Gilbert, dressed like a ghost, would move silently across the room and vanish without saying a word. Just when he was unable to bear "the detestable thraldom" of the Education Department, he (as his father had before him) inherited money. It was the happiest day of William Gilbert's life when he sent in his resignation. He then decided to devote himself to the practice of law.

He didn't get much "practice." In the four years from 1866 to 1870, he averaged one client every three months. However, he had no regrets, for now he had plenty of money. Nor did he have to report daily to an office. The lack of briefs was, to him, a blessing. It made it unnecessary to go into court, where he was not very successful.

It was not that he didn't enjoy the law, for he did. In fact, Gilbert had a great love for the legal profession and it shows in much of his writing. The trouble was that the man who became famous for his clever tongue never could think of what to say in the courtroom. Topsy-turvy Gilbert! In writing he was always able to put the right word in the correct place, but he was tongue-tied when wearing a lawyer's gown and wig. He did, however, eventually become one of England's finest after-dinner speakers.

Something was always happening in court to embarrass him. Once, convinced that a woman charged with being a pickpocket was innocent, Gilbert defended her as a dear, simple old lady. Her handbag, he informed the court, was always filled with religious books. The testimony of a few police officers soon convinced Gilbert that the bag was more often filled with articles taken from other people's pockets. This was bad enough, but when the judge found her guilty, the prisoner took off a shoe and flung it at Gilbert's head! It missed, but hit a reporter, and the young barrister claimed that was the reason for "the unfavourable light in which my search for the defense was placed in two or three of the leading papers the next morning."

Another time Gilbert was assigned to clear a woman who was accused of stealing a coat. Before he could open his mouth and address the court, she cried out that Gilbert was drunk and begged the judge not to hear him! None of these people ever paid Gilbert. Why should they? He had failed to clear them from the charges. The only time he was successful, his client, a Frenchman, threw his arms about the embarrassed young barrister and kissed him soundly on both cheeks. Yet, despite all these difficulties, Gilbert recalled his struggling days as a lawyer with pleasure in an extremely funny article written for the December, 1863, issue of *Cornhill*. In telling of his experiences, he dashed off one pun after another, explaining that he and his friend Felix Polter had both embraced the legal profession and were "patiently waiting for the legal profession to embrace us."

An honest man, Gilbert knew that he could do little for his clients because of his stagefright and lack of ability as a speaker. Then, too, he had nothing but unpleasant experiences in the courtroom. The result was that he lost all desire to make a living at the Bar. So, all in all, he found it far more pleasant to sit in his chambers in Clement's Inn than go into court. Gilbert was not idle as he sat. He made good use of his first purchase on being called to the Bar, "a quire or so of manuscript paper, a packet of quill pens, and a bottle of ink, a bundle of pencils and some wood drawing blocks."

His first successful writing as a professional was a translation of the laughing song from *Manon Lescaut*, which Madame Parepa-Rosa, who had known him from boyhood, was singing at the famous Promenade Concerts. The translation was printed in the program, and Gilbert, who made it a practice to attend the concerts nightly, looking over the shoulders of all who were reading his first real literary effort, often wondered what the concert-goer would do if he "knew the gifted creature who had written the very words he was reading" was standing beside him.

Gilbert's time was filled with writing humorous verse and illustrating them with weird drawings. These were, for the most part, rejected by editors. The struggling author, never one to admit defeat, decided to send his work directly to the owners of magazines whom he knew. They usually disagreed with their employees and gave orders that the pieces be printed—and, what was more important to their author, paid for. Gilbert knew this system annoyed the editors, but as he got his own way, he ignored their grumbling.

Hard as he tried, he could not sell anything to *Punch,* the famous English comic weekly. His contributions came back as fast as they were received. Gilbert, of course, took their rejection as a personal insult.

Once, at a dinner party, a guest asked the editor of *Punch,* "Mr. Burnard, do you ever get good contributions from outsiders for your magazine?"

"Why, that happens all the time," was the answer.

Gilbert, seated at the other end of the table, looked up and snarled, "Maybe you do, but they never appear!"

However, he was selling material to *Fun,* a comic magazine that was becoming very popular. His weekly assignment was a column of copy and a half-page drawing. Gilbert had no contract, but the editor assured him that his contributions would always be accepted. Before long, subscribers to *Fun,* on receiving the latest issue, would immediately look for the material signed "Bab," Gilbert's childhood nickname. There was nothing "Bab" didn't write verses about: police courts, theaters, art, fashions, politics, and the armed services. He poked fun at them all, and his drawings, malicious at times, sentimental at others, delighted Victorian England. Soon he was publishing his *Bab Ballads* in book form.

With the exception of the usual course in art offered every schoolboy, Gilbert never had received any specialized instruction in drawing. The lack of formal training made him feel that his illustrations were not too well done. In fact, in 1898, when the ballads were in their eighth edition, Gilbert was still apologizing for his lack of artistic skill, stating in the preface: "I have always felt that many of the original illustrations to the *Bab Ballads* err gravely in the direction of unnecessary extravagance. This defect I have endeavored to correct through the medium of two hundred new drawings which I have designed for this volume. I am afraid I cannot claim for them any other recommendation."

For once, Gilbert was too modest. In the first place, the original drawings were perfect. They caught completely the spirit of his verses. The redrawn illustrations, while good, lack the vigor of those which appeared in *Fun*. Strangely enough, Gilbert was wrong about everything connected with the ballads. He didn't think too much of the verses either. Everyone else has found in these delightful bits of "much sound and little sense," some of the best examples of nonsense verse in English. Never have these musical, humorous, nonsensical, madcap poems been equaled by any other writer. Gilbert, alone, considered the pictures "quite as bad as the ballads" but supposed "they are not much worse."

With money in his pockets, Gilbert decided he could now afford to get married. On August 6, 1867, he married Miss Lucy Blois Turner, the daughter of an officer in the Indian Service. The couple set up housekeeping, and Gilbert found that it was necessary to write and sell more material than ever before, in order to meet expenses. He worked long hours, and by the use of parody and pun, soon was out of debt. Being Gilbert, he was not satisfied, so he looked about for other outlets for his talents.

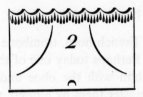

"A Wandering Minstrel, I"

—*The Mikado*

"THERE'S little time for a story, Arthur. I've got to go and rehearse the band. Besides, you've heard me tell a thousand times how your Aunt Elizabeth used to get a piece of candy from Napoleon every morning, and how the Little Corporal and I would take a walk every day. I'll wager you could tell the story of those days on St. Helena as well as I can. Come now, boy, hand me my uniform coat. A soldier in the British Army must never be late."

As he buttoned up his coat, Sergeant of the Band Thomas Sullivan saw the look of disappointment on his son's face. He smiled at the boy and promised, "I'll have a tale for you tonight while Mother's getting supper. Now, if you like, come along with me and join the rehearsal. Or perhaps you'd rather stay here and see what you can do with that old piano you've rebuilt. Seems to me you haven't composed anything for a month!"

It was a most difficult choice for eight-year-old Arthur Seymour Sullivan. What should he do? He had a wonderful idea for a piano composition. On the other hand, the band was such fun! Already he had taught himself how to play the flute, clarinet, French horn, trombone, alt-horn, euphonium and cornet. Perhaps today one of the friendly bandsmen would help him with the oboe and bassoon, for he couldn't seem to master them by himself. Quickly, he made up his mind, "I'll go with you, Father, and play the piano tomorrow."

Home after rehearsal and awaiting supper, the Sergeant kept his word. He eased himself into his chair, drew Arthur and Frederick, his eldest son, onto his lap, and with an Irishman's ability for spinning a tale, recalled the days of his childhood.

"I was there, as you know, because your grandfather had taken the King's Shilling, and after serving in the wars, went off to St. Helena as paymaster of the troops who were guarding Napoleon. The island was a wonderful place for a lad to grow up; you could explore the caves, swim in the sea, and watch the sailing vessels being refitted for the long trip to England. The whole of St. Helena was made by a volcano, and it was great fun to climb up the half-mile to the top of Diana's peak, the northern boundary of the crater. Then, too, we could walk about, looking at the various formations of lava, such as Lot's Wife and The Chimney. Yet, of all the memories I have of those happy days, boys, nothing is stronger than that of the sight of my father standing at attention, at the head of the Frenchman's casket. I can see it so plainly, the torches ablaze, the . . ."

"Supper is on the table and it will be spoiled, Thomas. No more stories for now. Come, eat, all of you."

"We're coming, Mother. Go wash yourselves, boys. I'll finish my tale another time."

The family sat down to supper. It was a simple meal, for the Sullivans were very poor. In fact, shortly after Frederick was born, they had so little money that Mrs. Sullivan, as well as her husband, was obliged to go to work. During those trying days, tiny Frederick was placed in a foster home. However, by the time Arthur was born on May 13, 1842, their financial condition had improved. By avoiding spending even one unnecessary penny, Sergeant Sullivan was able to keep his family together. It was difficult. An army bandmaster's pay was quite low. Nor did the Sergeant make much money from the private lessons he gave. He tried to increase his meager income by copying music or taking an occasional engagement in a theater orchestra as a clarinet player. Yet, hard as he worked, there was never enough cash to pay the bills. Despite this, the Sullivans were completely happy. They had no trips to Italy, no friends in high places. All they had was one another—and they wanted little more.

Supper over and the two boys tucked in for the night, Thomas Sullivan sat down to have a serious talk with his wife. She could, he knew, help him decide what to do about educating Arthur, for Mrs. Sullivan had been an assistant in a girls' school before her marriage. Despite her maiden name of Coghlan, she could, on her mother's side, trace her ancestry back to the famous and artistic family of Righi— a Righi had been Michaelangelo's chief assistant—but she was a practical woman, and Sergeant Sullivan wanted practical advice. For while he was delighted with Arthur's interest in music, he was not so sure that he wanted his son to become a professional musician. He knew from his own struggles how difficult a life it was—so the puzzled father turned to his beloved Mary and asked what to do.

By the time the elder Sullivans retired, plans for Arthur's schooling were complete. The boy was to go to a school or, as such establishments were called in those days, an "Academy," kept by William Pless in Bishop's Road, London. Here he would receive a general education and, as Thomas Sullivan said, "The music will take care of itself."

Arthur's schooldays were not like his future partner's. He was most happy and made friends among his schoolmates as easily as Gilbert made enemies among his. A rather delicate child, he was, nevertheless, full of fun. In fact, he often played truant. He would disappear for hours and spend the time in Westminster Abbey, wandering through the memorials to England's honored dead, and then return to Bishop's Road in time for supper.

It was during those days of fun, study and wandering about the streets of London that Sullivan formed the habit of writing letters. In later years he would write to millionaires, opera stars, dukes and even kings, and they would write to him. Now, as all schoolboys do, Arthur wrote to his mother, but not in the usual fashion of a youngster away from home. In those communications young Sullivan confided everything that happened, and he was always asking for advice. In one of his letters, he asked what to do about swapping his knife for a "little gold-pencil case which I have taken a fancy to." He could, he explained, get not only the case, but a *two-bladed* knife in the exchange. However, he would wait until he heard from home before going ahead with the transaction.

Arthur wrote to his father as well. Those letters were of a different sort. In every one he asked permission to join the Chapel Royal. His dominating ambition was to be one of the ten boys, called "Children," who provided the choral music for the religious services at St. James Palace, dressed in a brilliant tunic of scarlet and gold and knee-breeches. No other place in England seemed so wonderful to him—for in return for their singing, the choristers were fed, clothed and housed, given a good general education and offered one of the finest musical trainings to be had anywhere.

In every possible way young Sullivan tried to get his father's permission to apply for admission as one of the "Children." He begged, argued and implored, but the answer was always "No!" A clever lad, Arthur decided to try a new attack: one of Sergeant Sullivan's favorite composers was Henry Purcell, and the boy called his parent's attention to the fact that Purcell had been trained at the Chapel Royal. "That's very true," Thomas Sullivan wrote back, "but the Duke of Wellington is a famous man and he wasn't trained there!"

Nothing seemed to convince the Sergeant—no matter what Arthur wrote. In other matters Mr. Sullivan was far more agreeable. He gladly sent Arthur money for a chemistry set consisting, as a letter home explained, of "50 boxes like pill boxes, 12 small bottles, a glass measuring cup and a little book containing 100 experiments." However, along with the money for this purchase went a definite refusal of his son's latest request to become a chorister in the Chapel Royal.

Arthur would not give up the contest, however. Letter followed letter until at last his father consented. As he had said, "The music will take care of itself"—so perhaps it would be wiser to let his son follow his own wishes.

Overjoyed, Arthur set out with Mr. Plees, his schoolmaster, to see Sir George Smart, the organist at the Chapel Royal. Sir George was a busy man, but he graciously heard the youngster sing *With Verdure Clad* to his own piano accompaniment. When Sullivan had finished, the great man patted the boy on the head and told him to see the Reverend Mr. Helmore, who was in charge of the choristers.

The result of that interview was all Arthur could wish. There was one difficulty, however. Mr. Helmore had a rule that no boy could be admitted to the Chapel Royal after the age of nine, and this applicant was twelve. Finally, impressed by the boy's voice and amazed at his unusual knowledge of music, Mr. Helmore made an exception. People would always break rules for Arthur Sullivan. There was something about him that made all with whom he came in contact want to do him a favor. Two days after his admission, happily dressed in the gold-braided scarlet uniform of the Chapel Royal, Arthur sang the solo of Nares' *Blessed Be He* as part of the Easter Services. None of the other choristers were jealous that a new boy should be given such an honor—for in forty-eight hours he had made friends with them all. Arthur himself did not consider his performance worth writing home about—his letter was too full of his joy at being admitted to the Chapel Royal. The boy whose voice could reach to A or B flat had achieved his first ambition. From now on, success would follow success.

He was extremely happy. To be sure, sometimes as he and the other choristers were returning from a performance, their brilliant uniforms brightening London's dingy streets, the gangs at the corners would pelt them with snowballs, but he enjoyed returning the barrage. Arthur's sense of humor and lively personality made him the most popular of the "Children." Despite the fact that he was the newest member of the group, his advancement was rapid. It was not long before he was being given all the solos to sing and he was often sent out to entertain at private parties. These affairs gave him pocket money which he spent, not on sweets, but on music. His first contact with royalty came when he sang at the christening of the Duke of Albany. Queen Victoria was so pleased that she sent the Prince Consort to give the boy ten shillings. Years later, she would make him a knight.

His song at the royal christening was Michael Costa's anthem setting of the words, "Suffer little children to come unto me." This composer, born in Naples, Italy, was the leading musical conductor in England. Despite the fact that he had become a naturalized British citizen and had been knighted, he had never lost his accent. That is why Sullivan laughed to himself when, at rehearsal, Sir Michael called him from the loft and asked him to take more pains with his pronunciation. "Be sure," cautioned Costa, "that you sing: 'forbeed them not, for of sooch is the Kengdom of Haven.'" Sullivan often wondered if Her Imperial Majesty, Queen Victoria, would have liked his singing better if he had followed the composer's instructions as to pronunciation. At any rate, for weeks afterward, Arthur entertained his schoolmates with an imitation of the famous Sir Michael teaching a chorister of the Chapel Royal the proper way to pronounce various words.

Sullivan's closest friends at the Chapel Royal were François and Alfred Cellier, who were to be associated with him years later at the Savoy Theater. These three were the organizers of the Chapel Royal Choristers' Band. All the "Children" belonged, and with books for drums and tissue-paper covered combs, they loudly played the works written by their conductor and organist, Arthur Sullivan. Yet all was not fun. School hours were long and lessons difficult at the Chapel Royal, and Mr. Helmore knew how to use a cane if necessary, though on the whole he was a gentle man.

The Master of the Chapel Royal realized that Sullivan was more interested in music than in any other subject. He would often catch the boy daydreaming. "What are you doing, young Sullivan?" he would ask. "Thinking of music, sir," Arthur would reply. At once Mr. Helmore would give him a page of Latin to translate, or some geometry problem to work out. "Do you think," he would demand, "that you don't need an education?" If Thomas Sullivan had only known the treatment his son was to receive, he never would have held back permission for him to join the Chapel Royal. Mr. Helmore knew, however, that Arthur was a musical genius. Although the Master of the Chapel Royal directed Sullivan's mind into other fields, he made sure the boy composed something every week. Never, however, did Mr. Helmore show Arthur special attention or treat him differently from the rest of the "Children."

The months rolled on. While spending a vacation period at the country house of one of his chums, Sullivan showed his appreciation by writing a sacred song and dedicating it to his friend's mother. This work, *O Israel*, was sold to Novello, the famous music printer, and is Arthur Sullivan's first printed composition.

Arthur had, however, made money before this from his composing. The Dean of the Chapel Royal, the Right Reverend Dr. Bloomfield, was so delighted with an anthem Sullivan composed for use in the Chapel Royal that he patted the boy's curly head and gave him a sovereign. Arthur pocketed the sovereign and forced himself to smile at the pat on the head. It seemed as if someone was always patting him on the head, and he did not like it! One day a bishop, hearing Sullivan sing, was so amazed when he heard that the song had been written by the youthful singer that he also gave him a sovereign—but the quick-thinking youth avoided the customary pat by bowing low while expressing his thanks. His singing often brought him rewards. The Duke of Wellington, who, as Thomas Sullivan had cleverly pointed out, was *not* a Chapel Royal graduate, came up to Arthur one day after a service, chatted a while and gave him a gold piece.

Sullivan wrote his parents about these gifts and stressed the importance of the people who had praised him. Still friendly with everybody, he made a point of being gracious to important people. The older they were, the better Arthur got along with them. From these days at the Chapel Royal until his death, Sullivan was to mingle constantly with the famous and make friends with royalty. They, in turn, were attracted by him and gladly did everything they could for the bandsman's son.

In letters to Sandhurst, Arthur might write of simple things—"The cake is all gone and I soon shall be in need of another"—but for the most part his letters to his parents were filled with great names and they told of his earning extra money by singing. He sent some of his compositions home, asking if the Sergeant thought he could sell them. "I have," Arthur informed his father, "sold twenty-two shillings' worth here." Sullivan was still enough of a schoolboy to send home such news as the fact that Mr. Helmore stopped the fireworks on Guy Fawkes Day because he was in a temper—but the majority of Arthur's letters were about music—his solos and what the Duchess of Sutherland or Lord Bruce, the vice-chancellor, had thought of his singing.

It was not only titled ladies and gentlemen who petted and praised him. Sullivan's olive-colored face, dark, brilliant eyes and black curly hair, together with the heavy scarlet gold-braided coat of the Chapel Royal, caused many a teen-aged heart to flutter as he walked through London's streets. Then, too, frequently elderly women would ask and obtain permission from Mr. Helmore to take young Sullivan in their carriages to the afternoon services at St. Paul's. Affection and love were his for the asking, but he was more interesting in getting a ride than in those who offered it, for the boy was worn out with the constant rehearsing, study, composition and singing. Arthur was not a strong lad, and the ten-mile walk from the lodgings of the "Children" to the Chapel Royal and return wearied him so much that many afternoons he had to go to bed and rest.

Despite his run-down condition, Sullivan was always full of fun and a leader in the pranks of the choristers. Never in his letters home did he tell how tired he was. In fact, not once in a life which was often darkened with pain was Arthur Seymour Sullivan heard to complain.

In the early part of 1856, he had no time to feel ill. There was too much excitement. The Mendelssohn Scholarship, established in memory of the great composer, was to be thrown open to competition in London. Who could tell—perhaps the winner might be one of the "Children"! Sullivan decided to enter the contest. He had high hopes, but felt he had little chance of winning. Luckily he had, six weeks before, celebrated his fourteenth birthday, for no one under that age could enter. Arthur wrote home, "I stand a poor chance," explaining that there were seventeen boys entered in the competition, all older than he and all very clever. However, Arthur asked his father to come up to London and listen to him compete. The trip would not be wasted because Sergeant Sullivan could arrange to attend the grand rehearsal of Jenny Lind's concert while in the city.

Sergeant Sullivan was in the front row when the competition began. To his great joy, it ended in a draw between his son, the youngest entrant, and Josephy Barnaby, the oldest. Mr. Sullivan's joy turned to worry when the judges announced that there would be a second contest immediately. Nor was the father comforted when this test was over and the judges stated that they had not yet made up their minds, and would notify the winner by mail the following day.

There was no sleep for Arthur Seymour Sullivan that night. In a brief autobiography, written in 1899 for a long since vanished English weekly, *M.A.P.*, he recalled how he "spent the day in a fever of excitement. Every time I heard a knock at the door, my heart was in my mouth. The day wore on, but still no letter. Two o'clock came—three—four—I was beginning to lose hope. At last *rat-tat!* The postman's knock. It was unmistakable. I crept into the hall. The maidservant passed me by and went to the letter box. 'A letter for you, Master Sullivan,' she said. I took it from her, tore it open, and then—I had won it! I don't think I ever felt such joy in my life."

No letters home filled with names and self-praise now. All Sullivan could write about were his plans for the future. He was determined to make a career of music— "Nothing in the world would ever interest me so much. I may not make a lot of money, but I shall have music and that will make up if I don't."

The scholarship allowed Arthur to attend classes at the Royal Academy of Music, where he enrolled in courses comprising many unfamiliar subjects. Among them were Italian and the study of the violin. At the same time he kept up his duties at the Chapel Royal. The days and nights were filled with study and singing, but there was time for fun as well. Sullivan delighted his fellow students at the Royal Academy by playing strange sounds on their instruments, and turning comic songs into psalm tunes. He would turn his back to the piano and instantly name every note played for him. This ability to play musical jokes was one that was going to stand him in good stead later when he wrote music for Gilbert's humorous words.

Before the boy knew it, a year had passed. He had no reason to think the scholarship would be renewed. However, he took the examination again. For his entry he sang one of his own songs. When he had finished, Sir George Smart, who had carefully watched over him ever since the day Mr. Plees had brought Arthur to his house seeking a place in the Chapel Royal, forbade the boy to sing another note. Sullivan, writing home, explained to his mother that if Sir George had not stopped him, "I should have no voice at all." The reason for this was that young Arthur was going through the trying period of a changing voice.

The one song was enough, however. Sullivan was again awarded the scholarship. His work was so outstanding that the authorities began to talk of sending him to Leipzig for advanced study. The wife of the secretary of the Mendelssohn Scholarship Committee offered to teach him German, and he accepted. He disliked the language intensely, but soon was able to speak it fluently. Everything he did came easily and it was no surprise when it was announced that Sullivan was to be sent to Germany in September 1856.

Before Arthur left for Leipzig, Sir George Smart invited him to his house and gave him a final examination. The youth and the old master sat down and went over Sullivan's compositions: the overture, a sonata and all the songs. Sir George congratulated him and then gave him a test far more difficult than the one he had taken to win the scholarship. When they had finished, the old man knew that the sixteen-year-old youth was ready for anything the Leipzig Conservatoire might offer.

There was only one other ceremony to be held before Arthur Sullivan left for Germany. It was an ancient custom that every chorister, on leaving the Chapel Royal, should receive a gift of sixty pounds (currently $300) from the Queen, and that the Bishop of London present him with a Bible and Prayer Book. The only allowable reason for leaving the Chapel Royal was the breaking of a chorister's voice. Sullivan's voice had not completely changed. A rule was a rule—but Arthur's voice refused to obey. Yet, once again, Arthur Sullivan's case was made an exception. The sixty pounds were sent him by the Queen, and the Bishop duly presented him with the Bible and the Prayer Book.

With money in his pocket, his baggage full of original compositions, his mind filled with dreams, Sullivan set off for Leipzig.

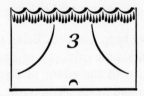

3

"A Je-ne-sias-quoi *Young Man"*

—*Patience*

ALL this time Gilbert's robe was gathering dust in a corner of the gloomy chambers in Clement's Inn, where the would-be lawyer waited for the clients who never came. Despite the fact that Gilbert had little opportunity to use his legal knowledge in the courtroom, it was not wasted. He relied greatly on his legal studies for material for his writings. In fact, some of his best *Bab Ballads* deal with legal matters. Lawyers for years have laughed over *Baines Carew, Gentleman*—the attorney who:

> *"When'er he heard a tale of woe*
> *From client A or client B,*
> *His grief would overcome him so,*
> *He'd scarce have strength to take his fee."*

Anxious to add to his income, Gilbert contributed articles and stories to dozens of magazines, and even acted as London correspondent of a Russian newspaper. Incidentally, he was not making one of his usual puns when he said that he was paid, and well paid, for everything he wrote for *Fun*. His income from his weekly contributions was quite large

25

and he should have been satisfied. Being Gilbert, he wasn't. Unable to stand a simple criticism of one of the *Bab Ballads,* he quarreled with the editor of *Fun,* flounced out of the office in a rage and never again wrote a line for the publication which had given him his start.

Years later, he was to draw upon the *Bab Ballads* for many of the plots of the Gilbert and Sullivan operas. In fact, many of the operas are merely expanded ballads, filled with additional puns and featuring Sullivan's delightful music. This was, however, far in the future. Now it was necessary to find another market for his musical, original and mirth-provoking verse. He had no difficulty. Editors gladly took everything he wrote, knowing how his sharp cuts at the customs of the day and his unequaled nonsense could fascinate Victorian readers.

Yet, Gilbert needed still more money to support himself and his wife. An opportunity to add to his earnings came when Robertson, the dramatist, unable to supply a play for the Christmas season of 1866, suggested to the management of the St. James Theater that the commission be given to Gilbert. When asked if he could have the piece ready in two weeks, the brash young author, who had never written a play for the professional theater, replied, "You'll have it in ten days!"

As a matter of fact, once he started *Dulcamara,* Gilbert found writing plays as easy as writing verse. True to his word, he delivered the script to the St. James Theater within ten days. He then made theatrical history by having it ready for production after only a week of rehearsals. In the excitement of getting the play written and ready for presentation, however, Gilbert for the first and only time in his life failed to arrange what the payment would be for his work.

When the time came to discuss terms and he was asked by the manager of the St. James Theater how much he wanted for *Dulcamara*, he really didn't know what to say. Gilbert tried to figure the value of the play on the basis of how much time he had spent writing it, but that didn't seem right. At last, he hit on a price, and years later ruefully recalled, "I modestly hoped that, as the piece was a success, £30 ($150 at that time) would not be considered an excessive price for the London right. Mr. Emden looked rather surprised and, as I thought, disappointed. However, he wrote a cheque, asked for a receipt, and when he had got it, said: 'Now take a bit of advice from an old stager who knows what he is talking about; never sell so good a piece as this for £30 again!' And I never have."

It did not occur to Gilbert that his play could fail, so he invited a few friends to join him at a midnight supper after the performance. It was a pleasant affair, but never again did Gilbert take it for-granted that his plays were going to be successful. As a matter of fact, he did not watch the performance on opening nights, but walked the streets of London, returning to the stage door of the theater from time to time, asking the doorman how the piece was going, vanishing quickly before he heard the reply.

From now on Gilbert would devote his time to writing for the stage. *Dulcamara* had assured his success as a playwright. One play after another came from his pen and was produced at London theaters. Most of his early works, like *Dulcamara*, which had parodied *Elisir d'amore,* were burlesques on operas. *La Vivandiere* was based on *The Daughter of the Regiment; Merry Zingara* was a parody on *The Bohemian Girl,* and there were others. Then came Gilbert's first real comedy, *An Old Score,* and when it was finished, he borrowed an idea of his father's—that of having a manuscript set up in type so that it could be easily read. Managers were attracted by the printed work and gave immediate consideration to Gilbert's manuscripts. As success followed suc-

cess, he no longer had to beg actors, managers and pro-
ducers to read his work; they asked him to provide them
with plays, offering payment in advance. It was not long
before Gilbert was considered a very important figure in the
theatrical world of London.

To be sure, the theater was not considered very important
in the England of Victoria's day. In fact, respectable folk
hardly ever went to a theater. They might attend a performance of one of Shakespeare's plays or take the children
to see a Christmas pantomime, but that was all. Going to
the theater was one of those things "nice" people didn't do.

It was Thomas German Reed who decided to do something about this situation. He knew that if he could overcome the Victorian attitude toward the word "theater" and
everything connected with it, he could reach thousands
who were hungry for entertainment. So Reed called his playhouse a "Gallery of Illustration" and avoided the use of the
works of writers who were well known and considered "vulgar." He presented instead light sketches and music. He
had hit on a magic formula. The "Gallery of Illustration"
was crowded night after night. Reed's establishment offered
Gilbert an ideal market for his work, and the latter wrote
many pieces for it. Most of these plays were charming comedies which delighted the audiences.

The music for Gilbert's frothy works was written by
Frederick Clay, who had the ability to turn out one song
after another. A happy-go-lucky chap, Clay sold all his
work at a flat figure—getting about twenty-five dollars for
each composition. Included in this unbusinesslike arrangement were three of the most famous songs of the Victorian
era: *The Sands of Dee, She Wandered down the Mountain
Side* and *I'll Sing Thee Songs of Araby*. Always giving parties to which he invited the theatrical and musical leaders of
London, Clay asked Gilbert to attend one of these affairs.

"You'll enjoy yourself, Gilbert," Clay promised. "Sullivan will play the piano for us."

"You don't think a musical evening is my idea of enjoyment, do you, Fred?" asked Gilbert. "I'll come on one condition—that you introduce me to this Sullivan." Clay promised, and Gilbert said he would attend. The composer should have realized that Gilbert was planning to play a joke on his fellow musician, for he was always playing jokes. What an opportunity this was! Gilbert planned to go to the party and pretend to be a musical expert, so he sat down at his desk with an encyclopedia in front of him. For hours he read everything the reference work contained about music. It was not easy reading for a man whose claim to musical knowledge was, "I know two tunes. One is *God Save the Queen,* the other isn't." By the time the evening of the party arrived, however, Gilbert was ready when Clay introduced him to Sullivan.

"I'm very glad to meet you, Mr. Sullivan," said Gilbert, holding out his hand, "for you will be able to decide a question which has just arisen between my friend Fred Clay and myself. I maintain that if a composer has a musical theme to express, he can express it perfectly upon the simple tetrachord of Mercury, in which (as I need not tell you) there are no diatonic intervals at all, as upon the much more complicated diapason (with the four tetrachords and the redunant note), which embraces in its perfect consonance all the simple, double and inverted chords."

The stunned Sullivan nervously shook hands and mumbled, "Well, Mr. Gilbert—that is—I would say—on the other hand—really now, I'm sorry, but I'll have to think the question over before I answer."

Gilbert nodded wisely. "Take your time, Mr. Sullivan, take your time. It is a matter on which I have spent considerable study and I would appreciate your opinion. There is no hurry. Whenever you are ready to tell me your feelings in the matter, I will be grateful. Meanwhile, what do you say, Clay, if we drop the matter?"

Poor Sullivan, he had no idea that Gilbert was joking! However, he must have thought about the question for years—for he never answered it. Not that it made any difference. Gilbert had forgotten all about his hoax the next morning.

A short time after Clay's party, John Hollingshead, a London manager, called Gilbert and Sullivan to his office and offered them a commission to write a comic opera. The pair collaborated on *Thespis*, which was produced during the Christmas season of 1871. It was not a success and the two men drifted apart, meeting once in a while, but with no desire to work together.

Gilbert was not too concerned with the failure of *Thespis*. What was one poor play among a long list of hits? Judged by any standard, he had won fame and fortune in the theater. The prices paid for his plays allowed him to go riding in the park, buy a small yacht and join several exclusive clubs, as well as to acquire an attractive home where he gave delightful parties for all the children in the neighborhood. The Gilberts never had any children of their own, but their house was the headquarters of all the youngsters in South Kensington. There was plenty of money to provide these young visitors with treats. For *Pygmalion and Galatea*, produced in 1871, Gilbert received $200,000 as against the $150 he was paid for *Dulcamara*, five years previously.

Secretly Gilbert was pleased that *Thespis* had not been a smash hit. He did not relish the idea of sharing fame or profits with anyone else. Nor did he want to be a co-author of a successful play. Why should anyone get the benefit of his abilities? There was just one thing that Gilbert gladly shared with others. That was his temper.

Always a fighter, he quarreled with managers, actors, costumers and stagehands. Once he knocked an actor down just as the man was about to make his entrance on the stage by means of a trap-door. The rest of the cast could not believe their eyes when, instead of the player they expected, Gilbert popped up through the floor and played the part as if it were his regular job. He was, incidentally, a fine actor and often appeared in performances for charities and benefits for members of the theatrical profession.

At a rehearsal of his play, *Broken Hearts,* Gilbert almost came to blows with John Hare, the leading man. Both Gilbert and Hare stormed out of the theater in a rage, and by sheer chance went to the same subway station for a train. They stood on opposite ends of the platform, glaring at each other, suddenly decided to shake hands, did so, rushed back to the rehearsal and found that the rest of the company had gone home!

When Clement Scott, the dramatic critic, referred to *Broken Hearts* as Gilbert's *Broken Parts,* the author was furious. The result was that he never spoke to Scott again. Yet when the critic was dying, the dramatist was a constant caller at the house and no one cried more at the funeral than he. Gilbert spent his life quarreling and making up. He was always hating someone, always repenting that hate. For hours he would scream, yell and rave at actors at a rehearsal, work them until they were ready to drop from exhaustion, and finally bring the session to a close by telling the cast how stupid it was. Then he would dig down in his pocket and give the actors and actresses money to pay their fares home, because, "I've kept you so late, you have missed the last bus."

It is difficult to decide whether Gilbert enjoyed the money he received from *Pygmalion and Galatea* as much as the opportunity it gave him to fight with Madge Robertson, the leading lady. They started out as great friends, but the actress had her own ideas how her part should be played and insisted on playing it her way. To Gilbert this was treason. He knew better than any actress! His revenge was typical. Night after night he would attend the performance, sitting in a stage box. Leaning over the rail, he would hang on every one of his words as spoken by the members of the cast until the moment when Miss Robertson came on stage. Then he would stand up, turn his back to her, talk to the others in the box at the top of his voice, making humorous remarks that forced them into gales of laughter. The acting in the box was oftentimes far more interesting than that which was offered on the stage. As a matter of fact, Gilbert did not get along with any of the famous actresses who played in *Pygmalion and Galatea*. He even warned one who dared to use her own gestures, instead of the ones he had suggested, that if she continued, "I give you notice that on Monday I shall apply for an injunction to prevent your playing the piece."

Gilbert's success as a playwright and his own ability as an actor convinced him that he was also an excellent dramatic critic. Sir Beerbohm Tree, one of the most famous Shakespearean actors of all time, asked Gilbert how he had enjoyed his performance as Hamlet. The reply was typical of Gilbert: "Well, my dear fellow, all I can say is I never saw anything so funny in my life, and yet it was not in the least vulgar." Sir Beerbohm should have known better, but he foolishly sent Gilbert tickets to see him play Falstaff, a part which made it necessary for him to wear a great deal of padding. That night, after the show, Tree again asked Gilbert what he thought of his acting. Gilbert glared at the actor, who was perspiring freely, due to his costume, and snapped, "Tree, I think the pores of your skin give a remarkable performance!"

When Gilbert heard that another famous actor was going to be starred in *Hamlet,* he said, "At last scholars can settle the question of whether Bacon or Shakespeare wrote England's greatest plays. Have both coffins opened and whichever has turned in his grave is the author!"

Gilbert's hot temper and domineering personality were making him one of the most cordially hated men in London. Deeply sensitive himself, he never cared how badly he hurt the feelings of others. He collected enemies just as some men collect coins and stamps, deliberately going out of his way to be disagreeable. Yet, he would suddenly make amends, and men to whom he had not spoken for years would be astonished by an invitation to have lunch with him.

Although Gilbert was selling plays of all kinds, he also found time to write many short stories as well. These tales dealt with supernatural beings and fantastic happenings. Like his poetry, his short stories were filled with terrible puns and peopled with outlandishly named folk who lived in strange geographic locations. Notwithstanding his desire to be a serious dramatist, he was never so happy or capable as when he was writing about honest smugglers, magic isles, happenings in Fairyland and adventures in Dreamland. Gilbert the lawyer, turned author, treated all this impossible material in as sober and logical a manner as if he were preparing a brief for a case in "Queen's Court, Common Pleas or Divorce."

It was the only way in which this material could have been written—and no one else could have done it but Gilbert, for he had discovered the Land of Topsy-turvydom and, as its king, found it a simple matter to obey the first and only law of that whimsical country: to allow only the impossible to happen. He was an impish ruler, full of wit and humor, as gay as a circus clown, more at home with

wicked fairies than with serious and honest folk. Gilbert
was, in fact, as topsy-turvy as his writings. As much as he
disliked most adults, he adored children. He enjoyed the
company of young and pretty girls, but had no use for old,
ugly women. He had quite a collection of animals and was
one of the first to breed ring-tailed lemurs in captivity. His
dogs had the run of the house, and he thought more of them
than he did of most of his visitors.

One day, a rather stout, gushy woman reporter, hoping to
make a good impression on him, remarked, as the dogs
leaped upon her, "See, Mr. Gilbert, how your dogs like me!"

"Why not?" snarled Gilbert, "It is rare that they see a
bone with so much meat on it!"

Unpopular as he was, Gilbert was successful in his writing. All of it—prose, verse and drama—brought him fame
and fortune. Most of the plays were money makers; there
was just one real failure, and the author said of it, "I called
it *Gretchen* and the public called it rot." None of his plays
were, to use the language of the theater, "smash hits." For
the most part they had long enough runs, but set no box-
office records. As a matter of fact, it is a wonder that any of
them were successful, for Gilbert, unable to get along with
his fellowmen, used the stage as a pulpit to preach to the
world. Angry with mankind's actions, he tried to change the
manners of the world through his plays, but the audiences
thought he was just being funny, and laughed at his tirades.
Meanwhile, they were paying for the chance to laugh, so
Gilbert made money, even though he failed to reform the
world.

Poor Gilbert! He never realized that, although he was
recognized as a very clever author of comedies, he was in
no way a really great dramatist. It was not until he was
willing to give up his serious ambitions and engage in fool-
ery, create preposterous situations and present absurd char-

acters that he was successful. In the world of commonsense he was only a peasant; in Topsy-turvydom, he was king.

Unhappy because the theatergoing public laughed at his theories, convinced that no critic in London was fair to him, yet making huge sums as he wrote prose, comedy, burlesque, melodrama and parody, Gilbert sulked. In order to revenge himself, he began to write bitter satire. Everyone thought that he was funnier than ever! His anger at the world grew greater, and the more he tried to show it in his writing, the greater became his reputation as a humorist. Topsy-turvy Gilbert, hailed as England's greatest writer of comedy, when he wanted to be considered a serious dramatist!

Yet, despite his reputation, his success and knowledge of the theater, Gilbert would not be remembered today if he hadn't teamed with Arthur Seymour Sullivan.

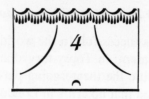

"Over the Bright Blue Sea"

—Pinafore

Y o u had better take a few thalers, Sullivan. You haven't a penny in your pockets. It's quite a distance to Leipzig and . . ."

"Please, sir, you've done quite enough. I don't know what I would have done but for your kindness. If you hadn't come to my rescue after my pocket was picked, I would have had to return to London. I simply can't borrow any more from you. Just as soon as I can, I'll return what I owe."

"You'll do nothing of the sort," the friendly traveler smiled. "Go on to your studies. I wish you the best of luck." The two shook hands, and Sullivan went off to the Conservatoire, arriving in Leipzig in September, 1858, without funds, but full of ambition.

Once in the old German city, steeped in musical tradition, famous for its Gewanhaus Concerts and the Conservatoire founded by Mendelssohn, Sullivan found his reputation had preceded him. Professors and fellow students alike knew all about him. Everyone expected great things from him. All praised him for his accomplishments back home and showered him with attention. As always, Sullivan found the approval of others most enjoyable. He thrived on praise as Gilbert did on censure.

It did not take long for the teachers at the Conservatoire to learn that their new pupil's reputation did not do him justice. Ignez Moscheles, head of the school, told everyone that the young Englishman knew more about playing and composing for the piano than any of the other students. Moscheles' opinion of his ability made Sullivan extremely happy, for the young Englishman had decided to become a conductor. He wrote to Sir George, telling him of his new ambition. The next post brought a letter in which the old master suggested that the change of plans did not meet with his approval. "There are now," he wrote warningly, "so many conductors that some of them are non-conductors."

Despite the disapproval of his old mentor, Sullivan did not give up the idea of being a conductor. Meanwhile, his instructors loaded him with work. As a matter of fact, they drove him continually. The faculty rejected most of his compositions, telling him he could do better. Instead of discouraging him, this treatment spurred him to do better work. Never so happy as when writing music, he enjoyed his assignments. The more difficult the task, the more pleasant he found it. As long as he was at the piano keyboard or setting notes on paper, he was happy. Music was his whole life—and Leipzig's whole life was music—he wanted nothing more. He did not have a single worry, save money. In a school where most of the students were poor, Sullivan was the poorest of them all.

There was little money to be had from home. Sullivan tried to save as much as he could. He kept a careful record of his expenses each month, setting down every groschen he spent. The only time his accounts did not balance was in December. That was the month in which he gave gifts to all who had entertained him. It was a long list, for almost everyone in Leipzig had been hospitable to the attractive young Englishman.

It was a struggle to make his allowance last. Midwinter had arrived before Sullivan started the fire in the room for which he paid five thalers a month. In order to save as much money as possible, he suggested to a fellow student that they room together.

"We'll save money that way, John. We're spending four thalers a month for breakfast and six and a half thalers for dinner. We simply can't cut down any more on those items. But if we room together, we can save on rent. Look here, we'll only need one fire, then at night when we are working, we can both use the same light. What do you say?"

"It's a grand idea, Arthur. Just the thing. You haven't figured the cost of our suppers, though—how about them?"

"Well, you see, I don't have to buy many. I get so many invitations. One evening I go to a professor's house. Another time I go to one of my friends in the city. Then, too, I go to the Barnetts quite often."

Indeed he did. Except when working at his music, Sullivan was never so happy during his student days as when he was at the home of Clara and Rosamund Barnett. Nor were the Barnetts any less happy to have him. Both girls were madly in love with the curly-headed young man from London. Sullivan, on the other hand, was not half so interested in them as he was in the Sunday evening supper parties given by Mrs. Barnett.

Always fond of food, it took dozens of Mrs. Barnett's jam tarts and three or four pieces of her pie to satisfy Sullivan's appetite. An excellent cook, Mother Barnett was delighted when this satisfactory guest showed that he appreciated her skill by not leaving a single crumb on his plate. Moreover, since she enjoyed the young man's company almost as much as her daughters, she, like so many others, made an exception in his case. It was a rule in the Barnett household that students at the Conservatoire were welcome only on Sunday nights. Sullivan alone, of all Clara's and Rosamund's school chums, was permitted to come to supper any evening he wished.

The Barnett girls were not the only ones who found Arthur Sullivan a most attractive young man. His sense of humor, good looks and pleasing personality made him the most popular date at the Conservatoire. The fact that the Englishman had no money didn't bother the girls a bit. There were free concerts to attend, museums to visit, walks in the country and tea parties galore. Clara Barnett, however, was not content to share Sullivan with anyone else. The trouble was, Arthur enjoyed flirting with Rosamund, while he considered Clara nothing but a child.

"I'll know what I'll do," Clara confided to her mother. "I'll write a string quartet. Then he'll pay some attention to me. Right now, all he thinks about are his music and Rosamund. I'll show him. You wait and see!"

"Go ahead, dear," advised wise Mrs. Barnett. "I know you can do it."

After weeks of struggle, Clara succeeded in finishing her composition. It was the greatest thrill of her life when Sullivan exclaimed, "Well done, little girl!" Clara was so happy she forgave the "little girl"! In her biography, written years later, she said that Sullivan's praise gave her far greater pleasure than any that came to her when critics all over the world acclaimed her voice.

Then one day Sullivan called to take Rosamund to a tea party. Mrs. Barnett informed him that her older daughter was ill. Always gallant and charming, he suggested that perhaps Clara would like to go.

"I think I can," the young lady hesitated. "Mother, have we any plans for this afternoon?"

Smiling at her daughter's technique, Mrs. Barnett replied, "Well, Sister, there's nothing so important that it can't be skipped. You may go if you wish."

Clara was overjoyed. She was to have Arthur all to herself for a whole afternoon! As quickly as possible, she put on her hat and gloves. Mother Barnett called her back, "You had better take a coat, Clara. It may be colder before you come home." Clara rushed into the house. "Darling," she whispered to her mother, "don't you know that this is my opportunity? Why do you make me waste even a single minute? Oh, I know the only reason he is taking me is that there is no one else for him to flirt with, but that isn't going to prevent me from enjoying myself."

At the party, Sullivan was most gracious, paying attention to no one but his companion, and as the two exchanged confidences and small talk, Clara was sure that from now on Sullivan was hers and hers alone.

On the way home, walking hand in hand through the almost deserted streets of Leipzig, Sullivan agreed that it would be wonderful to spend part of the summer vacation at the Barnetts' summer home in Schandu. He promised that he would. Clara could hardly wait to tell her mother and sister the news. "You can have him," Rosamund laughed as she snuggled deeper into the pillows. "I've decided that Arthur is not my type." Now vacation could not come fast enough for Clara!

Everything went according to plan. Sullivan arrived at Schandu bearing a gift for his hostess and affectionate greetings for the two girls. A round of summertime fun began. True to her word, Rosamund made it plain that she was not the least interested in Sullivan. As a result, Clara had him all to herself. Then one day, while leading her idol to a romantic spot, her dreams were shattered. The pair met a party of English tourists, among whom were two extremely pretty Irish colleens. Sullivan immediately lost interest in Clara. She had to go home alone, and in tears.

Yet, within a month, Sullivan again ruled Clara's heart. Back in Leipzig, he set her quartet for four-stringed instruments and, aided by three of his fellow students, played it one Sunday at the Barnett home before the jam tarts and tea were served. Clara, again sure that Arthur was all hers, was extremely happy. Surely the setting of her quartet was proof of his love. The most brilliant and hard-working student at the Conservatoire had taken time to score her composition. Clara was positive that Sullivan's flirting days were over. He loved her and her alone!

Poor Clara! The work on the quartet was nothing but a typical gesture on Sullivan's part. The unhappy girl was forced to spend all of her student life watching him flirt with every newcomer at the Conservatoire. She took it upon herself to warn Madeline Schiller, whom Sullivan was dating quite frequently, that "Arthur can't be true to any girl." Madeline agreed, but said that she didn't mind. "You see, she explained, "I always think of him as the L.G.D."

"What do you mean?" demanded Clara. "L.G.D.?"

"The Little Gay Deceiver!" was the laughing reply.

Busy as he was, flirting with the girls, Sullivan spent most of his time studying. By now his work had so improved that less and less of it was being turned back for rewriting by his teachers. His compositions were featured at the Gewandhaus Concerts and he conducted them in great style. His scholarship was renewed and he worked harder than ever. In addition, the directors of the Conservatoire, knowing the young man from England had barely enough money to cover his food and lodging, excused him from paying certain school fees. There were not enough hours in the day for Sullivan to accomplish all he wished to do. Then, before he knew it, it was time to go home. Before he left Leipzig, he finished his music to *The Tempest* and conducted the piece with great success at a Gewandhaus Concert. Then he said good-by to friends and faculty and set out for London.

Sullivan arrived home in April, 1861, his student days over, but never to be forgotten. After a joyful reunion with his parents, he went to see Sir George Smart. The old master welcomed him, expressed his pleasure and satisfaction at the reports sent from Leipzig, and then asked, "Now, what are your plans?"

There were plenty of plans, but the most important thing was to make a living. Sullivan was on his own now. As much as he liked music, he disliked teaching, yet how else could he make money? So in the *Musical World* of May 11, 1861, appeared the following notice: "Mr. Arthur Sullivan begs to inform his friends that he has returned from Germany. All communications respecting pupils, etc., to be addressed to his residence, 3 Ponsonby Street, Pimlico."

Sullivan waited in vain for pupils while he watched his money vanish. In order to meet his living expenses, he took the post of organist at St. Michael's Church. Careful as he was, the nineteen-year-old musician found that the salary paid him did not provide him with sufficient income. Worried about the future, he turned to his old master, Mr. Helmore, for help. That kindly gentleman offered him an assistantship at the Chapel Royal. Sullivan gratefully accepted the position, but soon found teaching elementary school subjects to the choristers a wearisome task. Bored, he forgot his troubles by turning proverbs upside down and setting them to music: "Policy is the best honesty"—unknowingly training himself for his future collaboration with Gilbert.

Meanwhile, Sullivan became acquainted with most of musical London. Old friends introduced him to new ones. Jenny Lind, the most famous singer of her day, became quite fond of him, and watched over him as if she were his mother. "You work too hard, Arthur," she kept scolding. "You don't eat enough and you worry too much about the future."

Sullivan agreed, but as he had barely enough money to pay his rent, he could not afford to eat heartily. Nor did it look as if he were ever going to have any money. Seeking a means to add to his income, he began to compose popular songs. Most of them were sickly-sweet love ballads, but they delighted Victorians. During this period of his career, he put his name to any composition which he could sell. *O Mistress Mine, The Willow Song* and others of that type brought him the same amount of money as his famous *Orpheus with His Lute*—ten guineas (about $50). Such payment was ridiculously low, but as it never took Sullivan more than an hour or two to compose the words and music to a song, it was an easy way to make a living.

One evening George Grove, secretary of the famous London musical center, the Crystal Palace, attended a concert at St. James Hall. During the intermission he looked over the audience, and turning to his companions, asked, "Who is that engaging young man over there? Do any of you know?" Someone followed the direction of the pointed finger and said carelessly, "Oh, that's Arthur Sullivan. You know, the chap that won the scholarship. He's just back from Leipzig. Would you like to meet him?" Introductions followed, and from that time on, George Grove was Sullivan's friend and constant musical adviser.

"Arthur," said Grove one day, "this business of selling your songs outright must stop. From now on, demand a royalty for every copy sold. You'll get a royalty, never fear, and then your money worries will be over."

Sullivan wasted no time in following Grove's advice. The composer demanded and received a royalty from his publishers. Still there was not enough money coming in to allow him to devote his time to the composition of serious music. Recognizing his protégé as a musical genius, Grove was anxious to help him all he could. With financial difficulties out of the way, chances were that the young man would create something worth-while. So it came about that Grove invited Sullivan to come and live with him.

"It's no favor," Grove insisted. "I've a big house and hate to live alone."

Sullivan gratefully accepted the offer, and for the first time since he had returned from Leipzig was able to begin the task of rewriting the score of *The Tempest*. Free from worry, he worked on his music until two o'clock every morning. Soon the score was finished. Grove immediately made arrangements for the presentation of the composition at the Crystal Palace. Musical London, anxious to hear the first work of the Mendelssohn Scholarship winner, turned out in large numbers. *The Tempest* was a success and had to be repeated. Fame had come to Arthur Sullivan.

At the close of the performance the second night, Charles Dickens came backstage and congratulated Sullivan. A few months later the composer and the novelist went to Paris together. It was a wonderful trip. Dickens knew every street in the French city and made an excellent guide. Sullivan's fame gave the pair an opportunity to meet many well-known singers and composers. The outstanding event of their visit occurred when the young Englishman played *The Tempest* four-handed with the aged Rossini. When they had finished, the composer of *The Barber of Seville* and *William Tell* shook hands with Sullivan and said, "You should try to write a grand opera, my boy." Before long Queen Victoria would suggest the same thing to Arthur Sullivan. On his return to London, the composer decided to take Rossini's advice. Grove was enthusiastic, but too many things interfered with Sullivan's ambition. There was a commission to write ballet music for Covent Garden; Robert Browning, the poet, asked him to set a friend's verses to music; and a trip to Ireland inspired Sullivan to write a symphony. In addition, Sullivan wrote a *Wedding March* for the Princess of Wales, and as a result formed a friendship with the Duke of Edinburgh which was to last a lifetime.

H. F. Chorley, the leading music critic of London, brought Sullivan the book of his light opera entitled *The Sapphire Necklace*. It was an uninspiring work, but he wrote the music for it out of friendship. At last the project was given up. Chorley repaid Sullivan for his work, however. Unable to accept a commission from the promoters of the Birmingham Festival because he had no libretto, Sullivan asked Chorley what he should do. In reply, the critic sat down and produced the book of *Kenilworth, a Masque of the Days of Queen Elizabeth,* based on Scott's novel. The resulting cantata was a great success. There were very few in England now who did not feel that Sullivan was the hope of English music. Then came the performance of his *Symphony in "E" Flat* at the Crystal Palace. Jenny Lind appeared on the program as a favor to her young friend, and Sullivan chalked up another triumph. The Committee of the Norwich Festival requested a composition. Sullivan accepted the commission, but once again was at a loss for an idea.

Try as he would, he could get no inspiration. He walked the streets of London for hours. He sat down at the piano and improvised, wrote long letters to friends in Germany and talked endlessly with Grove. He composed pages and pages of music, played them, tore them up and brooded on his inability to create something worth while. The Norwich Festival was planned for October—September came and he had nothing to show for his hours of toil.

"Don't worry so, Arthur," his father consoled him. "Keep

at it. Something will come along that will give you an idea."

Something did. On September 22, just three days after giving his son this advice, Thomas Sullivan died. Stunned, Arthur Sullivan could not write a note. Then—and Sullivan was always to get inspiration from grief—on the evening of the funeral, the composer sat down at his desk. For the next twelve days he was rarely to leave it. Finally, he finished his work for the Norwich Festival. It was *In Memoriam,* dedicated to his father. Produced on October 30, 1866, the work was very warmly received by the audience. The crowds were so large that Sullivan, who was conducting his own composition, had to pay for the tickets he wished to give his friends. There were no worries about the future now. Sullivan was ready for anything the years might bring.

It was Grove—and Grove was always helping Sullivan —who arranged a meeting between his young friend and Tennyson. The idea was that the Poet Laureate would write a cycle of twelve songs, and Sullivan would set them to music. Composer met poet, and during their talk Tennyson was lectured about the proper rhythm to use! The two set to work. When *The Window, or the Song of the Wrens* was published, it was against Tennyson's wishes. The poet was not pleased with what he had done and he offered Sullivan a large sum not to issue the book. Proud of his association with the Poet Laureate, the composer refused. This caused strained relations between the two men, which ended only when the poet wrote a letter apologizing for his actions. All this unpleasantness was unnecessary, for so few people bought the volume that it was not worth the trouble it caused.

Meanwhile, Arthur Lewis, at whose home it was the delight of artists and royalty to gather in order to produce amateur shows, suggested to Sullivan that the composer and

Frank Burnard write a musical piece for one of the meetings. The two set to work at once. The result was *Cox and Box,* which proved too good for amateur enjoyment alone. Offered to the management of the Adelphi Theater, it was accepted. But there was one difficulty. Sullivan had written out only the melodies. For the original production he had improvised as the performance proceeded. Now a full score was needed.

There was just a week in which to score completely *Cox and Box*—the Adelphi had announced the opening date of the piece. Seven days in which to do a month's work! Sullivan called for two music copyists. As fast as the composer wrote a page, they snatched it from his hands. Sleep was forgotten. The task was finished the morning *Cox and Box* was to be produced; within an hour after the last note was written, the orchestra was in rehearsal!

After a long run at the Adelphi, *Cox and Box* was put on by the German Reeds, who had given Gilbert his first audiences. Reed suggested to Burnard and Sullivan that they try their hand at a longer work. They did and produced *The Contrabandista.* It took them sixteen days to write it, and it ran three months!

There was plenty of money in Arthur Sullivan's pockets now. In celebration, the composer set sail for the Continent. Accompanied by Grove, Sullivan went to Vienna, where the two dug deep into the dusty and musty files of Spina, the music publisher. To their great joy, they discovered forty songs of Schubert that had never been printed, and the lost parts of *Rosamunde.* Young Sullivan and the elderly Grove were so delighted that they actually danced with joy, astonishing everyone by their actions. Then they sat down, completely out of breath, and copied the music that had been lost for sixty years.

The friends went on to Leipzig. Five years had passed

since Sullivan had been to a Gewendhaus Concert. Now he was the main attraction. Before townsfolk, students and members of the Conservatoire faculty, he directed *In Memoriam,* and, as he wrote his mother, "Everyone of note came and congratulated me, and I think it has laid a firm foundation to a good reputation in Germany." After a few days in the city where he had studied, Sullivan and Grove left for Paris and a visit to the Exhibition for which the composer had done much of the music.

All this time he was not neglecting the field of popular songs. In addition, he wrote hymns, anthems and part songs. An invitation to compose a work for the Three Choirs Festival at Worcester, England, in 1869 resulted in his oratorio, *The Prodigal Son.* Sim Reeves, who was to make the work famous, failed to appear the night of the performance, as did Mademoiselle Titiens, who was advertised to sing the other leading role. The substitutes were very poor, but the music was favorably received, and Sullivan was commissioned to write another oratorio for the Festival of 1873.

Then music suddenly became unimportant. Strangely enough, this indifference had its origin in Grove, as did so many of Arthur Sullivan's actions. Grove introduced the composer to Scott Russell, who was not only on the Board of Directors of the Crystal Palace, but also was a noted engineer, the builder of the *Great Eastern,* the most famous steamship of all times. For good measure, he was the father of three extremely beautiful daughters. Always attracted by a pretty girl, Sullivan was immediately drawn to one of the sisters. This was not a flirtation, as in Leipzig, the passing fancy of a summer day while visiting Schandu with the Barnetts, or the devoted affection of a son—this was love.

As was usual in the case of any woman to whom Sullivan was attentive, there was a response. Within a few weeks it was understood among members of Sydenham society that "Sullivan and the Russell girl are engaged." To be sure, there was never a formal announcement of the intended marriage. It was just taken for-granted that the composer and the daughter of one of England's most distinguished families would wed.

Blinded in love as he had been clear-eyed in flirtation, Arthur Sullivan never thought for a moment that anything would happen to prevent his marriage. For that matter, there was no reason for his thinking any such thing. He had, from his days at the Chapel Royal, got along extremely well with those of rank and wealth. So he found nothing but inspiration in this, his first real love. The result was a long list of love songs.

For several years the situation remained unchanged. Then suddenly the understanding between Sullivan and Miss Russell ended. A wandering minstrel was a welcome addition to the music room of a cultured Victorian family, but marriage into such a family was definitely out of the question for a mere minstrel. There was in good Queen Victoria's England a strong feeling that ability was not equal to ancestry.

Sullivan did not have time to suffer over his lost love. The Franco-Prussian War kept the composer busy doing relief work. Her Royal Highness wrote asking for a complete set of his compositions. Socially, Sullivan was more active than ever. He became very friendly with the exiled Empress Eugenie of France and walked with Napoleon the Third, as his father had walked with Napoleon the First. The Prince Consort asked Sullivan to help him correct the errors in the royal attempts to write music. In between these activities, Sullivan composed, conducted and dined with his many friends.

It was a full life. There were so many demands on his time

that he did not know which way to turn. Despite the fact that his health was beginning to suffer because of overwork, Sullivan probably would have continued in the pattern he was following, except for one thing. He decided to work with Gilbert again!

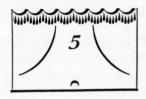

"So Go To Him"

—Patience

FOUR years had passed since Gilbert and Sullivan had joined forces and produced *Thespis*. In that space of time, both men had become famous: Sullivan was now England's greatest composer, Gilbert her best known and most successful dramatic author. Then one day Richard D'Oyly Carte, known to those in the theater as "Oily Carte," a genius in theatrical management, suggested to Gilbert that the partnership be revived. At any other time Gilbert would have refused, but circumstances played into Carte's hands. Resting on Gilbert's desk was the libretto of an extremely funny mock trial the author had developed from a piece furnished for the April 11, 1868 issue of *Fun*. He had originally offered it to Carl Rosa, who had studied with Sullivan at Leipzig, and who was now manager of a troupe which produced operas in English. Rosa was married to Mademoiselle Parepa, the opera star, who had been a friend of the Gilberts for years and for whom the author had done his first professional writing—the translation of the laughing song from *Manon Lescaut,* which the singer had used at the Promenade Concerts. Rosa saw great merit in Gilbert's manuscript and realized it contained an excellent part for his wife. In fact, the operatic impresario liked the libretto so much that he decided to set the piece to music himself. All plans were abandoned when Parepa-Rosa died suddenly, and the manuscript was returned to Gilbert.

Never one to waste anything he had written, the dramatist agreed to Carte's suggestion that the partnership of Gilbert and Sullivan be revived. To be sure, Gilbert was not too happy about the idea of collaborating with Sullivan. The author would have preferred working with Clay or Reed, for his association with the composer had not resulted in a success, and Gilbert despised failures. However, anxious to dispose of his libretto, he consented to team with Sullivan if Carte would make all the arrangements. The manager, who needed a short piece to fill out the program he was offering at the Royalty Theater, lost no time in making an appointment with Sullivan.

Carte had not earned his nickname for nothing. It was not long before his persuasive manner and personal charm had nearly convinced Sullivan that only in Gilbert's manuscript would the composer find an opportunity to utilize his musical skill to its utmost. It was Sullivan's knowledge of Gilbert's temper that prevented him from consenting immediately to Carte's proposition. Memories of the author's biting remarks and tantrums during the production of *Thespis* made Sullivan hesitate to accept Carte's commission. Too much of a gentleman to tell the manager his real reason for refusing, the composer expressed doubts that the proposed work would have any box-office value. "I'm not at all sure that Gilbert and I can write anything as successful as you suggest," Sullivan objected, "I feel that Gilbert and . . ."

"Gilbert and yourself," interrupted Carte, "will become the talk of the theatrical world when this piece is produced. There's no doubt about it, Sullivan, no doubt at all. Your musical talents, combined with Gilbert's ability to write lively, humorous verse, will make an ideal combination. Nor do I think that this is going to be a temporary association. In fact, I'll stake my professional reputation that you two will find a permanent collaboration an ideal arrangement, and will, in time, be considered the outstanding writer-composer team in England!"

Sullivan laughed heartily at Carte's enthusiasm. "Now wait a minute, Carte," he interposed. "I know that no man in London has a better reputation for picking winners in the theatrical world than you have, but really now, don't you think what you're suggesting is rather farfetched?"

"Not a bit," rejoined Carte. "I certainly do not. I think I know what the public wants and I know that you two can supply it. Theater-goers would welcome comedy operas written originally by Englishmen. The public has had enough of importations from France with translations by hack writers. However, I grant that much of what I am talking about lies in the future. Right now the question is: will you write the music for this piece of Gilbert's?"

Still thinking of his previous association with Gilbert, Sullivan refused, but Carte paid no attention to his objections. By the time the manager left the composer's rooms, Sullivan had agreed to Carte's proposal and an appointment had been made for Gilbert to call and to discuss the proposed work. The night the two were to meet, a severe storm blanketed London, but that did not prevent Gilbert from trudging through the snow-packed streets to see Sullivan.

Stomping into the composer's rooms, Gilbert shook the snow from his fur coat, nodded "hello" to his host and growled, "Where do you want me to sit?" Sullivan pointed to an easy chair by the fire. Gilbert strode over to it, reached into his pocket and pulled out a sheaf of tattered paper and sat down. "Are you ready?" he queried. Then, without waiting for a reply, he began to read the libretto of *Trial by Jury*. As he read, his nose wrinkled with disgust at his own words, and he snorted disdainfully at his puns. From time to time he would lift his eyes from the manuscript to scowl at Sullivan as if he were daring his listener to make a comment. As fast as he read a page, he would crumple it into a ball and stuff it behind him. Finally he was finished, and glaring at the composer he snarled, "Well, don't sit there like a store-window dummy! Tell me, what do *you* think of it?"

Once again Sullivan could not answer a question of Gilbert's. This time it wasn't because he didn't know the proper reply; it was because he was doubled up in silent laughter. Never had he heard anything so witty as the libretto Gilbert had just read to him! At last, wiping the tears from his eyes, Sullivan was able to assure the belligerent author that he was positive that together they could produce a sensation. The composer promised Gilbert that he would devote all his time to writing the necessary music and would have it ready soon. Sullivan kept his word, and *Trial by Jury* was in shape for presentation at the Royalty Theater within three weeks of the night that Gilbert paid his call on the composer.

In order to advertise the piece, Carte announced in the Royalty program that there was "In preparation, a New Comic Opera composed for this Theater by Mr. Arthur Sullivan." Both Carte and Sullivan soon found out that this was a mistake. Gilbert, on reading this announcement, stormed into the office of the theater where Carte and Sullivan sat talking. The author loudly berated Carte for omitting his name and accused Sullivan of trying to take all the credit for their joint production. When Gilbert ran out of abuse and breath, Carte managed to convince him that no deliberate oversight was intended, that his name had been omitted due to a printer's error. This error, Carte went on to explain, had been discovered before Gilbert's visit, and next week's program would carry the author's name. Still grumbling, Gilbert stamped out of the theater. Carte rushed a messenger to the printer ordering him to make the necessary addition to the program. The result was another mistake: the author's name appeared as "W. C. Gilbert"! Already angry at the omission of his name, Gilbert was furious on seeing it misspelled. He charged into Carte's office like a wounded elephant. The manager had to close all the doors leading to his office in order to muffle the author's roars, so they would not disturb the audience in the theater. How Carte managed to quiet Gilbert is unknown, but he did. However, by the time the opening night came, Gilbert's name was correctly spelled. Incidentally, Sullivan's name came before Gilbert's on the program, the only time in their entire collaboration that this order was followed.

The audience at the Royalty Theater saw a typical English courtroom when the curtain rose on *Trial by Jury* on the evening of March 25, 1875. A breach of promise case is about to be tried. While waiting for the arrival of the learned judge, the jurymen are flirting with the girls who crowd the courtroom. Their chattering is stopped by a pompous usher who demands, "Silence in Court!" In a solemn manner, the usher warns the jury that they must be absolutely fair during the trial. The defendant, Edwin, who is being sued by Angelina, has, he announces, been "summoned by a stern subpoena" and his side of the case must be heard. Angelina is a sweet, simple girl whose heart has been broken, the usher points out. Then he reminds everyone that Edwin is a ruffian, but warns the jury that:

> *"From bias free of every kind*
> *This trial must be tried!"*

Edwin enters the courtroom and attempts to explain his actions. The jurymen pay no attention to him, but read newspapers during his testimony. The judge then enters and announces:

> *"If the time you'll not begrudge*
> *I'll tell you how I came to be a judge."*

When the judge finishes, the jury is sworn in. At this point Angelina, dressed as a bride, accompanied by bridesmaids, dances into court. The judge gives a note to the usher to deliver to the prettiest of the bridesmaids, but changes his mind and sends it to Angelina instead, for he admits, "Never, never, never, since I joined the human race. Saw I so exquisitely fair a face."

Meanwhile the case continues, Angelina's lawyer calling attention to the fact that his client had been shamefully deserted by Edwin and that it was:

> *". . . doubly criminal to do so,*
> *For the maid had bought her trousseau."*

In order to settle the question of damages, Edwin offers a compromise. Suppose he marries Angelina today and marries his new love tomorrow? At first this seems a solution, but Angelina's counsel, after consulting his law books, announces:

> *"In the reign of James the Second,*
> *It was generally reckoned*
> *As a very serious crime*
> *To marry two wives at one time."*

Nor is Angelina satisfied with Edwin's offer. She insists that she loves no one but he and hopes that the good and kind men of the jury will remember the position he has put her in when:

> *". . . you I'm addressing, are busy assessing*
> *The damages Edwin must pay!"*

There doesn't seem to be any solution to the problem as the lawyers and their clients object to every suggestion the judge makes. At last, losing his temper, the jurist tosses his books and papers into the air and sings:

> *"All the legal furies seize you!*
> *No proposal seems to please you,*
> *I can't stop up here all day,*
> *I must shortly go away.*
> *Barristers, and you, attorneys,*
> *Set out on your homeward journeys;*
> *Gentle, simple-minded usher,*
> *Get you, if you like, to Russher;*
> *Put your briefs upon the shelf,*
> *I will marry her myself!"*

With this announcement the curtain falls.

Trial by Jury was an immediate success. The cantata, originally planned as a curtain raiser, soon became a featured after-piece. Englishmen, who held a fair trial as a fundamental right of all men, laughed heartily at Gilbert's satire on justice and happily hummed Sullivan's tunes. The antics of Frederick Sullivan, the composer's older brother, who played the learned judge, caused even staid members of the bench to smile. To be sure, there were those who complained that Gilbert's plot brought ridicule to the legal profession, but Carte, Gilbert and Sullivan paid no attention to these complaints. Why should they? The theatergoing public was fascinated by *Trial by Jury,* delighting in a chorus which sang "trial at law" instead of "tra la la," and proved it by crowding every performance. Carte had been correct when he had interviewed Sullivan. He did know what people wanted for theatrical entertainment, and Gilbert and Sullivan could furnish it. Now about eighty years old, *Trial by Jury* still makes people laugh and probably will continue to do so forever.

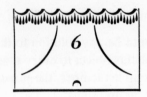

6

"In a World That's All Our Own"

◯

—*Pirates of Penzance*

CARTE, who had forged the links in the chain which bound Gilbert and Sullivan together, was not content with the success of *Trial by Jury*. He knew that this brief skit, written and composed by these two men, outstanding in their chosen fields, was nothing but a sample of what they could create together. In order to make sure that none of his rival managers would secure their services, he put Gilbert and Sullivan under a contract which left them free to engage in any activity they chose, but stipulated that any comic opera composed and written by the pair was to be produced by Carte. Once he had made sure that Gilbert and Sullivan could not write a comic opera for any other manager, Carte, never one to take chances with his own money, set about forming a company to produce any work the collaborators might prepare. It was difficult to secure financial backing, but finally Carte was able to interest some music publishers in his venture. With the money he raised, he formed the Comedy Opera Company and that organization took over the lease of the Opera Comique in 1877. The manager announced his plans to reporters, and theatrical London and the theatergoing public anxiously awaited developments.

There were none. Gilbert and Sullivan had no piece ready for production. Far from it. If they had been allowed to follow their own wishes, they never would have written another comic opera together. The pair had signed Carte's contract as a matter of course; he was responsible for *Trial by Jury,* had lived up to all agreements—but that didn't mean they were going to collaborate. Both Gilbert and Sullivan had other ambitions. They were, as we have seen, successful men in various fields. Why should they risk their reputations writing comic opera? Carte alone realized that Gilbert and Sullivan's great work lay in the future, and that their past triumphs were nothing compared to the fame they could achieve if they specialized in comic opera. While Carte was content that Gilbert and Sullivan should win fame, he wanted some of the money their joint productions would earn. So he kept hounding the pair, asking when they would have a piece ready for the Opera Comique.

"I don't want to write any more libretti," growled Gilbert in answer to Carte's request. "Look what happened when *Trial by Jury* was produced. You left my name out of the program announcement, and then spelled it wrong when you did use it. W. C. Gilbert, indeed! Rest assured, Carte, I don't fancy that middle name of mine, Schwenck, but at least it doesn't begin with a 'C.' Then, too, the critics gave Sullivan all the credit for the success of the peace—all I got was jeers for making fun of the dignity of the British Bar. Moreover, I don't like comic opera, for the music drowns out my words, which are far more important than any tune! No, no more comic opera for me! I want to be remembered for my serious plays, like my dramatization of *Great Expectations,* or my original works such as *Tom Cobb* and *Sweethearts,* for example . . . although I'll grant you can make more money producing comic operas."

Carte felt the author might agree if Sullivan should approach Gilbert tactfully with the suggestion that they begin work on a new production. However, the manager found the composer no more anxious to write comic opera than Gilbert was. Sullivan frankly told Carte that a life spent in writing scores for comic operas had no appeal, but he was more pleasant in refusing the manager's request than his future partner had been.

"You see, Carte," he smiled charmingly, for Sullivan was always charming to important people, "I'm really a very lazy chap. When I feel well, I'm apt to run over to the Continent with one of my friends, like the Duke of Edinburgh, and never think of music. I can, strangely enough, compose only when I am suffering from the stone in my kidney and drugs won't dull the pain—and writing music is so much effort at such times that I would rather spend my time with an overture or something else worth while than with a comic opera."

"I understand perfectly," replied Carte smoothly, "but your work comes so easily—and, after all, you make much more money with a comic opera than with a serious composition and . . ."

"Then, there are my friends," Sullivan broke in. "Most of them seem to feel I am wasting my talents writing light music. Even the Queen, God bless her, who asked me to help her husband, Prince Albert, with his musical endeavors, has hinted that she thinks I should confine myself to themes that will uplift British music. As a matter of fact, I would rather be remembered as a classical composer than anything else. You'll just have to wait until I feel in the mood to collaborate with Gilbert again—though, naturally enough, I won't promise I ever will."

Meanwhile, the stockholders in the Comedy Opera Company were asking Carte when they might expect some return on their investment, and other embarrassing questions.

Fearful that his backers might withdraw, Carte tried harder than ever to get Gilbert and Sullivan to agree to write another comic opera together. It was not long before he wished Gilbert's ambitions to be a serious dramatist and Sullivan's friends among the royal family were at the bottom of the English Channel! Daily, for two and a half years, Carte either spoke or wrote to Gilbert and Sullivan, begging them to consider his proposition. During this time, Sullivan became Principal of the National Training School of Music and received the honorary degree of Doctor of Music from the University of Cambridge. When not engaged in teaching, he toured England from one end to the other, conducting orchestras. As he traveled, the composer was not idle, but filled his time by writing more sticky love songs for the romantic-minded piano-playing maids of the day. There were times, however, when he was tempted to listen to Carte's frantic pleas.

All thoughts of working with Gilbert vanished, however, when his brother Fred, who had made such a success in *Trial by Jury*, fell ill. Arthur Sullivan, who loved his family greatly, gave up all his engagements to sit beside Fred's bed. For three weeks, Sullivan waited for the end. It was soon apparent that death would release the composer from his vigil. One night he happened to pick up a book of poems to help him pass the long hours until morning. One verse greatly appealed to him as he kept watch over his brother. He set it to music. When dawn broke, he had finished his task—the music for *The Lost Chord*, a song which rates a place on any "All-Time Hit Parade." Musical experts agree it is one of the six most popular songs ever written.

It was Sullivan's lifelong friend, Mrs. Pierre Ronalds, one of the most famous beauties of the Victorian Age, who made the song popular when it was first published. This American woman, whose love of England was so great that she separated from her husband because he refused to live there, had been introduced to London society by the exiled Empress Eugenie of France. Mrs. Ronalds' personality charmed everyone, even imperious Victoria. The Queen overlooked the fact that Mrs. Ronalds had left her husband, and granted the Boston belle a private audience—and, what is more, *stood* for an hour chatting with her! Sullivan's introduction to this beautiful woman and singer of great ability came from the Duke of Edinburgh. Immediately the composer and "the permanent ambassadress of the United States at the Court of St. James" became fast friends. The pair met daily if Sullivan were in town. If he were out of London, Sullivan wrote or telegraphed Mrs. Ronalds every day.

On Sundays, at her charming house at No. 7 Cadogan Place, Mrs. Ronalds held a *salon* which was attended by society, members of royalty, and famous artists. It was at one of these gatherings that the beauty from Boston's Beacon Hill sang *The Lost Chord,* and the Prince of Wales summed up the feeling of her listeners when he said, "I would walk the entire length of the British Empire to hear Mrs. Ronalds sing that song." Royalty's opinion was backed up by a rush of commoners to the music shops to buy copies of the sheet music.

Years later, in Sullivan's drawing room, before a gathering of musical greats and the cream of London society, the first phonograph record ever played in England was heard. It was the sweet voice of Mary Ronalds singing *The Lost Chord.* Sullivan, incidentally, gave the song's best singer the original manuscript, and when she died, Mrs. Ronalds' will directed that it be buried with her.

For weeks after his brother's death, Sullivan was unable to do any composing. He refused all professional engagements and did not leave his rooms even to take a walk. Friends tried to convince him that brooding over Fred's death was undermining his own health, but he paid no attention. Staying in his study, the composer did very little but cry—and answer letters from C. L. Dodgson (Lewis Carroll), who was trying to interest him in writing a score for a dramatization of *Alice in Wonderland.* Sullivan offered his correspondent one excuse after another, and finally bluntly informed the great mathematician that he wasn't the least bit interested in writing the music Dodgson's play required.

Meanwhile, Gilbert, weary of Carte's continual prodding, had consented to write a libretto for use by the Comedy Opera Company. Never one to hesitate in borrowing ideas from anyone, including himself, Gilbert decided to use a story he had written for a magazine many years before and transform it into a full-length opera. The original story, *An Elixir of Love,* was one of the dozens he had dashed off in the days when he was writing as much verse and prose as possible in order to earn the money he needed to set up housekeeping. As might be expected, *An Elixir of Love* was an upside-down tale and had for its central idea a theme that was very dear to Gilbert—the use of a love-philtre. Once Gilbert had agreed to furnish Carte with a work, the manager spent all his time trying to convince Sullivan to join his former collaborator. Carte was successful, and by the time Gilbert had the piece ready for the scoring, Sullivan was actually anxious to begin his share of the work. He was still suffering from the shock of his brother's death and found it extremely difficult to get into the routine of composition. For a time it was impossible for him to write the music of a single song. The musician would have given up the commission if there had been any need for an early delivery of the score, but there wasn't—Gilbert and Carte were engaged in the first of a long series of heated discussions about the actors who would play the various parts, and the best method of producing the opera. As a result, Sullivan had ample time to compose his music.

It made no difference to Gilbert that Carte was considered one of the most capable theatrical managers in England. The author had very definite ideas about stage direction and play production, and refused to allow Carte to offer even a suggestion. Gilbert wasted no time in making his viewpoint clear to Carte, who was worn out between the demands of his backers, Sullivan's inability to compose, and Gilbert's temper. One argument followed another, and it was not long before Carte realized that so far as Gilbert was concerned, all the manager had to do was to confine his activities to business matters—the author would take care of everything else.

Asked by Carte whom he was planning to star, Gilbert replied, "There aren't going to be any stars in this company, and I wish I didn't have to have a tenor. Tenors can never act, and they are the curse of light opera. I'm going to put George Grossmith in the leading part—oh yes, I know all he has ever done professionally is to give drawing-room shows and entertain Y.M.C.A. gatherings, but he's the man I want."

"Grossmith!" exploded Carte. "What are you thinking of, Gilbert? I won't stand for it!"

"Then sit down and I'll tell you a few things. Who is writing this opera, who is directing it, who is designing the costumes and the scenery? I am! So you stick to the business end of the production, let Sullivan confine himself to his music, and I'll run things otherwise. By the way, you might as well hear this now as later. I'm giving Rutland Barrington the part of the vicar."

"Barrington! Why, he can't even sing!"

"That's not important. Barrington is a great big hulk of a man who never thinks for himself and will do whatever I order without asking a single question—my idea of a perfect actor. Moreover, he ought to make an excellent vicar, he's the son of a churchman!"

"Perfect actor indeed! What's being the son of—well, at least you'll let me have something to say about the chorus. After all, I've studied music, written songs and operettas, and feel that Sullivan and myself . . ."

"Can stay out of it," interjected Gilbert. "I don't want trained singers. I want amateurs who can be turned into professionals, not professionals who act like amateurs."

Gilbert absolutely refused to listen to a single suggestion offered by Carte. Feeling that Sullivan would support him in his contest with Gilbert, Carte went to the composer and asked him for help. The manager told Sullivan all that had happened and suggested that Sullivan should insist that the author leave the hiring of the chorus to others. Sullivan listened to Carte, but refused to help him. Secretly the composer welcomed the idea of Gilbert choosing the ladies and gentlemen of the chorus, for it would save him many a weary hour of listening to auditions.

"I am in no physical condition to battle with Gilbert," Sullivan explained. "My dear brother's death seems to have dulled my brain. I never could find answers to Gilbert's cutting remarks—even if I wanted to. No, Carte, I'm afraid you'll have to give in to his demands, or fight him alone. I simply can't help you."

Even if Sullivan had been in excellent physical condition, he knew that he was no match for Gilbert. The composer recalled, all too well, the reply of the dramatist to one of the principal actors in *Thespis*, who, on being corrected, attempted to put Gilbert in his place by saying, "I, sir, am not a member of the chorus!" "No," Gilbert had snapped in reply, "you are not, but you would be if your voice were strong enough!" Sullivan also remembered the time when one of the ladies in the chorus had complained to Gilbert that one of the men in the company had put an arm around her and called her, "a dear, little thing." Quickly Gilbert had replied, "Don't give the incident another thought, he really couldn't have meant it!" With memories like these, it was no wonder that Sullivan was perfectly willing to confine himself to his music and let Carte fight Gilbert without his help.

It was not long before Carte realized that Gilbert was a master of stagecraft and decided that perhaps it was best, after all, to leave the details of the production to him. Meanwhile, there were matters which Carte alone could handle, so he set to work. First, he had to convince his backers in the Comedy Opera Company that Gilbert's judgment in casting Grossmith and Barrington was excellent! Then there was the problem of hiring a theater, and after much consideration, Carte took a lease on the Opera Comique. The question of choosing a name for the opera was settled in a conference attended by Gilbert, Sullivan and Carte. It was decided to call the work *The Sorcerer,* as one of the leading characters was John Wellington Wells, the head of the "firm of J. W. Wells and Company, the old-established sorcerers in St. Mary Axe." At last, all was ready, and on the evening of November 17, 1877, the curtain went up on what Carte had advertised as "An Entirely Original Modern Comic Opera."

The Sorcerer opens with all the tenants and friends of Sir Marmaduke Pointdextre gathered on the lawn of Sir Marmaduke's mansion to witness the marriage of His Lordship's son, Alexis, to the beautiful Aline, daughter of Lady Sangazure. Everyone is delighted at the marriage and all are happy except Constance, daughter of Mrs. Partlett, the pew-opener of the village church. For Constance is in love with the village vicar, Dr. Daley, who considers her nothing but a child, even though Mrs. Partlett insists that she has grown up. The vicar refuses to pay any attention to the mother's statements, however.

Once Alexis and Aline are married, Alexis tells his new wife that he has some very definite ideas about marriage. People, he says, should marry only for love and not because of social position, wealth, or because they are the same age. In order to test this theory, he hires Wells to brew a teapot-ful of "patented Oxy-Hydrogen Love-at-first-sight Philtre" and serve at least one cup of this drink to all the wedding guests at the reception.

Wells does as he was ordered and everyone falls into a drugged sleep lasting twelve hours. When they awake, the philtre begins to work immediately. Men and women fall in love with the first person of the opposite sex they see. As a result, Sir Marmaduke swears devotion to old Mrs. Partlett. Dr. Daley and Aline find themselves madly in love, Constance and the notary who drew up the marriage contract are greatly attached to each other, while Lady Sangazure insists that Wells marry her. Frantic, Alexis asks Wells to undo the damage his love potion has caused. The sorcerer explains that the only way to break the spell is for Wells to sacrifice himself to the great god Ahrimanes. After some natural hesitation, the man of magic weaves a spell and vanishes in a cloud of smoke and brilliant flame—and immediately the villagers and guests are freed from the charm. They then pair off properly and the curtain falls as all enjoy the gay wedding festival.

Sullivan had not been too sure that the work was going to be a hit. Only a few days before the opening night he had written, "I am putting the last few bars to my opera, and tomorrow begin the scoring. I have been slaving at this work, and I hope it will be a success. Everything at present promises very well. The book is brilliant, and the music I think very pretty and good. All the company are good and like it very much."

The composer need not have worried. Not only did the magic elixir of John Wellington Wells, the "dealer in magic and spells," influence the company on the stage, but infected the audience, and all London was charmed. To be sure, during its run of six months, there were times when business was bad. Carte's fellow directors of the Comedy Opera Company wanted to end the run of *The Sorcerer;* but the astute manager knew that they had a good thing and insisted on keeping the piece running. After much discussion, the directors agreed. *The Sorcerer* was played until May 22, 1878, a total of 175 performances, and it made a profit.

Thanks to Carte's judgment, everyone was happy, the librettist, the composer, the directorate of the Comedy Opera Company, and the members of the cast who didn't have to worry about an engagement for a whole theatrical season. But, above all, the theatergoing public was overjoyed. In *The Sorcerer* they had found wit and humor, gay and sparkling tunes, excellent direction, and a superior company of actors.

The approval of Gilbert and Sullivan's light opera marked the beginning of one of the most important chapters in the history of the theater. In *The Sorcerer* the partners had discovered a formula that they would use successfully for years. In all their works they would give to their audiences a young couple in love, a pair of elderly folk and a comic character. They would then place them in fairylike surroundings and make them say clever things to delightful music. The new pattern they had cut was just the style the public wanted, and they could and would give it to them. Forgotten for the time being were classical composition and the writing of serious dramas—the world of Topsy-turvy-dom had been discovered, and Gilbert and Sullivan meant to mine all its riches.

Flushed with success, Sullivan went to Paris, where his joy in travel and association with important people was slightly marred by almost daily reports from Carte that the directors of the Comedy Opera Company wanted to close the Opera Comique, and what the manager was doing to keep the theater open. Sullivan's worries about the future vanished, however, when the postman brought him a bulky envelope. On opening it, the composer found the script of Gilbert's *H. M. S. Pinafore*. Included was a brief note in which the author expressed the hope that Sullivan would find the work of interest.

Sullivan was enthusiastic when he finished reading his partner's libretto. Losing no time, he immediately began to write music for the piece, despite the fact that he was suffering terribly from his backaches and at times fainted with pain, as he sat at his desk. However, he was able to compose a breezy score to launch Gilbert's ship, and rehearsals got under way at the Opera Comique.

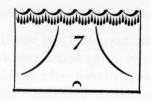

"That Infernal Nonsense Pinafore"

—*Pirates of Penzance*

Pinafore has its origin in three places: The *Bab Ballads,* Gilbert's knowledge of the sea and ships, and a children's book written by Dr. Gilbert (one of those illustrated by his son), called *The King's Middy.* Of the three sources, the *Bab Ballads,* many of which were about the sea and sailors, furnished most of the material on which the opera was based. Gilbert, always stealing from himself, used ten of the ballads in writing *Pinafore.*

The main idea of *H. M. S. Pinafore, or The Lass That Loved a Sailor—An Entirely Original Nautical Comic Opera in Two Acts,* as the piece was announced on the opening night, came from the pages of *Fun*:

> "Kind hearted Captain Reece, *R. N.*
> *Was quite devoted to his men,"*

a typical Gilbertian verse which told how Captain Reece of the Royal Navy supplied feather beds, warm slippers and hot water bottles to his crew, and hired a valet to take care of their uniforms. The poem related in great detail how the captain, anxious to do all in his power to make his men

70

happy and contented, asked the tars if there was anything they desired. One of the sailors offered the opinion that it would be very friendly-like if Captain Reece's "ten female cousins and a niece, six sisters and an aunt or two" could be united to "unmarried members of the crew." The good captain agreed that it would and arranged the weddings at once. Moreover, he took for his own wife the widowed mother of his coxswain—an elderly woman who made her living doing washing for the ship's officers.

This was Topsy-turvydom at its best, and Gilbert made the most of it. With his verse about Reece as a basis, all he had to do to make a full-length opera was to lift some characters from other *Bab Ballads,* add the young couple in love demanded by light opera tradition, and use the recent appointment of W. H. Smith, a publisher, to the position of First Lord of the Admiralty, as part of the plot. Mr. Smith, an excellent businessman, knew nothing about ships, the sea or sailors, and there was something Gilbertian about the fleet of the world's greatest sea power being commanded by a man who had absolutely no knowledge of naval affairs!

In its final form, the story told in *Pinafore* is merely the same tale presented in *The Sorcerer.* The only real difference is in the setting. Instead of watching the village folk of Ploverleigh, the audience sees what happens on the decks of a ship named after the low-necked, sleeveless apron that was so popular for children in the days of Queen Victoria.

When the curtain rises, showing *H. M. S. Pinafore* tied up in Portsmouth Harbor, we learn that Josephine, the beautiful daughter of Captain Corcoran, commander of the vessel, has fallen in love with handsome Ralph Rackstraw, a foremast hand. Josephine, a proud and haughty beauty, promises her father that she will never let Ralph know that he has won her heart. After all, Ralph is nothing but a common sailor, while Josephine is a captain's daughter! Captain

Corcoran is delighted with Josephine's attitude, for Sir Joseph Porter, First Lord of the Admiralty, has asked his permission to seek her hand in marriage.

Despite her promise never to let Ralph know how much she loves him, Josephine cannot forget him. She pays little attention to the pompous Sir Joseph, who goes about his duties surrounded by "his sisters and his cousins and his aunts." The First Lord, thinking Josephine is awed by his superior position, assures her that she need have no fears, for "love levels all rank." This statement is all that Josephine needs to hear in order to follow the dictates of her heart. She rushes to Ralph and tells him that now that Sir Joseph has officially announced that love should know no barriers caused by rank or wealth, she cannot hide her feelings. Overjoyed, Ralph takes Josephine in his arms and they make plans to elope that very night. Ugly Dick Deadeye, the mate of the *Pinafore,* overhears their plot and immediately reports their plans to Captain Corcoran. In a furious rage, the captain rushes on deck in time to prevent the elopement, and in his anger says, "damme," an oath which so shocks Sir Joseph that Corcoran is ordered to his cabin in disgrace. Ralph, brave sailor that he is, frankly tells the First Lord that he loves Josephine and she loves him. Now the easily-shocked ruler of the Queen's navy loses *his* temper and commands that Ralph be placed in a dungeon cell under a marine guard.

While all this excitement is taking place, Little Buttercup, a bumboat woman, who sells "sugar and 'baccy" to the sailors, has been on board. She stops Sir Joseph and informs him that when she was "young and charming" she "practised baby farming" and during this time she was given two tiny babies to rear. One was of noble birth, the other a commoner. Little Buttercup tearfully confesses to Sir Joseph that she mixed the babies up, and the truth is, Ralph is really the captain, and the captain is really Ralph. On hearing this, the First Lord orders Ralph and Corcoran to exchange ranks. Now that he is a captain in the Royal Navy, Ralph is free to marry Josephine. Sir Joseph is no longer interested in the young lady, for while he feels that "love levels all rank," it doesn't lower his enough to marry a common sailor's daughter! The First Lord decides to marry Hebe, one of his cousins. Corcoran proposes to Little Buttercup, as the curtain falls on the entire cast singing:

> *"For he is an Englishman,*
> *And he himself hath said it,*
> *And it's greatly to his credit*
> *That he is an Englishman!*
> *But in spite of all temptations,*
> *To belong to other nations,*
> *He remains an Englishman!"*

In *Pinafore* Gilbert and Sullivan are at their best. The audience is asked to believe that two babies are exchanged in the cradle and, years later, when their paths cross, one has a daughter old enough for the other to marry—and the audience does so without any question! For as we watch the antics of the folk who appear on the *Pinafore*'s decks, they do not seem fantastic and strange; all we are conscious of are Gilbert's extremely funny lines and Sullivan's entrancing music. Incidentally, to those who know music well, the score of *Pinafore* is as much a burlesque on the traditional techniques of the writers of Italian opera as the plot is a satire on the most sacred thing in England—the Royal Navy.

Long before the opening night of *Pinafore*, May 25, 1878, it was impossible to secure a seat at the Opera Comique. Those who had heard and seen *The Sorcerer* and *Trial by Jury,* which was all London, were most anxious to see Gilbert and Sullivan's new work. The fortunate ticket-holders who packed the theater were delighted with *Pinafore*. They laughed heartily at Gilbert's puns and jokes and left the Opera Comique whistling and humming Sullivan's tunes. Naval men, annoyed at the fact that the opera made fun of Her Majesty's fleet, had to admit that every rope in the rigging of the *Pinafore* was correctly hung, and that the sailors' costumes were perfect in every detail. It was no wonder. Gilbert had spent several weeks on board Nelson's famous flagship, the *Victory,* which was tied up in Portsmouth. With permission of naval authorities, the author had made careful drawings of every detail of the quarter-deck. From the drawings he reproduced the famous man-of-war, first in a small model, and finally as a stage set. As for the sailors' costumes—there had been no possible chance of an error—Gilbert had ordered them made at the same establishment that made uniforms for the British Navy. Yet, despite the first night success, *Pinafore* almost sank as soon as it was launched.

It wasn't the fault of the opera or the players—it was the weather. London was experiencing one of the hottest summers in its history. No one wished to go to the theater in the unbearable heat. . . . Victorians did not enjoy the benefits of air conditioning! The Comedy Opera Company seemed doomed. Ticket sales at the box office dwindled to almost nothing. Carte's fellow directors, as always, lacking faith in the manager's judgment, wanted to close the Opera Comique. Carte argued that *Pinafore* had been favorably received by both critics and the public and once the weather turned cooler, the opera would play to capacity audiences. During the conference held to decide whether to put *Pinafore* into drydock or not, a delegation representing the members of the cast entered Carte's office. Anxious to keep their jobs, the players offered to help keep Gilbert and Sullivan's boat afloat by taking a one-third reduction in salary. As the members of the chorus were only getting the equivalent of $12.50 a week, this was no small sacrifice. Moreover, it was a great tribute to Gilbert, who had worked them unmercifully, that they wished to remain under his direction.

For they were definitely under Gilbert's direction. The author never let any member of the cast think or act for himself. To Gilbert, actors and actresses were mere puppets, and he alone had the ability to pull the strings. Every gesture they made, every step they took, had been Gilbert's idea. With the aid of the model he had made from his drawings of the *Victory,* and with blocks of wood of different colors, representing principals and chorus, he had carefully worked out all the stage "business." For hours Gilbert had arranged and rearranged the two-and-one-half inch blocks, representing the ladies of the company, and the three-inch tall blocks, representing the men. Let anyone else dare to have ideas on how the cast should be placed in the various scenes!

Few dared. Only rarely did an actor find courage enough to express his own opinions. One old-timer, who thought Gilbert's suggestions as to where to stand were wrong, leaned over the footlights and said, "Mr. Gilbert, I think you are wrong. I have been on the stage quite long enough . . ."

"Quite," snapped Gilbert, interrupting him, "you certainly have!" and fired the suggestion maker immediately.

Gilbert's tongue was always lashing somebody or something. His wit was never still. During a rehearsal of *Pinafore,* Gilbert told Barrington, who was playing Captain Corcoran, to "walk slowly toward left stage, then sit on the skylight pensively."

Barrington, who was Gilbert's idea of a perfect actor because he never had an idea of his own how a part should be played, followed instructions. The skylight, not strong enough to support Barrington's one hundred and eighty-five pounds, collapsed.

"My good fellow," screamed Gilbert, "I said pensively, not *ex*pensively!"

During one rehearsal, no matter how many times he instructed the crew and Sir Joseph's sisters, cousins and aunts on the proper method of arranging themselves in groups of twos, Gilbert found that one sailor always ended up with a girl on each arm.

"NO-NO-NO!" Gilbert bellowed. "Can't you do anything correctly? Look, two ladies and one man make THREE! I WANT TWOS! You can, I trust, count? Very well, then, let's try it again."

The chorus went through the action once more, and again, because one of the sailors was missing from the rehearsal, ended their evolutions with the same result: there were two girls paired off with one man. Gilbert jumped out of his seat in the first row and made for the stage, waving his arms in the air. Before he could reach the unfortunate members of the cast who expected to be pommeled by their irate director, Richard Barker, the stage manager, managed to explain to Gilbert that because one chorister was missing, it was impossible to secure the grouping desired. At once Gilbert was pacified. Turning to the badly frightened chorusman who had a girl on each arm, Gilbert smiled and apologized, "Now I see what the trouble is. You've just come into port after a long voyage and couldn't wait to see all your lady friends! Barker, if our crew is incomplete, I suggest you send out a press gang."

Gilbert alone was allowed to make jokes as the rehearsals for *Pinafore* proceeded, and there were strict rules to be followed by all who associated with him. Julia Gwynne, who was in time to rise from the chorus of *Pinafore* to the position of leading lady in many of the later operas, recalled that once during a lull in rehearsal she was standing with the rest of Sir Joseph's cousins, when Barker called her to his desk. "Gwynne," he accused, "I just saw you smiling. What have you got to say?"

"Smiling, sir?" stammered the singer nervously. "I don't think so. It must have been my usual pleasant expression you saw."

"No doubt it was," replied the stage manager. "I noticed that expression. You're fined a half-crown for laughing during a rehearsal!"

In his own quiet way, Sullivan demanded as strict attention to details as did Gilbert. Sullivan asked for, and got, as firm a discipline as his collaborator, but he was usually more considerate of the cast. If a member of the chorus went off key, the composer would stop the rehearsal and make the offender repeat as a solo the note on which he had gone astray. He did not bully the singer, but made it plain that the correction had been made in an impersonal manner. Sullivan could, however, be as cutting as Gilbert. Once, when Grossmith finished a solo, Sullivan got up from the piano and applauded. Grossmith was delighted until he heard what Sullivan was saying, "A wonderful tune, my boy. Now, would you mind trying mine?"

Then there was the incident during a full rehearsal. George Powers, who was playing the part of Ralph Rackstraw, confirmed Gilbert's opinion of tenors and lingered over-long on a high note. Sullivan tapped his baton on the stand, stopping the orchestra and tartly remarked, "That's a fine note, Powers, but please don't mistake your voice for my composition!"

Despite the verbal blows of the librettist and composer, the players at the Opera Comique were extremely happy in their association with the Comedy Opera Company. That is why when it was rumored that Pinafore was to be taken off the stage and the company dissolved, they offered to work for less money in hopes of saving their engagement. The money they contributed did little to help meet expenses, however. The temperature went higher and higher and ticket sales went lower and lower. No one was surprised when the notice that *Pinafore* was to close in two weeks was posted on the call-board backstage. Then Sullivan, who was conducting the Promenade Concerts, made an arrangement of *Pinafore* music and included it on one of his programs. Those who heard the tunes enjoyed them greatly. Anxious to hear more of Sullivan's music, many of them braved the heat and went to the Opera Comique. Overnight the weather turned cooler, and more and more people went to see *Pinafore*. The closing notice was taken down, and as August drew to an end, Gilbert and Sullivan's opera was one of the greatest hits in the history of the English theater.

Still the good ship was not sailing smooth seas. Carte, weary of the constant conflicts with his co-directors and sure that in Gilbert and Sullivan he had a chance to make a fortune (which he did not wish to share with anyone), decided to dissolve the Comedy Opera Company. Both Gilbert and Sullivan encouraged him. They, too, were tired of the methods of Carte's backers. After much negotiation, it was settled that when the company's lease on the Opera Comique ran out, Carte would pay off his fellow-directors, and Gilbert and Sullivan would be under his sole management.

There was another matter that demanded attention. America had gone *Pinafore* mad. In New York City alone, eight theaters within five blocks of each other were playing the opera. Hurdy-gurdies tinkled Sullivan's tunes in the streets of every American town. Managers were putting on *Pinafore* with crews composed of Chinese, Indians, Negroes, church choirs, college glee clubs, amateurs, all-girls and children. There were dozens of parodies: *His Mud Scow*

Pinafore, T.P.S. Pinafore, H—ear M-e S-hout Pinafore or the Girl Who Sassed a Sailor and *H.M.S. Needlefore, or The Lass Who Loved a Tailor,* to name but a few. It was even being played in German (*Ihrer Majestat Schiff Pinafore*), and the thousands of New Yorkers who were of German origin were delighted with *Gennant Butterblum.*

As there was no copyright agreement between England and America, Gilbert and Sullivan, to say nothing of Carte, received no royalties from any production of *Pinafore* in the United States. Music publishers were making fortunes by the simple means of having an agent send them one of the scores printed in London, reprinting it without credit, selling thousands of copies. Carte, too good a businessman to allow a situation of this nature to continue, sailed for America in early July, 1879. He would, he assured Gilbert and Sullivan, do something about the pirates who were scuttling the good ship *Pinafore.*

Carte left Michael Gunn in charge at the Opera Comique, confident that his assistant was capable of handling anything that might arise until his return. It was only a matter of a few weeks before the lease on the theater would expire and all arrangements were complete for the transfer of the Comedy Opera Company's properties to the new organization. Carte was barely on the high seas when the directors, who by now realized that they were giving up a very profitable enterprise, dismissed Gunn. They also announced that D'Oyly Carte was no longer manager of the theater and went to court to make their actions legal. Their demands were denied. Still they refused to abandon the ship. On the last night of the lease, July 31, 1879, the 374th performance of *Pinafore,* a mob of fifty thugs, hired by the directors, stormed into the theater through the stage door, intent on stopping the show and carrying off the scenery and stage "props."

The appearance of the thugs caused a riot to break out backstage. Soon it was impossible for the audience to hear the performance because of the noise. Sir Joseph's sisters, cousins and aunts, waiting in the wings to make their entrance, fled screaming to the safety of their dressing rooms. The crew of the *Pinafore* tried vainly to repel the boarders, aided by the stage hands. Alfred Cellier, who had been a fellow student with Sullivan at the Chapel Royal and who was conducting the opera, tried to quiet the audience. Some were fleeing to the exits, while others were standing in their chairs in order to get a better view. Someone yelled "Fire!" and the panic might have been worse if George Grossmith hadn't gone before the curtain and frankly explained what was happening. Grossmith could hardly be heard, for the battle on the decks of the *Pinafore* was getting more violent every minute. Barker, the stage manager, was thrown down a flight of stone steps. The actress playing Little Buttercup used her natural stoutness and her padding to block one of the doors. Finally, the extras who played the marines turned the tide. They were forcing the roughnecks from the premises with the bayonets they used to guard Ralph as they marched him off to the dungeon cell when the police arrived. Quiet was restored and the performance went on, ending with an after-piece called, appropriately enough, *After All!*

The following Monday, Gunn, the former directors of the Comedy Opera Company, the marines and all the rest were in the Bow Street Police Court. Charged with assaulting Barker and creating a disturbance, the directors offered a very poor defense. The judge found them guilty and went on to say that in his considered opinion the whole affair was a deliberate attempt to rob Carte, Gilbert and Sullivan of their property.

Carte's former partners, smarting from the verbal thrashing given them by the judge and wishing they were getting the $2500 weekly that had been their share of the profits of *Pinafore* (they had each, originally, only advanced that amount), were determined to save something from their sinking ship, so they offered their own version of *Pinafore* in a theater next to the Opera Comique.

Gilbert and Sullivan immediately placed the following notice in all the London papers:

"In face of the fact that our opera, *H. M. S. Pinafore,* is being played at another London theatre, we, as the author and composer respectively of the above-mentioned opera, feel it due to ourselves and to the Company of the Opera Comique to state that the performances at the Opera Comique are conducted by artists, operatic, dramatic and orchestral, who were selected by us for the purpose of representation, and whose exertions have contributed so largely to the exceptional success of the Opera: that the Opera as performed by the Opera Comique is, and always has been personally superintended and sanctioned by us in every detail; that we have superintended the rehearsals of no other London Company whatsoever; and that the Opera represented at the Opera Comique is played with our entire concurrence and approval."

This statement, plus the fact that the production offered by the former directors of the Comedy Opera Company was a very ragged one, was enough to sink the rival craft. Meanwhile, the "Pinafore Riot," as it was called, proved to be an excellent advertisement, and it became more difficult than ever to secure seats for any performance at the Opera Comique. Carte had returned from America by this time. The manager told Gilbert and Sullivan just what was happening overseas and suggested that the partners, Cellier and some of the leading players of the Opera Comique Company go to America and put on an authorized version of *Pinafore*.

Gilbert thought this an excellent idea. "I will not have another libretto of mine produced if American managers are going to steal it," he thundered. "It's not that I need the money so much, but it upsets my digestion." Sullivan, always happy when traveling, was willing to go, but he was in very poor health. The operation he had had two years previously had done little to improve his condition. All during the writing of his music for *Pinafore,* the composer had been in agony. "Never," he had written, "was music composed under such distressing conditions." It was not like Sullivan to complain, so the pain he was suffering must have been exceptionally severe. All his life he was tormented by the ache in his back and found comfort only when he took morphine. Another operation, undergone shortly after the "Pinafore Riot," brought him temporary relief, and after a period of rest, he felt equal to the journey across the Atlantic.

It was early in the morning of November 5, 1879, that the *Bothnia* docked in New York, with Gilbert, Sullivan, and some of the *Pinafore*'s crew on board. Despite the fact that both the composer and author were excellent sailors, Gilbert owning his own yacht and Sullivan cruising constantly with rich friends and members of the royal family, they had both suffered from seasickness on the voyage. As a matter of fact, the *Bothnia* had had an exceptionally rough trip. When he felt more like himself, Gilbert remarked that a mistake had been made and evidently "Britannia did *not* rule the waves!"

Waiting for Gilbert and Sullivan to land was Fred Clay, who had introduced them. Clay greeted the partners warmly

Cover of musical score of **H. M. S.** Pinafore, *by Gilbert and Sullivan*

Sir W. S. Gilbert

Sir Arthur Sullivan

Mr. Richard D'Oyly Carte

Souvenir programs for Princess Ida *and* The Mikado *for*
D'Oyly Carte's Savoy Theatre

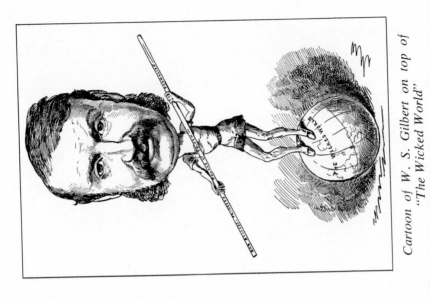

Cartoon of W. S. Gilbert on top of
"The Wicked World"

"I Never Saw That Pin-afore."

One of the many American cartoons
popularizing Pinafore

Henry Lytton as Gama in Princess Ida

Leo Sheffield as the Grand Inquisitor in The Gondoliers

HOLLIS ST. THEATRE

ISAAC B RICH
PROPRIETOR
&
MANAGER.

View of Ladies'
Reception Room.

Program cover for a performance of The Mikado at the
Hollis St. Theatre in Boston for Monday, February 22,
1886, showing Ladies' Reception Room

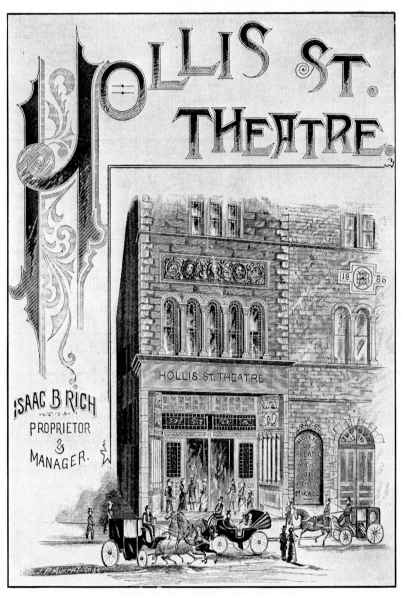

*Program cover showing exterior of the Hollis St. Theatre
where Gilbert and Sullivan played for weeks on end*

STANDARD
THEATRE.

FIRST PRODUCTION IN THIS CITY

Of an Entirely New and Original Nautical Comic Opera,

H. M. S.

PINAFORE

COMPOSED BY ARTHUR SULLIVAN.
WRITTEN BY W. S. GILBERT.

*ORIGINALLY PRODUCED AT THE "OPERA COMIQUE," LONDON, LAST MAY, AND
WHERE IT IS NOW ENJOYING A MOST PROSPEROUS RUN, HAVING
ALREADY BEEN PLAYED NEARLY*

Three Hundred Consecutive Nights.

A. S. SEER, Theatrical Printer, 26 Union Square, New York.

*Cover of program for the first "legitimate" production of
H. M. S. Pinafore in New York. Original is from the fascinating Gilbert and Sullivan collection of the author*

Cover for music for The Pirates of Penzance *Quadrille*

At 8, a New and Original Vaudeville,
By FRANK DESPREZ,
Music by EATON FANING,
called

MOCK TURTLES

Mr. Wranglebury ... ... Mr. C. POUNDS
Mrs. Wranglebury ... ... Miss MINNA LOUIS
Mrs. Bowcher ... ... Miss BRANDRAM
Jane ... ... Miss SYBIL GREY

✸✸✸✸✸✸✸✸✸✸✸✸✸✸✸✸

At 8.40

PATIENCE

Or, Bunthorne's Bride.

Written by W. S. GILBERT, Composed by ARTHUR SULLIVAN

Reginald Bunthorne ... Mr. GEO. GROSSMITH
  A Fleshly Poet
Archibald Grosvenor, Mr. RUTLAND BARRINGTON
  An Idyllic Poet
Mr. Bunthorne's Solicitor ... Mr. G. BOWLEY

Col. Calverley ... Mr. WALTER BROWNE
Maj. Murgatroyd Mr. FRANK THORNTON
Lieut. the Duke Mr. DURWARD LELY
of Dun-table   *Officers of Dragoon Guards*

CHORUS OF OFFICERS OF DRAGOON GUARDS

The Lady Angela Miss JESSIE BOND
The Lady Saphir Miss JULIA GWYNNE
The Lady Ella   Miss FORTESCUE
The Lady June   Miss ALICE BARNETT
  Rapturous Maidens   AND
Patience ... A Dairymaid ... Miss LEONORA BRAHAM

CHORUS OF RAPTUROUS MAIDENS

ACT I.

EXTERIOR OF CASTLE BUNTHORNE

ACT II.

A GLADE.

Conductor ... ... Mr. FRANK CELLIER.
Stage Manager ... ... Mr. W. H. SEYMOUR.

The Opera produced under the personal direction
of the Author and Composer.

NEW SCENERY BY H. EMDEN.

The Æsthetic Dresses designed by the Author, and executed
by Miss Fisher. Other Dresses by Messrs. E. Mosss & Son,
Messrs. G. Hobson & Co., and Madame Auguste.

THE DANCES ARRANGED BY MRS. J. D'AUBAN.

✸✸✸✸✸✸✸✸✸✸✸✸✸✸✸✸✸✸✸✸

NO FEES OF ANY KIND.

Programmes are provided, and Wraps and Umbrellas taken
free of charge. Any attendant detected in accepting money
from visitors will be instantly dismissed: the public is
therefore requested not to tempt the attendants by offering
them gratuities.

✸✸✸✸✸✸✸✸✸✸✸✸✸✸✸✸✸✸✸✸

The Refreshment Saloons are under the direct control
of the Management, and everything will be found to be
of the best quality.

Acting Manager ... *Mr. GEORGE EDWARDES*

Inside of program for Patience, which followed "a New and Original

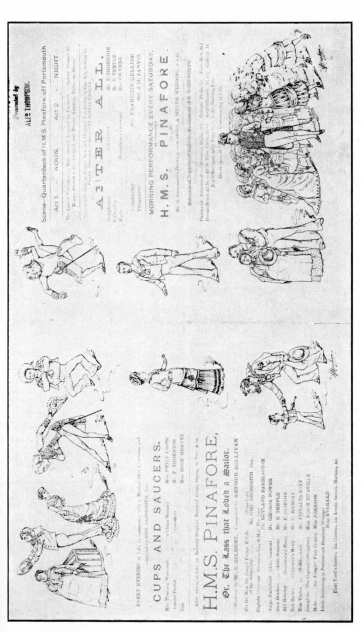

Inside of program for H. M. S. Pinafore, "commenced" by a Musical Sketch about two "China Maniacs," entitled Cups and Saucers, and "concluded" by a Vaudeville Act, After All, at the Opera Comique, in London

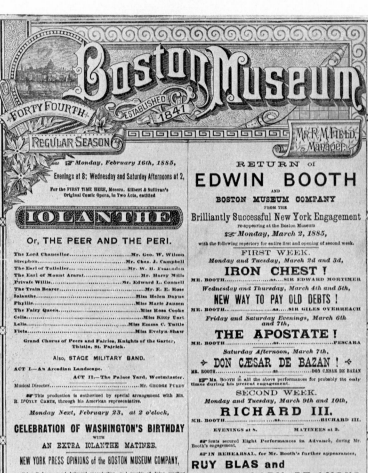

Program of the Boston Museum announcing Iolanthe, *for Monday, February 16th, 1885*

Page from The Illustrated Dramatic Weekly, published in New York in 1879, picturing two unusual "court" scenes from Trial by Jury

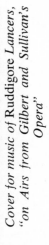

Cover for music of Ruddigore Lancers, "on Airs from Gilbert and Sullivan's Opera"

Cover for piano music from Iolanthe. *This was printed in full color, with intricate decorative borders around the music, and measures 10½″ by 13½″*

and gave them all the news about *Pinafore* while the customs officials examined Gilbert and Sullivan's baggage. Clay, Gilbert and Sullivan left the dock just as Clay reported, "There are nearly fifty companies playing your piece. Those formed after six o'clock last night are not included in my count!"

So great was the *Pinafore* rage, explained Clay as the trio set out for their hotel, that newspaper editors had forbidden quotations from it in their columns. There was, he informed his friends, a most popular game in America: every time anyone used a line from *Pinafore* in conversation, he had to pay a fine. "Why just the other day, it happened to me," recounted Clay. "I went to church with old Sam Barlow— you chaps know Sam, don't you?—and when the minister ended his sermon by saying, 'For He Himself hath said it,' Barlow, without thinking, muttered, 'And it's greatly to his credit' and had to hand me half a dollar for quoting you men!"

Gilbert and Sullivan laughed at Clay's stories. "See, Sullivan," Gilbert chuckled as they entered their hotel and were surrounded by reporters, "even old friends of ours like Clay are making money on *Pinafore* and not offering us a royalty. It is just as well we made this trip!"

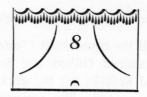

"Everything Is a Source of Fun"

—*The Mikado*

WHEN Gilbert and Sullivan arrived at their hotel they found the lobby crowded with reporters assigned to interview the famous pair. Several hours passed before the partners could go to their suite and relax. The creators of *Pinafore* had been asked hundreds of questions by newspapermen who realized that their editors and readers would want to know everything about the Englishmen. New York newspapers carried long stories about them the next day, but the best of all the interviews was the one which appeared in the New York *Herald*. Here it is, exactly as it was published in the editions of November 6, 1879. Remember, as you read it, that newspaper reporters in those days were supposed to use as many flowery adjectives as possible, and that journalists rarely got a chance to interview famous foreigners seventy-four years ago. You might find it fun to compare this interview with one in your local paper and see how reporting styles have changed. The unknown reporter who wrote this piece of "copy" has, however, given us a wonderful word picture of Gilbert and Sullivan as they looked to the Americans who had gone *Pinafore* mad.

"The appearance and manner of the two famous Englishmen greatly belie the published accounts which have found their way across the ocean, and which represented more especially Mr. Gilbert, as a man of austere and haughty temperament. On the contrary, two more amiable, modest, simple, good humored and vivacious men could not easily be imagined. They fairly brim over with animation, high spirits and the jolliest kind of bonho-mie, and it would appear to the most indifferent observer that they must shed gladness upon any company in which they hap-pen to be.

"Mr. Gilbert is a fine, well-made, robust man apparently 45, above the medium stature, with the brightest and rosiest of faces, an auburn mustache, and short 'mutton chop' whiskers, tipped, only slightly with grey, large clear blue eyes, and a forehead of high, massive, and intellectual cast. His voice has a hearty, deep ring, and his utterance quick and jerky—as though he were al-most tired of this business of saying funny things, which every-body more or less expects of him. Mr. Sullivan is quite different. In his appearance gentle feeling and tender emotions are as strongly expressed as cold, glittering, keen-edged intellect is in that of Mr. Gilbert. He is short, round and plump, with a very fleshy neck, and as dark as his collaborateur is fair, with a face of wonderful mobility and sensitiveness, in which the slightest emotion plays with unmistakeable meaning. With all this Mr. Sullivan, who keeps a monocle dangling over one eye while the other twinkles merrily at you, and whose dark whiskers and hair have an ambrosial curl, is also something of a polished man of fashion.

"The conversation of course turned upon *Pinafore* and Gilbert and Sullivan agreed in expressing their surprise at its enormous success in this country.

" 'It is rather hard,' said Gilbert, with great good humor, 'when one has done for years serious work—work at least, aim-ing to be so—to find after all that a frothing trifle like this should here so far exceed in its success the work which one has held in far more serious estimation. For we really had no idea it would be such an extraordinary success, you know.'

"Mr. Sullivan cordially chimed in with this sentiment and alluded to his oratorios and other compositions of a more classical and ambitious style, which, he was constrained to acknowledge, had not met with anything like the popular success that *Pinafore* has enjoyed.

" 'Under what inspiration was it composed?'

"Mr. Sullivan laughed and replied that during most of the time in which he wrote the score for *Pinafore* he was seriously ill, and often in great pain when he composed the merriest melodies in that tuneful little work.

" 'Did those striking airs occur to you spontaneously, or did you have to search for them, as it were?'

" 'Oh, it's a great mistake to suppose that the music of an opera bubbles up like a spring,' was the composer's reply, 'we have to dig for music like a miner for his gold. It won't do for a miner to expect the gold to come up spontaneously. He has to dig deep for it and so we, also, have to dig for our musical treasures.'

" 'And the words?' the reporter queried, turning to the author, 'how was it they were so closely wedded to the musical idea?'

" 'We have been working together harmoniously for the last seven years,' was Mr. Gilbert's reply, 'and have learned to understand each other so thoroughly that even the faintest suggestion of the one meets with a ready and sympathetic response from the other. In all this period of active-cooperation it has never once occurred that we have disagreed as to the way in which an idea should be carried out, be it either poetically or musically.'

" 'Did you expect these familiar quotations from *Pinafore* to become the popular catchwords which they now are?'

" 'Never!' was Mr. Gilbert's serious and emphatic reply.

" 'What! Never?'

" 'Well, very seldom,' the author laughingly assured, 'as I once innocently said before to a gentleman who asked me the same question and who laughed uproariously, he thought it so funny. But seriously speaking, I had no idea that these few jocular expressions would pass into the small currency of daily conversation. Had I sat down with the mechanical effort to coin a popular catch-word I probably should have failed completely.'

" 'And how is it that *Pinafore* has not been as great success in England as it proved in this country?'

"Mr. Sullivan took up the question and replied: 'Oh, it has been a very great success. In London it has been running 500 nights, and it was played in four theatres at one time. In the provincial theatres it has been a continual attraction for the last year and a half or more.'

" 'And,' added Mr. Gilbert, 'remember that it is the only operatic work by a native author and composer which ever kept the British boards over three weeks.' "

Thanks to the columns of "copy" turned out by the reporters, everyone in New York knew that Gilbert and Sullivan were in town. Crowds waited outside their hotel to see the author and composer of *Pinafore* and followed them as they walked through the streets. Society folk and theatrical personalities invited them to dine, and it soon became impossible for them to plan a single hour of relaxation in their hotel suite. Everything they wore, said, did or ate was commented upon in the newspapers. Even Sullivan, who delighted in being the center of attraction, became weary of being a public figure and longed for "a little rest and quietness, but I fear it is out of the question here."

It was. There were not enough hours in the day to meet people, attend testimonial dinners, talk to newspapermen and rehearse a company for a production of *Pinafore*. Worn out from meeting so many people, Sullivan plaintively wrote in his diary, "Where do these Americans end?" There was never to be an end. The social round took more and more of Gilbert's and Sullivan's time. They were given a dinner by the Lotus Club, and were introduced as "two gentlemen we have long known, with whom we are intimately acquainted, but whom we have never met." The Lotus Club numbered among its membership some of the most impor-

tant men in America, and Gilbert, by now an excellent
speaker, seized the opportunity to complain, in an extremely
funny speech, about the lack of an international copyright.

"We propose," Gilbert told his distinguished audience,
"to open here on the first day of December, at the Fifth
Avenue Theatre, with a performance of—*Pinafore*. I'll not
add the prefex initials, because I have no desire to offend
your republican sympathies. I may say, however, that I have
read in some journals that we have come over here to show
you how the piece should be played, but that I disclaim both
for myself and my collaborateur. We came here to teach
nothing—we have nothing to teach—and perhaps we
should have no pupils if we did! But apart from the fact that
we have no copyright, and we are not yet managers in the
United States, we see no reason why we should be the only
ones not permitted to play the piece here!"

Nor did his hosts, who included among others, Chauncey
Depew, former Secretary of State; Whitelaw Reid, America's leading newspaper editor; and John Hay, who had
served as private secretary to Lincoln during the War Between the States and who was to negotiate the treaty which
made the Panama Canal possible. These men, like the rest
of America, could hardly wait for Gilbert and Sullivan to
launch their own version of how the good ship *Pinafore*
should be sailed.

As the two men were leaving the Lotus Club dinner, one
of the club members, a judge, came up to them. "Gentlemen," he said, "it is my sincere wish that some time during
your stay in New York you will be arrested and brought before me in Police Court! Nothing would give me greater satisfaction than dismissing the case in return for the pleasure
Pinafore has given me!"

Despite the demands on their time, Gilbert and Sullivan
spent long hours getting their "authorized production" of

Pinafore ready. Everything was shipshape by the evening of December 1. New Yorkers who knew every line and note of *Pinafore* as played by American companies impatiently awaited the opening night. Suddenly, the jinx that seemed to hang over Gilbert and Sullivan's vessel, appeared again. The members of the orchestra at the Fifth Avenue Theater, who were getting $17.50 a week, walked out. The musicians demanded more money on the grounds that *Pinafore* was not comic, but *grand* opera! Sullivan was prepared to put down this mutiny by accompanying the singers on the piano, with Cellier at the harmonium, a small organ. This plan did not have to be carried out, however, for the union ruled that the musicians had signed a contract, and they had to abide by it.

From then on, all was smooth sailing for *H. M. S. Pinafore*. If the opening night performance was not particularly good, it was in no small way due to an extra member of the *Pinafore*'s crew. This tar was none other than Gilbert himself, who thought the best way to keep his eye on a company composed of English stars and an American chorus was to be on the stage as much as possible. It is extremely doubtful that Gilbert tried to sing, however! When the curtain fell on the last act, the author, no longer in the uniform of a British sailor, stepped forward to the footlights and told a wildly cheering audience that, "It has been our purpose to produce something that should be innocent, but not imbecile."

Pinafore as produced by Gilbert, with full orchestration directed by Sullivan, was so different from the pirated versions that the public flocked to the opera as if it were a new piece. Nor did the average theatergoer content himself with seeing but one performance. As the dramatic critic of the Boston *Advertiser* wrote on May 31, 1879: "Ten performances in all is not a high average for those who have surrendered themselves completely to the attractions of *Pina-fore;* while the number of those who have seen and heard the opera five times or more certainly amounts to the hundreds in Boston alone. It is merely a question of means and opportunity when one will stop."

It looked like the opportunity to stop would never come. *Pinafore* was a mania and there was no cure. Theatergoers would attend the Gilbert and Sullivan directed version, then go to one of the pirated productions to compare the two, and return to see the authorized version again and again. In Boston and other cities, the public went regularly and faithfully to the presentations offered in various theaters, storing up notes for comparison when the authentic ship would be berthed locally. Women were buying Pinafore stockings and toilet water: schoolboys who sat on tacks placed on their chairs by fellow-students would complain loudly, "I never saw that pin-a-fore!" while political cartoonists used the characters from the opera and Gilbert's lines to help elect their candidates. Never, no, never had the American public acted this way about a theatrical production.

Naturally enough, there were those who did not like the piece. One critic called it "a frothy production destined soon to subside into nothingness." The review of the authorized version that appeared in the *New York Dramatic Mirror* found little to recommend to playgoers. The *Mirror* thought the chorus poorly trained, and the review must have put Gilbert into a rage when he read, "The chorus was not so well trained as the one which formed the distinctive feature of the Philadelphia Church Choir Company." Nor did Sullivan fare much better in this fault-finding review. "He is not," said the *Mirror*'s critic, "a brilliant or picturesque conductor and is apparently not on familiar terms with the music which he claims as his own." While Gilbert was furious at this criticism, Sullivan merely laughed and said, "So he wants a picturesque conductor, does he? Very well, watch me tomorrow night."

The next night Sullivan waved his baton in wide arcs, stamped his feet, and bobbed his head from side to side in time with the music. "See, Gilbert," he chided his partner, "I only need to be told what is wrong about my direction, and I immediately correct it."

"If you think you looked like a picture tonight," snapped Gilbert in reply, "all I can say is you were an overdeveloped one!"

"That's true," agreed Sullivan, "but it's a picture no one will ever see again. It was fun though—the members of the orchestra thought I was having a fit!"

Playgoers paid little attention to those reviewers who found fault with *Pinafore,* and more and more people went to see the cargo Gilbert and Sullivan had loaded upon their famous ship. The official version brought the partners a fortune, although pirate-dominated crafts still sailed the stage of hundreds of theaters. In fact, Gilbert and Sullivan's production of their own work was so successful that more managers than ever were inspired to present the opera. Meanwhile, college professors were giving scholarly lectures on the reasons for the popularity of *Pinafore*—managers not interested in reasons, but in money, looked around for novel ways to present the piece. One production was given in the New York Aquarium, with a background composed of fishtanks! All over the country, real ships were built on artificial lakes, the audience listening to performances of *Pinafore* from their seats on the shore. The German version of the piece had been so successful that in Reading, Pennsylvania, *Pinafore* was offered in Pennsylvania Dutch, Sir Joseph's announcement that he is "the monarch of the sea" being changed to *"Ich bin der kaybich frim der meet."*

The opera furnished professional funnymen with an endless source of material for filling their columns. Unfortunately, they used the same jokes over and over, until one humorist was forced to admit:

> *"We never tried to spin afore*
> *A yarn which has been spun afore;*
> *But when we pun on Pinafore,*
> *It seems we've heard the pun afore."*

In dozens of papers the story appeared about the pilot in Newport, Rhode Island, who, on learning that *H. M. S. Pinafore* was soon to arrive in that city, rowed miles out to sea in order to get the job of piloting her into the harbor! A Boston paper printed the tale about the man who walked up to the box office of the theater in which an English company was playing grand opera, and asked, "Is the Queen in?"

"Queen who?" queried the puzzled ticket seller.

"Why, Queen Victoria, of course."

"No, sir," came the bewildered reply.

"Isn't this Her Majesty's Opera Company that is singing here?" was the next question.

"Certainly."

"Well, isn't the old lady traveling with her own show? I've come all the way to Boston from Maine to see her, and all I've got to say is I'm mighty disappointed. However, I'll go down to the wharf and see Her Majesty's Ship *Pinafore,* because I know that's in town!"

Newspaper poets had fun with the opera. This is a sample of their work:

> *"O Sullivan and Gilbert,*
> *You've much to answer for;*
> *We've no desire to kill, but*

We'd like to 'take the law'
On you for daring to concoct
H. M. S. Pinafore.
Our managers have got the craze,
Their cry is still for 'more';
Such fights for 'singing chambermaids'
Were never seen before—
For on nearly every stage is heard
'H. M. S. Pinafore.'"

Big Business took notice of *Pinafore*—a manufacturer announced that he had orders for one hundred thousand hand-organs that would play nothing but tunes from the opera. Up the Hudson River, at the United States Military Academy, West Pointers were marching to Sullivan's music played in march tempo. While learned professors attempted to explain the reasons for *Pinafore*'s popularity, it would have been difficult to find anyone who was really interested in what they were saying about the philosophy to be found in the opera. People just wanted to hear and see the piece over and over again. Henry Ward Beecher, one of the most distinguished ministers of the day (he was the brother of Harriet Beecher Stowe, who wrote *Uncle Tom's Cabin*) while lecturing in Philadelphia on the evils of amusements, stressed the fact that he had never, no, never, been inside a theater in his life. Yet it caused no comment when, two hours later, the great preacher was seen sitting in a stage-box, enjoying a performance of *Pinafore*. Everyone in America was going to see Gilbert and Sullivan's comic opera, so why shouldn't Mr. Beecher?

Perhaps it was Reverend Beecher's attendance that inspired the owners of the Philadelphia theater to send Gilbert and Sullivan a royalty. This gesture was followed by a similar one on the part of the music publishing firm of Oliver Ditson of Boston, who sent with the money a letter, "hoping that an international copyright law would soon be enacted." *Pinafore* had not only won the hearts and filled the minds of Americans, but it had opened their pocket-books as well!

The hopes of the Ditson Company that an international copyright law would prevent theatrical pirates from stealing Gilbert and Sullivan's work was appreciated by the English-men, but such hope was in vain. Gilbert, Sullivan and Carte found that the law was all on the side of the pirates. The trio's lawsuits, aimed at stopping the theft of their work, be-came as mixed-up and as topsy-turvy as any Gilbert and Sullivan opera. One judge sided with them, another sided with the pirates. The result was the partners lost thousands of dollars in royalties and could do nothing about it.

Gilbert's bitter tongue and Sullivan's mild manner were little help to the lawyers who were representing them in the lawsuits brought against the theatrical pirates who had seized *Pinafore*. As a result, Carte decided to handle all the legal details and to testify in court. Always an excellent businessman, the manager used the lawsuits to get as much publicity as possible for *Pinafore,* and the authorized version of Gilbert and Sullivan's work became more popular than ever. American correspondents of London papers kept their editors informed on the progress of the various lawsuits and told how it had become an American custom to see *Pina-fore*. These dispatches made Englishmen who had not yet seen a performance of the opera in its homeland rush out to buy tickets. *Pinafore* was the most talked about theatri-cal production on both sides of the Atlantic.

Nor was news about Gilbert and Sullivan's comic opera confined to American and English papers. The New York representative of the Paris *Temps* cabled a story about the theatrical entertainment everyone in America was seeing so many times. According to a newspaper columnist of the day, this cable, literally translated, read as follows: "The Vessel of Her Majesty, the *Pinafore* we are informed, is sung everywhere; the troupes of Christian minstrels, a pious opera corps, sing it; never in the country of the English language have there been seen a like vogue and fury. It is a satire on, or rather a picturesque tableau of the English navy and amuse greatly the public which sings everywhere, 'I call myself the little buttercup.' " True or not, this account was humorous enough to please even Gilbert!

Many American managers, anxious to make a fortune from *Pinafore,* approached Gilbert and Sullivan with suggestions for improving their work. One of these managers had a serious talk with Gilbert, hinting that he would be willing to back an American version of the opera. "Now all you've got to do, my friend, is make a few changes. That H. M. S. can become U. S. S., then pull down the English flag and run up the good old Stars and Stripes," he said. "Instead of anchoring your boat off Portsmouth, wherever that is, berth your ship near the Jersey shore. Swap that First Lord of yours for our Secretary of the Navy, and all that's left to do is change that song to 'He is an American.' "

Strangely enough, Gilbert didn't fly into a rage at the suggestion. He merely nodded and said, "I'd like to do what you ask, but I'm afraid I couldn't. There are too many difficulties. You see, I don't know your Yankee speech well enough, although—let me see—I could, I suppose, say:

> *"He is Ameri-can*
> *Tho' he himself hath said it,*
> *'Tis not much to his credit*
> *That he is Ameri-can—*
> *For he might have been a Dutchman,*
> *An Irish, Scotch or such man,*

> *Or perhaps an Englishman.*
> *But in spite of hanky-panky,*
> *He remains a true-born Yankee.*
> *A cute Ameri-can!"*

"Say, that's wonderful," approved Gilbert and Sullivan's would-be partner, not realizing that the author was making fun of him. "That's just the stuff!"

"I'm afraid not," replied Gilbert as he walked away. "I don't think that sort of thing would make for good relations between England and America."

Gilbert wasn't always so gentle when dealing with Americans. One night at dinner a woman who knew even less than he did about music—which is saying a good deal—mistook him for the composer of *Pinafore* and babbled on about how much she enjoyed the music of Bach. "Dear, marvelous Bach!" she trilled. "How I enjoy his music! Tell me, if you please, just what is dear, dear Bach composing now?"

"Bach, madame," shouted Gilbert in his best quarter-deck manner, for he was exceedingly angry that he should have been taken for the composer, not the author of *Pinafore,* "is not composing anything these days! I would venture, as he died in 1750 and it is now 1879, rather than composing, he is decomposing!"

Sullivan was also having trouble with Americans. Everyone had been most cordial to him at the concerts he had conducted up and down the Atlantic seaboard, but he found American women "most unattractive." He frankly said so in many of his speeches! Instead of making them indignant, this attitude made the ladies more determined than ever to impress him, and Sullivan received more invitations to dinners, balls, parties and teas than he could possibly accept. Only once was his judgment of the American people as being "most wonderfully kind and hospitable" in error. One night the lady he was delegated to escort to dinner drew herself up haughtily and stated, "I refuse to dine with a common musician whose tunes are heard in every street!" Sullivan's hostess was speechless, but the composer merely laughed and thought of his devoted friends among the royal family of England and the other great houses of Europe. He went into the dining room alone.

Gilbert and Sullivan had, however, much more to do than talk to Americans, go to one party after another, or count the receipts from *Pinafore*. The partners, with Carte's help, were busily devising a plan to scuttle the pirates who were robbing them. At last they had one. Instead of first presenting their next opera in England, they would introduce the piece simultaneously in England and America. If their scheme was successful, the opening night audience in New York would, as it left the theater, hear that the opera had been seen and heard a few hours previously in England. Let the pirates find a way to get around this plan! So, satisfied that at last they had developed a method of protecting their property, Gilbert and Sullivan set to work to smooth out the rough spots in their new work, *The Pirates of Penzance*.

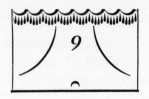

9

"*Source of Infinite Merriment*"

○

—*The Mikado*

A PLAQUE set into the wall of number Forty-five East
Twentieth Street, New York City, marks the location
of the hotel in which Gilbert and Sullivan stayed during
their first visit to that city. It reads:

ON THIS SITE
SIR ARTHUR SULLIVAN
COMPOSED
"THE PIRATES OF PENZANCE"
DURING 1879

As a matter of fact, this inscription is not absolutely true.
Sullivan had brought the music for the second act of *The
Pirates* from England with him, but when he unpacked his
luggage he found that he had carelessly left all his music
for the first act on the desk in his London apartment. Therefore it was only the forgotten music that the composer rewrote in the long vanished hotel on East Twentieth Street.
He did, however, completely score the opera in New York
City.

It was not easy for Sullivan to work during this period.

The composer was not well and had to force himself to set Gilbert's words to music. Sullivan was not getting enough sleep; during the day he helped supervise rehearsals of the second act of *The Pirates,* which meant that he had to work on the music of the first act at night. The only way Sullivan could meet the demands of this routine was to take a short nap following rehearsals, and then, after a brisk walk with Gilbert, lock himself in his hotel room and drive himself to the task of completing the music for *The Pirates.* Rarely did Sullivan get to bed before dawn, and then he was so weary he could not sleep. It was no wonder that he wrote to his mother, "The last three weeks have been imprisonment with hard labour."

Gilbert had as much to do as Sullivan. Despite the fact that he had written a great deal of the new opera in England, there still remained the task of cutting, rewriting and expanding his libretto. Unlike his partner, Gilbert found New York an excellent place in which to work, but then, writing always came easy to him. As a result, while Sullivan was toiling far into the early hours of the morning, Gilbert, accompanied by Fred Clay, was enjoying himself at dinners, parties and receptions.

Everyone was curious about the new opera. Theatergoers, who by now were slightly weary of *Pinafore,* were anxious to see a fresh Gilbert and Sullivan production. Theatrical managers were inquiring of Carte when the piece would appear. The partners refused to discuss their work with anyone. As a result, rumors flew all over New York. Reporters, unable to get Gilbert, Sullivan or Carte to talk about the coming production, or even tell its name, wrote columns of copy which, even if not true, helped to advertise the opera. The less information the partners gave out, the greater became the interest of the public. Still the trio remained silent—and were asked more questions than ever.

Truth to tell, they didn't know the answers. Gilbert, dissatisfied with his own work, had decided to eliminate some of the characters in the opera and add others. This meant much rewriting of both words and music, so it was impossible to tell when the piece would be ready for production. The thought of what had happened to *Pinafore* made them extremely careful about what they said to theatrical folk or newspapermen. Long before Gilbert and Sullivan had even thought of coming to America, the London correspondent of *The New York Times* had asked Sullivan for information about the comic opera the partners were writing. "Is it true," asked the newsman, "that the idea of your next piece is a sort of dramatized *Bab Ballad,* in which six burglars and six policemen appear?"

"That," said Sullivan, handing the correspondent a cigar, "was an idea we had for a short piece; but we have introduced it into the latter part of the new opera, which will be in two acts, like *Pinafore*. The notion chiefly develops a burlesque of Italian opera. It is a mere incident. An old gentleman returns home in the evening with his six daughters from a party. Nice bit of soft music takes them off for the night. Then a big orchestral crash, which introduces six burglars. They commence their knavish operations in a mysterious chorus, lights down. Presently, the old gentleman thinks he hears someone stirring; comes on; of course, sees nobody though the burglars are actively at work. The only noise is the sighing of the wind, or gentle evening breeze. The old gentleman and the burglars perform a bit of concerted music, and in due course the six ladies enter. The six burglars are struck with their beauty, forget their villainous purposes and make love . . . then there is a rescue by policemen and other humorous conceits of Gilbert's, which I hope and believe will be as funny as anything in *Pinafore* or *The Sorcerer*."

Anxious reporters, told by their editors to get information from the Englishmen or lose their jobs, used this interview between Sullivan and the *Times* correspondent as the basis for their daily reports on the activity of the partners. Since only the newspapermen knew that the composer had been interviewed five months previously, the general public thought they were getting the latest news from the Fifth Avenue Theater. Everyone was satisfied that the new opera was going to be about a gang of burglars! As a matter of fact, this belief was not completely in error. Originally, Gilbert had planned to call the work *The Robbers.* While in America, he changed his mind and transformed his second-storymen into pirates. The author wasn't telling newspapermen of the change, however—he, like Sullivan and Carte, was too afraid of theatrical pirates!

So Gilbert said as little as possible (which was a most difficult thing for him to do) and merely smiled when asked if the rumors about the new opera were true. Sullivan did not have time to talk to reporters, nor to anyone else. The composer stayed in his hotel room every minute he was not at the theater, composing music for the songs Gilbert had added during the rewriting of the piece. Carte, when approached by reporters, merely looked wise and said that he was so busy making arrangements for the new opera's tour of America that he had no time to answer questions. However, the manager did use the interest of the newsmen to continue his fight for an international copyright. He told his interviewers that he was trying to make all arrangements "through Mr. Ford of Philadelphia . . . for he is the only American manager to pay us a royalty and I would like to return the compliment." The reporters found they had to be content with the story of the burglars, which by now most of them had come to believe.

Meanwhile, Carte, still engaged in lawsuits in hopes of

getting legal judgments against the managers who had produced their own versions of *Pinafore,* gave out interview
after interview on his feelings about Americans who were
legally free to steal the work of English authors and dram-
atists. As *Princess Toto* was being produced at the Standard
Theater, Gilbert, anxious to fill all the seats, would gladly
talk about that work written by Fred Clay and himself.
But neither Gilbert nor Carte would say a word about the
new Gilbert and Sullivan production, except to mention
that it was nearly ready for presentation.

It was, for after once again stealing from himself, this
time from his unpublished work, *Our Island Home,* Gilbert
had completed the libretto of the new opera to his satisfaction. Sullivan, on the verge of a breakdown, had written
all the music except the final orchestration. Now full rehearsals could begin at the Fifth Avenue Theater.

Carte had brought players over from England for the
leading parts in Gilbert and Sullivan's new work. All that
had to be done, so far as casting was concerned, was to
secure choristers and people for the minor roles. Gilbert,
always preferring untrained actors so that he himself could
train them to act, wrote the advertisement that announced:
"Amateurs, desirous of adopting the lyric stage, should report to Steinway Hall and ask for Mr. R. D'Oyly Carte."
The author made it clear that "applicants must possess good
voices, a knowledge of music, and be young and of good
appearance."

Hundreds of young men and women answered the advertisement. Many of them had sung in *Pinafore* productions given by schools, churches or clubs. Here and there
in the long lines waiting for the auditions to begin could be
seen the faces of well-known singers like Blanche Correlli
and Henri Laurent, who had no idea Gilbert would hold
their experience, training and proven talent against them.

For hours the tryouts continued, each singer running through the scale and singing a bar or two of his favorite song. Between fifteen and twenty men and women an hour were heard by Carte. Try as the manager did, there was no way in which he could speed up the process. For days he sat on the stage of Steinway Hall and listened to stage-struck youngsters and ambitious amateurs, jotting down on the slip of paper that contained each applicant's name and address, notes about voice and personal appearance. Most of these notes were brief: "ancient and feeble"; "pretty, but poor voice"; and, most often of all, "N.G."

"I shan't," he told the ever-present reporters, "engage more than five out of this whole lot. The best are a shade poorer than my chorus in London. I think I will be able to get a good chorus here, nevertheless. It won't be for lack of rehearsing. We are very particular about our rehearsals. We stage them each day for six weeks, from eleven in the morning until four in the afternoon. I'm sure you'll be satisfied."

While Carte was having trouble choosing choristers, Sullivan was also having difficulties. The musicians at the Fifth Avenue Theater, still angry at the composer for having refused to pay them higher salaries during the run of *Pinafore,* pointed out that Sullivan was England's most famous composer, and thus there could be no question but that the new piece was *grand,* not *comic* opera.

Sullivan, being Sullivan, was of course flattered that these men called him England's greatest composer. He was, however, not willing to pay double salaries in return for their judgment of his work. After listening to the spokesman for the group, Sullivan tapped his baton against the conductor's stand for silence, and looking severely at the members of the orchestra, announced: "Gentlemen, just before leaving England I ended an engagement as conductor of the finest band in the British Empire—that at Covent Garden. I have with me the names and addresses of every member of that organization. All of them, I am sure, will be delighted to play under me here in America. All I have to do is to send a few cables and they will be here on the next boat. Until they arrive, Mr. Cellier and myself will accompany the opera by piano and harmonium. Of course, it goes without saying that rather than take this step, I would prefer you to reconsider your demands."

The orchestra reconsidered. Sullivan, always a gambler, had bluffed its members completely. It would have been impossible for him to round up the entire musical ensemble of Covent Garden—but how were American musicians to know that? The musicians were correct, however, in saying that there was music equal to any in grand opera in the score of *The Pirates*—the second act finale is as rich and full-bodied as anything ever heard when grand opera is sung.

Incidentally, "it is greatly to the credit" of the orchestra that, despite their continual conflict with Sullivan over salaries, not one member accepted the offers of large sums of money for the music to the new piece made by those who wished to steal Sullivan's work. The partners took no chances, despite this loyalty, however. Both the words and music to the new opera were kept in manuscript form because, according to American law, once a dramatic work appeared in print, it became public property. Sullivan himself collected each music part after every rehearsal and locked them in the theater safe. This same system of protecting the music was carried out after the opening night, and all during the run of *The Pirates* in America.

Gilbert took complete charge at rehearsals and soon had the company letter perfect in their parts. After six hours of telling the cast where to stand, how to walk, sit on a bench and speak their lines clearly, the author was the only one in the theater who was not exhausted. The longer the rehearsal and the more Gilbert shouted and raved, the greater was his enjoyment. Sullivan, on the other hand, found no pleasure in the task of training the orchestra and the singers. Always inclined to leave difficult duties until the last possible minute, he had to stay up all night before the opening performance of the opera, working on the overture. The result was that the composer went to the Fifth Avenue Theater on December 31, 1879, suffering from weariness. Sullivan could hardly see the score he had written, but as the first night audience laughed even more heartily at *The Pirates* than they had at *Pinafore,* he felt himself responding to the enthusiasm and soon was wide-awake. There was no doubt of the success of *The Pirates*—the audience stood on its chairs after the finale and roared for Gilbert and Sullivan to make an appearance. They did—and were recalled nine times!

The Pirates of Penzance, or the Slave of Duty is, of course, merely *Pinafore* on land instead of on the sea. The main difference is that in *The Pirates* Gilbert makes fun of the police and the army, rather than the navy. When the curtain rises, we see a bit of the rocky coast of Cornwall, where the famous Pirates of Penzance are celebrating the twenty-first birthday of their young apprentice, Frederick. The pirates are singing and dancing, laughing merrily, but become gloomy when Frederick tells them that now that he is "out of his indentures," he must carry out his duty and wipe out the entire band. This act, the lad assures the pirates, is a most sorrowful and difficult task, because he loves every one of them!

If it hadn't been for Ruth, a nursery maid who was slightly deaf, Frederick never would have been raised as a member of a pirate crew. Ruth had misunderstood her instructions, and instead of apprenticing Frederick to a *pilot,* indentured him to a *pirate*. The boy knew that his nurse had not carried out his father's orders, but being a youth with a wonderful sense of duty, he felt he had to live up to the terms of the agreement. Now, twenty-one and a free man, Frederick feels obliged to exterminate his life-long comrades.

Strangely enough, the pirates, including their king, agree with Frederick that he must do what his conscience tells him. These pirates, it can be seen, are most unusual ones. They never attack a band smaller than themselves (so are usually defeated), nor, being orphans, will they hold an orphan for ransom. Every sailor knows this, so it seems to the pirates that the entire British merchant marine is composed of nothing but orphans!

Frederick says farewell to his former comrades and is about to leave when Ruth asks if she may accompany him as his wife. The boy, who has never seen another woman, is about to agree, when a group of beautiful maidens, all sisters, stumble upon the pirates' lair. Frederick immediately realizes that Ruth is old and ugly and refuses to marry her. He falls in love with Mabel, one of the sisters. The pirates are just about to carry off the other girls when Major-General Stanley, their father, appears. Stanley claims that he is an orphan and that "these girls are all that I can call my own." So the pirates, true to their code, allow him and his daughters to escape. Frederick leaves with them.

As the curtain rises on the second act we see Frederick preparing to march with a troop of policemen against his former friends and tutors. Suddenly, the Pirate King, accompanied by Ruth, enters the Major-General's garden and the pirate chief explains that he has been rereading Frederick's indentures. Frederick, the pirate chieftain points out, was apprenticed until his twenty-first *birthday*, not his twenty-first year. "Thus, if we go by birthdays, you're only five and a little bit over!" he claims, for Ruth has reminded the pirates that Frederick was born in leap year. Young Frederick, always anxious to answer the call of duty, agrees that he still is bound by his indentures and that his rightful place is with the pirates. Tearfully he explains the situation to Mabel and returns to Penzance. Now, as a member of the pirate band, he is, by his sense of duty, forced to announce that the Major-General is no orphan—and moreover, never was one! Stanley, Frederick tells his companions, lied to protect himself and his daughters.

On hearing this news, the pirates are furious. The band plans a midnight raid on the Major-General's castle. With drawn swords, they enter the garden and are met by the police who admit, "a policeman's lot is not a happy one," but they have to do their duty. In stern tones the officers demand that the pirates yield to them in the name of Queen Victoria. Brutal men though they are, the pirates respect their queen and surrender at once. Just as they are being hauled off to prison, Ruth informs the policemen that "they are no members of the common throng, they are young noblemen who have gone wrong." This makes a difference! They are not pirates, but peers. Major-General Stanley refuses to press charges against them, the pirates are released from custody and the opera ends with Stanley's suggestion to his former enemies that they:

> *"Resume your ranks and legislative*
> *duties*
> *And take my daughters, all of*
> *whom are beauties."*

New York audiences were quick to see the similarity between Gilbert and Sullivan's new opera and their previous production. Gilbert had merely turned the female relatives of Sir Joseph into Major-General Stanley's daughters, little

Buttercup into Ruth, Sir Joseph into the Major-General; and had caused all the other folk from *Pinafore* to appear, with different names and claiming different titles. No fault was found with Gilbert's use of old material, however. Everyone was delighted that the Englishmen had written another opera cut from the same pattern as their first success. As had been the case with *Pinafore,* the songs and lines from *The Pirates* soon became parts of everyday speech, and every time one met an officer of the law, it was considered absolutely necessary to hum, "A policeman's lot is not a happy one."

A few newspaper critics saw flaws in the opera and pointed out minor things in the production that they did not like. Very little attention was paid to the reviews of these fault-finders, and enthusiastic audiences crowded the Fifth Avenue Theater night after night. Incidentally, the opera has always been a great favorite in America and is, of course, the only one of the Gilbert and Sullivan series that had its first real performance on this side of the Atlantic. One of the songs from *The Pirates,* the famous chorus of the pirates which they sing as they march into Major-General Stanley's garden, has become a most important part of American folk music. Only the way it is sung at club meetings, parties and picnics does not mention piracy—it informs the world:

> *"Hail, hail, the gang's all here*
> *So what the heck do we care?"*

A performance of *The Pirates* was given at the Bijou Theater, Paignton, on Tuesday, December 30, 1879, to protect the English copyright. Gilbert would have been livid with rage if he had seen it, for it was a very unfinished production. One of the *Pinafore* touring companies, dressed in their sailor costumes, with scarfs around their necks and on their heads to repesent pirate dress, acted and sang the opera with parts in their hands. However, thanks to this makeshift arrangement, *The Pirates* was the property of Gilbert, Sullivan and Carte on both sides of the Atlantic.

One of the actors in this copyright performance at Paignton was Richard Mansfield, who played the Major-General. No one in the company, or in the audience of fifty, realized that Mansfield would be famous some day, not as a singer in operetta, but as a great dramatic actor, winning international fame in the title role of Rostand's romantic play, *Cyrano de Bergerac,* and in the dual parts in Robert Louis Stevenson's *Dr. Jekyll and Mr. Hyde.*

On the morning of January 1, 1880, Gilbert, Sullivan and Carte looked forward to the best year they had ever known. *Pinafore* was playing to crowded houses in London, *The Pirates* was a great success, and all day long telegrams were arriving from theatrical managers all over the United States, asking the trio to send a company to play the new work. Carte read the telegrams, smiled and said, "I guess we've scuttled the pirates, gentlemen." Indeed they had; there was no chance of stealing Gilbert and Sullivan's work. More and more requests for touring companies of *The Pirates* piled up in the office of the Fifth Avenue Theater and the partners made plans to send out at least three troupes to play the piece. Within a week, arrangements were complete and the three companies were engaged. It was a mad whirl. Cellier, Gilbert and Sullivan worked day and night drilling the casts, for despite the fact that they had tried to protect the copyright by an American *première,* they knew that there were managers who would not hesitate to produce an unauthorized version of *The Pirates* in towns far from New York. The sooner the official touring companies were ready, the less danger there would be from these theatrical pirates.

Even in New York, despite the copyright, the new opera

was by now bringing money into the pockets of others than the Englishmen. The locking up of the music each night had prevented a wholesale printing of the score by Americans, but long before the official score was issued, *Recollections of the Pirates of Penzance* was offered to the public by an enterprising music publisher who had sent musicans with good memories to listen to the opera night after night, so that they could crudely reproduce Sullivan's work. This theft of his music caused Sullivan to lose some of his appreciation of American hospitality. Normally gracious, he picked up a copy of the *Recollections,* tore it in half and muttered, "A free and independent American citizen ought not to be robbed of his right of robbing someone else!"

Once the excitement of the opening of *The Pirates* was over, Sullivan almost gave in to the pain and exhaustion that sapped his vitality. If the composer had acted wisely, he would have frankly explained his condition to Gilbert and Carte and gone to bed for several weeks. Instead, he dragged himself to the rehearsals of the touring companies, devoting hours to the training of the singers. In addition, he spent almost every evening at some social function, meeting hundreds of important people and charming them with his looks and personality. The strain was too great. One day, Gilbert went into Sullivan's hotel room and found his partner unconscious on the floor; yet that very night Sullivan was the main speaker at a banquet! The composer refused to stop and kept going by drawing on his last ounce of energy and the dubious comforts of morphine.

While Sullivan was suffering, Gilbert was enjoying himself. The author was as excited as a schoolboy given an unexpected holiday from classes. There were three companies to rehearse! Three groups of actors to train in the proper way to perform on a stage. Gilbert made the most of his opportunity. He bullied, glowered, shouted, demanded and screamed—and got what he wanted from the casts. During one of the rehearsals, the tenor who was singing the part of Frederick missed a cue and was not on stage to answer Mabel when she sang, "Frederick here, oh joy, oh rapture! Summon your men and effect their capture," with the line, "Beautiful Mabel, I would if I could, but I am not able." Quickly Gilbert stepped from the wings and took the missing tenor's part, singing, "I'd sing if I could, but I am not able." The chorus, appreciating the situation, laughed as they sang their required line, "He would if he could, but he is not able."

All was not fun, however. When an actor said, "I haven't done that before, Mr. Gilbert," the coach roared, "No, but I have!" Another actor, not quite understanding directions, politely inquired, "I beg your pardon?" Without a second's hestitation,Gilbert replied, "I accept your apology for being stupid. Now let's get on with the rehearsal!"

At long last, the companies were ready for their tour of America. The money was going to come to the Englishmen for their pirates, and not going to those who pirated the Englishmen! Gilbert and Sullivan, satisfied that they had done all they could to protect their work, planned a tour of western America and a trip to Cuba. Carte spoiled their hopes of a vacation. The manager reminded them that *The Pirates* had to be made ready for a spring production in London. "We have been in this country long enough," said Carte flatly. Sullivan would have time to give a few more concerts in and around New York, but Gilbert and Sullivan had to be at the Opera Comique by March. That, Carte made clear, was an order.

Sullivan gave his concerts. Everywhere the composer went he was honored. Then Gilbert, Sullivan and Carte journeyed together to Buffalo, New York, where they organized another company to play *The Pirates,* and visited

Niagara Falls. Carte and Gilbert returned to New York City, while Sullivan traveled on to Ottawa, Canada. It was mid-February when he arrived, and the city was covered with snow. There were no difficulties for Sullivan, however. A sleigh met him at the station and took him to Government House, where he stayed with Princess Louise and her husband, the Marquess of Lorne, Governor-General of Canada. Now, for the first time in months, Sullivan was completely happy. Americans were kind, hospitable and friendly—but here in Canada he was the guest of royalty! So he enjoyed himself thoroughly, even going tobogganing, receiving so many bumps that he wrote home, "I wasn't sure whether I had my body on or left it behind." The days passed quickly, and all too soon Sullivan had to rush back to New York.

Everything was in perfect order at the Fifth Avenue Theater and reports from touring companies were excellent. Even Carte, the astute businessman, felt that their American affairs were in satisfactory condition. The manager, looking forward to the profits from the English production of *The Pirates;* Gilbert waiting for a reunion with his wife, of whom he was very fond; and Sullivan, anxious to see his mother again, all went aboard the *Gallia* and set sail for England, on March 3, 1880. Gilbert, Sullivan and Carte had conquered America. Could they do as well in their native land?

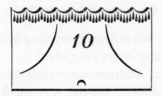

10

"I Am an Intellectual Chap"

—*Iolanthe*

THE day after the *Gallia* docked, Gilbert, Sullivan and Carte met by agreement at the Opera Comique to inspect the theater, examine the books and find out what had happened while they were in the United States. Richard Barker, the stage manager who had acted so heroically during the "Pinafore Riot," greeted them warmly and gave them a full report of all that had occurred during their absence. "The only thing I've done without your permission, Mr. Carte, is to borrow an idea from those theatrical pirates you had so much trouble with overseas," stated Barker.

"What idea did you borrow?" inquired Carte.

"That of having a children's company play *Pinafore*," explained the stage manager, "and it has worked out very well. We trained a group of youngsters—I tried to follow your system of stage directions, Mr. Gilbert, and sincerely hope you won't think their performance slipshod—and I think you'll find no fault with the way we adjusted your music to young voices, Mr. Sullivan. The production has delighted audiences. You'll find proof of this when you check the ticket sales for the dates on which the children played, Mr. Carte. We sell out everything in the house when the juvenile company offers *Pinafore*."

While Carte and Sullivan congratulated Barker on the initiative he had shown, Gilbert was silent. "I'll tell you what I think of what you've done after I see these youngsters of yours perform," the author muttered. The next evening, accompanied by his wife who was his constant companion, he watched the children present a sparkling performance of *Pinafore,* and despite the fact that he felt no one could train actors as well as he, went backstage and told Barker, "You've done an excellent job." While he was talking to the stage manager, the childless Mrs. Gilbert was inviting the entire company to a fancy-dress party. Both of the Gilberts enjoyed having a houseful of young guests and would spare no expense to entertain them lavishly.

The author's praise of Barker's stage-direction did not stop with his compliment. Gilbert called a special rehearsal of the senior members of the *Pinafore*'s crew and after it was finished suggested, "You all had better plan to attend several performances of the juvenile company. There isn't one of you that couldn't learn something from watching Barker's troupe!" The children's production of the operetta was so successful that in later years it was revived many times. The youngsters always drew full houses. There was only one person in the whole of England who found fault with the youthful actors.

That sole critic was Lewis Carroll, who had never forgiven Sullivan for his refusal to write the music for the author's dramatization of *Alice in Wonderland.* Whenever the children's production of *Pinafore* was revived, Carroll would write long letters to the newspapers, complaining about the idea of "innocent children" learning to paint their faces. Newspaper editors learned to expect a letter from Carroll just as soon as it was announced that a company of youngsters was to present the operetta. Before they read the letters, the journalists knew that Carroll would object to the fact that the child playing Captain Corcoran had to say "damme," which was, according to the writer, "sad beyond words." More than ten years after the original children's production, the great scholar was still writing letters bewailing the fact that young people were being ruined by Gilbert and Sullivan. In one letter to the papers, Carroll complained, "How Mr. Gilbert could have stooped to write, or Sir Arthur Sullivan could have prostituted his noble art to set to music, such vile trash, it passes my skill to understand." Carroll, alone of all the stiff-necked Victorians, felt that playing in *Pinafore* meant ruination to any child. All the others of his generation welcomed the chance to pay to hear what the creator of *Alice* considered "vile trash."

While the original children's production was closing the run of *Pinafore,* rehearsals for *The Pirates* were in full swing. Gilbert and Sullivan devoted all their time to getting the piece ready. In less than a month from the day they landed, the partners had the operetta prepared for presentation. On April 3, 1880, *The Pirates of Penzance* was offered to a capacity audience. The work was an immediate success and it ran for almost four hundred performances.

With nothing to prepare for Carte, both Gilbert and Sullivan were free to turn their talents to other fields. The composer, despite his great success in light opera, had not forgotten the ambitions of Leipzig. So he gladly accepted an invitation to write a full-length work for the Leeds Music Festival. As usual, Sullivan had difficulty in finding a suitable theme. Finally, he decided to use *The Martyr of Antioch,* a religious drama by a former dean of St. Paul's Cathedral, as the basis of his composition. The only trouble was that the work in its original form could not be used as an oratorio. Sullivan asked Dean Millman's heirs for permission to take selections from *The Martyr* and change them into suitable form. The request was granted. Now the problem was, who was to do the rewriting?

Sullivan knew that he was not capable of the task. After much thought, he decided to ask Gilbert to put Millman's drama into verse. Sullivan had hesitated to ask his partner because he thought the author would refuse the assignment. Sullivan need not have worried. Gilbert still had ambitions to become a serious dramatist and was tremendously flattered that his associate thought enough of his ability to ask him to write religious verse. Gilbert wasted no time, he set to work at once. Rewriting the highly spiritual work of the Dean was a strange assignment for a master of comedy; but there was not a hint of the *Bab Ballads* in the finished work. Gilbert realized exactly what Sullivan wanted and gave it to him. The result was a perfect blending of words and music. When *The Martyr of Antioch,* dedicated to the Princess of Wales, was produced, the oratorio was hailed as a masterpiece.

This acclaim of his composition was all Sullivan needed to make up his mind to desert the field of popular music. For years the composer had wanted to achieve fame as a creator of serious music. *The Martyr* was proof that he had been wasting his talents. As he read the critics' praise and accepted their personal congratulations, Sullivan decided that he would never write another comic opera score. To be sure, he had made a fortune with Gilbert's frothy plots, but everlasting fame was more important. Sullivan had another reason for wishing to break with his partner. Gilbert, who, as he bragged, knew no music, had been annoyed at hearing Sullivan's tunes played everywhere he went in the United States. These sparkling airs, Gilbert was sure, never would have been written were it not for his verses. Angry that Sullivan was getting so much publicity, the author relieved his feelings by making jokes at his associate's expense every time the pair appeared at a social or business gathering. Everyone who heard Gilbert thought he was just being funny, but the author's humor was sharp and cutting. Sullivan, being a gentle soul, could not develop an armor strong enough to ward off the blows. If it hadn't been for the fact that Gilbert and Sullivan rarely met in London, there might have been a break-up of the partnership right after their arrival in England. However, since the two men never came in contact with each other, except at infrequent business conferences, and it looked as if *The Pirates* would run forever, there was no business to discuss. So there was no opportunity for Gilbert to hurl taunts at Sullivan.

The composer's ambitions and hurt feelings were not the only reasons why he was thinking of breaking with Gilbert. Sullivan's friends among royalty, newspaper critics, and English men of music, all told him that he was wasting his talents and time in writing light opera. Joseph Barnaby, whom Sullivan had defeated for the Mendelssohn Scholarship, and who was now a famous orchestral conductor, wrote his former competitor that *The Martyr* was a work "which is a credit to England." Sullivan made up his mind that from now on he was going to devote himself to classical music. Mentally he wrote identical letters to Carte and Gilbert—"it has been a most profitable and pleasant an association and I am very grateful to you, but from now on, I feel it necessary that I . . ." Then Gilbert called and outlined his idea for a new operetta, and Sullivan, always willing to take the easier way, forgot his ambitious plans and sat down to discuss *The Pirates'* successor.

At first Sullivan was disturbed about his partner's proposed plot. The dramatist, again rummaging around in the *Bab Ballads* for inspiration, had discovered in one of the most satirical of the lot, *The Rival Curates,* the theme of his new work. The composer, listening as Gilbert outlined his libretto, recalled the complaints made against *The Sorcerer* because of the use of a vicar as a comic character. What would happen if the partners produced a comic opera which would really offend church members? Perhaps, in the back of his mind, Sullivan was wondering if the piece would hurt the sale of the hymns he was writing. At any rate, the worried Sullivan was prepared to argue against using Gilbert's latest idea.

Before Sullivan could point out his objections to the plot, Gilbert decided that his idea might be offensive. Not that the author had decided to discard *The Rival Curates,* for he never wasted anything he had written. His problem was to find some means of using his original thought in a different form. He did not have far to look for a solution to his problem. England in general, and London in particular, was in the midst of an aesthetic craze. Led by the poet-dramatist Oscar Wilde, young men were letting their hair grow long, dressing in knee-breeches and wearing sunflowers in their lapels. Girls, attired in the flowing draperies of ancient Greece, talked about things being "too, too utter." At Oxford and Cambridge, the most famous universities in the British Empire, students gave up cricket and punting and spent their time writing poetry, collecting china and talking about "high art." So Gilbert turned his curates into poets, and wrote the new operetta as a satire against Wilde and his followers.

There was no need of a new attraction at the Opera Comique. *The Pirates* was making money every week. Gilbert, however, was never one to dally, once he had made up his mind to write a poem, short story, play, or comic opera. Now that he had decided what form the next production was to take, he immediately set to work to finish the piece. Sullivan, always a spasmodic worker, decided to go to Nice, a famous French health resort on the Mediterranean, for the Christmas holidays. He remained there until the middle of January, trying to compose, but finding that "the sunshine and my natural indolence prevented my doing any serious work." He might have added he was spending too much time at the gambling tables at Monte Carlo, for there was nothing Sullivan enjoyed so much as betting on a horse race, or risking money on the turn of a wheel. The composer would watch the ball bounce along with straining eyes, willing it to fall on his number. Hours would pass as he sat at the roulette table, forgetting to eat and the need for sleep. Sometimes it was only when he had spent every cent he had with him that he realized the passage of time. One night, after losing a very large sum of money, Sullivan staggered exhausted from the gaming casino and remarked to a friend, "They have taken every note I had with me."

"Cheer up, old boy," came the soothing reply, "there are thousands of more notes where those came from."

There were, but Sullivan, while appreciating the pun, was not in the mood for work. He just wanted to drift along. Offered a chance to invest in a street-car company in Turin, Italy, he went to that city, hoping to make an easy and quick fortune. The promoters who had invited him to join in the venture were unable to get a permit to operate; so, deeply disappointed, he left the ancient Italian city and went on to Paris. In his suitcase was Gilbert's libretto, but so far as the composer was concerned, it was excess baggage. There was too much to do in the gay metropolis on the Seine to spend time writing music. Carte, always the businessman, wrote and reminded him that *The Pirates* would not run forever, and that Sullivan had best return to England and get down to work.

Other matters demanded his attention as well. The lawsuit that the three partners were bringing against the directors of the Comedy Opera Company was at last coming up for trial. Sullivan had to attend conferences in the office of the trio's solicitor, Charles Russell. In addition, a performance of *The Martyr* was booked for Albert Hall, and the composer had weeks of rehearsals ahead. Between training his singers, coaching the orchestra and discussing the law suit, he pleaded that he had no time for light opera. To be sure, he did write a few numbers, but for the most part he paid little attention to Carte's demands.

On March 10, 1881, the case against the Comedy Opera Company directorate was tried. Theatrical folk from all over England filled the courtroom in anticipation of Gilbert's performance in the witness-box. Everyone knew the author was never so brilliant as when answering the questions of a lawyer. Gilbert did not perform. Mr. Russell wisely refrained from calling the author to the stand. As a matter of fact, the barrister won the case for Carte and his associates without calling a single person to testify. The judge's decree that the former directors of the Comedy Opera Company had lost the case meant that there was now no question that Gilbert, Sullivan and Carte were the sole owners of *Pinafore*. Unfortunately for both the pride and pocketbooks of the triumvirate, American managers were not affected by this decision.

While Sullivan had been vacationing in France and Italy, Gilbert had been devoting long hours to rehearsing the Opera Comique Company. As fast as Sullivan had sent a number to the theater, it had been given to the cast to learn. The trouble was that the composer had not written many compositions. Gilbert was frantic as he looked at the calendar on his desk. Both the author and Carte begged Sullivan to devote more time to scoring the new operetta, but their requests went unanswered. Suddenly, Sullivan realized that there were but ten days before the scheduled opening of the piece. Always at his best when working under pressure, he sat down to his desk. Night after night he worked, slaving until the hour when most people were rising. He could do nothing during the day, as he was helping rehearse the company and training the singers. The members of the orchestra sat idly in the theater—they did not have a single sheet of music to play—Sullivan was too busy writing numbers for the stars and chorus to provide them with parts. It was the day before the opening when the composer finally passed out his score and then spent all night drilling the musicians. Everyone connected with the production felt the strain and was extremely nervous during the first performance. When the curtain fell at the Opera Comique on Saturday, April 23, 1881, the cast, Carte, Gilbert and Sullivan knew that their worries were groundless. In "An Entirely New and Original Aesthetic Opera in Two Acts, Entitled *Patience, or Bunthorne's Bride,"* they had another great success.

It could not have been otherwise. *Patience* contains some of the best verses Gilbert ever wrote and a great deal of Sullivan's finest music. The operetta, written to ridicule a passing fad, has, strangely enough, worn remarkably well. The aesthetic craze has been forgotten, Oscar Wilde's sunflower faded these many years, but still *Patience* attracts large audiences whenever it is played. Its score, containing such songs as *The Soldiers of the Queen* and *Love Is a Plaintive Song,* is known by thousands, and what junior high school choral practice class has not learned to sing *The Magnet and the Churn?*

The action of *Patience* takes place on the green in front of Castle Bunthorne. As the curtain rises, we see a group of twenty maidens who tell us that they are "lovesick all against our will and twenty years hence, we shall be, twenty lovesick maidens still." The reason why they are, and will be lovesick, they explain, is that they are all in love with Reginald Bunthorne, a "fleshly poet," who refuses to pay any attention to them. The gloom of these lovely ladies is deepened when Lady Jane, an elderly admirer of the poet, announces that he has given his heart to Patience, the village milkmaid. None of the girls can understand this action, for Patience is not interested in either poetry or art.

Patience herself knows or cares nothing for Bunthorne's affection. She is far more thrilled over the news that the 35th Heavy Dragoon Guards are coming to the village. Normally, the other maids would be just as excited as Patience, for most of them had fallen in love with the handsome soldiers during a previous visit. Now, every girl in the entire countryside feels that no soldier can compare with a poet, nor a uniform with flowing robes. When the Dragoons arrive, the village girls give them a cool reception. Meanwhile, a group of Patience's friends convince the milkmaid that if she doesn't want people to think she is selfish, she must fall in love.

A most generous girl, who has an absolute horror of being considered ungenerous, Patience seeks someone to love. While looking, she meets Archibald Grosvenor, an "idyllic poet," who had been a childhood playmate. Poor Archibald! A most attractive young man and perfect in every respect, his misfortune lies in the fact that every woman he meets falls madly in love with him. Patience is no exception, and she and the poet plan to be married at once. Just as they finish making all the arrangements, Patience remembers that her friends told her that love demands sacrifice—and as neither she nor Archibald can find a single flaw in each other, there is no sacrifice. Tearfully the lovers part.

All this time Bunthorne, who has been jilted by the milkmaid, is trying to make up his mind which of the lovesick

maids he should marry. Finally, he decides, "by the advice
of my solicitor," to raffle himself off "in aid of a deserving
charity." There is a rush to buy tickets, each girl hoping that
she will be the one lucky enough to win Bunthorne, who is
"such a judge of blue-and-white, and other kinds of pottery,
from early Oriental down to modern terra-cotta-ry." Arrangements for the drawing are complete when Patience
rushes in and announces that she will accept Bunthorne's
proposal, for "a maiden who devotes her life to loving *you*,
is prompted by no selfish view!"

Now that Patience has consented to marry Bunthorne,
the village maidens return to their old loves, the Dragoons.
The happy couples are singing of their love when Grosvenor
appears, reading aloud from his poetry, which is so pure
and simple, that "to appreciate it, it is not necessary to think
of anything at all." Such verse is, of course, "too, too utter,"
and once again the girls desert the soldiers and flock around
a poet. Only Lady Jane remains true to Bunthorne.

During the second act, Patience and Grosvenor admit
that they are still in love with each other, "but it cannot be!"
Bunthorne, jealous of his fellow poet's popularity with
women, informs his rival that he will make him the victim
of a terrible curse if he does not cast aside poetry and become "a commonplace type, with a stick and a pipe." Grosvenor, tired of his own verses and the girls who follow him
everywhere, gladly agrees to stop writing poetry. Meanwhile, the Dragoons, in the hope of regaining their lost
loves, have transformed themselves into aesthetics. The
soldiers have even shed their brilliant uniforms, which have
been as "successful in the courts of Venus as on the fields of
Mars," and appear in the dress of Oscar Wilde. Their knee-
breeches, velvet coats and berets are making a tremendous
impression on the girls when Grosvenor appears dressed as
a "matter-of-fact young man." Immediately the maids ex-

perience another change of heart: if Archibald Grosvenor, the perfect man who is never in error, feels it right to desert art, the girls are compelled to do so as well. Flowing robes are exchanged for modern dress, knee-breeches for uniforms. Patience pairs off with Grosvenor, each Dragoon embraces one of the village belles, leaving Lady Jane as the only woman not betrothed. This situation is taken care of by the Duke of Dunstable, commander of the Dragoons, who asks her to marry him, leaving Bunthorne without a bride (despite the sub-title of the operetta), as the curtain falls.

By now the pattern is recognizable. Little Buttercup, Ruth and Lady Jane—all stout elderly ladies, the chorus of lovesick maids, Major-General Stanley's daughters and Sir Joseph's sisters, cousins and aunts. *Patience,* like its sister operettas, displays the same folk from Topsy-turvydom, and they act as Gilbert's creations always do when they hear Sullivan's music.

Patience played to a completely filled theater every night. Carte, Gilbert and Sullivan were making a fortune. The trio could have made even more money if the seating capacity of the Opera Comique had been larger. Carte was too good a businessman to let such a situation continue, so he decided to move the operetta into a larger playhouse. After weeks of negotiations he failed to find a suitable location, so he went looking for a site upon which to build his own theater, which would be devoted to playing nothing but the light operas of Gilbert and Sullivan! Finally, Carte found a piece of land in the district in which he wanted to build, and work was begun on the building which was to give its name to all the Gilbert and Sullivan series—the Savoy. From the Savoy, too, has come the name by which all those who have ever been members of a D'Oyly Carte Company are called, or who make it a practice to attend performances of the productions, year after year—Savoyards.

The Savoy was the most moden playhouse of its day. It was, for example, the first public building in the world to be lighted by electricity. There were many other features, and the best account of them is the one D'Oyly Carte wrote himself:

TO THE PUBLIC

"LADIES AND GENTLEMEN,—I beg leave to lay before you some details of a new theatre, which I have caused to be built with the intention of devoting it to the representation of the operas of Messers. W. S. Gilbert and Arthur Sullivan, with whose joint productions I have, up to now, had the honor of being associated.

"The Savoy Theatre is placed between the Stand and Victoria Embankment, on a plot of land which I have purchased, and is built on a spot possessing many associations of historic interest, being close to the Savoy Chapel and in the 'precinct of Savoy' where stood formerly the Savoy Palace once inhabited by John of Gaunt and the Dukes of Lancaster, and made memorable in the Wars of the Roses. I have used the ancient name as an appropriate title for the present one.

". . . The Theatre is large and commodious . . . and will seat 1,292 persons. I think I may claim to have carried out some improvements deserving special notice. The most important of these are in lighting and decoration.

"From the time, now some years since, that the first electric lights in lamps were exhibited outside the Paris Opera House, I have been convinced that electric light in some form is the light of the future for use in theatres, not to go further. The peculiar steely blue colour and flicker which are inevitable in all systems of 'arc' lights, however, make them unsuitable in any but large buildings. The invention of the 'incandescent lamp' has now paved the way for the application of electricity to lighting houses, and consequently theatres. ". . . has enabled me to try the experiment of exhibiting this light in my theatre. About 1,200 lights are used, and the power to generate a sufficient current for these is obtained from large steam-engines . . . placed on some open land near the theatre. The new light is not only used in the audience part of the theatre, but on the stage, for footlights, side and top lights, etc., and (not of the least importance for the comfort of the performers) in the dressing rooms—in fact, in every part of the house. This is the first time that it has been attempted to light any public building by electricity.

". . . the ornament consists entirely of delicate plaster modelling, designed in the manner of the Italian Renaissance. The main colour-tones are white, pale yellow, and gold—gold used only for backgrounds or in large masses, and not—following what may be called for want of a worse name, the Gingerbread School of Decorative Art—for gilding relief work or mouldings. The back walls of the boxes and the corridors are in two tones of Venetian red. No painted act-drop is used, but a curtain of creamy satin, quilted, having a fringe at the bottom and a valance of embroidery of the character of Spanish work, keeps up the consistency of the colour-scheme. This curtain is arranged to drape from the centre. The stalls are covered with blue plush of inky hue, and the balcony seats are of stamped velvet of the same tint, while the curtains of the boxes are of yellowish silk, brocaded with a pattern of decorative flowers in broken colour.

"To turn to a very different subject. I believe a fertile source of annoyance to the public to be the demanding or expecting of fees and gratuities by attendants. This system will, therefore, be discontinued. Programmes will be furnished and wraps and umbrellas taken charge of gratuitously. The attendants will be paid fair wages, and any attendant detected in accepting money from visitors will be instantly dismissed.

"The theatre will be opened under my management on Monday next, October 10th, and I have the satisfaction to be able to announce that the opening piece will be Messer. W. S. Gilbert and Arthur Sullivan's opera *Patience* which, produced at the Opera Comique on April 23rd, is still running with a success beyond any precedent.

"The piece is mounted afresh with new scenery, costumes and

increased chorus. It is being again rehearsed under the personal direction of the author and composer, and on the opening night the opera will be conducted by the composer.

"I am, ladies and gentlemen, your obedient servant,

"R. D'OYLY CARTE"

The theatergoing public could not wait for the opening of the Savoy, but old-timers in the show world laughed at Carte. They were sure the electric lights would fail, and felt that he was a fool not to charge for programs and checking. For Carte to attempt to run the refreshment stands himself, instead of renting them and being assured of an income, seemed to theatrical managers plain stupidity. "He'll lose every cent he has," asserted a rival impresario. "Imagine paying salaries high enough so that ushers and checkers don't have to depend on tips!" Carte paid no attention to his critics but supervised the furnishing of his theater. Nor did he answer those who called him foolish for planning to give to every patron a beautifully designed booklet, printed in color, illustrated with scenes from the Gilbert and Sullivan operettas, instead of the cheaply printed programs for which a fee was charged at all other London playhouses. Incidentally, these booklets today are prized possessions of those who collect Gilbert and Sullivan material.

While the Savoy was being made ready for *Patience,* Gilbert, of course, was busy checking on the new costumes, scenery and properties to be used in the new theater. The author could always find something to do and was happiest when busy. Sullivan, on the other hand, could always find an excuse for not working and liked nothing better than assigning someone to take over his duties. So the composer delegated Cellier to rehearse the orchestra and new choristers, and went off with the Duke of Edinburgh, "the sailor prince," on *H. M. S. Hercules,* to visit St. Petersburg, the city in Russia now called Leningrad, and cruise the Baltic

Sea. Sullivan and Victoria's son had become close friends during the organization of the Royal College of Music, and the composer and His Royal Highness often spent hours talking about the future of music in England. Sullivan warned the Duke that he was taking the trip with one thought in mind—not to have anything to do with music during the entire voyage—but in two days he was leading the tars as they sang songs from *Pinafore!*

When the *Hercules* docked at Copenhagen, the King of Denmark was waiting for his visitors. His Majesty was not so anxious to greet his cousin, the Duke, as he was to meet Sullivan! A great admirer of the composer's work, King Christian had ordered his court orchestra to plan to give one concert a week of nothing but the Englishman's music. The party from the *Hercules* was entertained royally. Following a state dinner, they went on to Cronstadt, on the Gulf of Finland, where the vessel was moored among a large fleet of Russian men-of-war. Another round of parties began and then the Duke and his guest went aboard the Czar of Russia's private yacht for a trip to St. Petersburg. Soon Sullivan, who during his American visit had been turned down as an escort into dinner "because he was a common musician," was residing in an Imperial Palace reserved for the personal guests of the ruler of Russia! The composer, writing home, said that he found "everything very comfortable, though plain, but no baths!"

One of the highlights of the visit to St. Petersburg was the concert given by the Imperial Chapel Choir. Dressed in red and gold uniforms, which reminded Sullivan of his Chapel Royal days, the singers thrilled the visitors with their voices. Sullivan took careful notes all during the performance, and much of his later music shows the influence of what he heard that night. Then came another state dinner, more music by Arthur Sullivan, and after a courtesy call paid by their Imperial Majesties on board the *Hercules,* the English squadron set sail for Keil, Germany.

Sullivan went below and wrote a long letter to his mother, telling her everything that had happened in Russia. Busy as he was with his composing and his social life, he never neglected her. He had tried in vain to convince her to come and live with him and share his success, but she refused, stating that she was perfectly happy if he would write to her when he was away and come and see her often when he was in London. As there was nothing that meant more to him than his mother's happiness, Sullivan always complied with her wishes.

When the *Hercules* docked at Keil, the vessel was met by Prince William of Germany, whose military ambitions when he became Kaiser William II brought about World War I. The German prince was also an admirer of Sullivan, and as the composer got into the royal carriage, His Royal Highness bowed low and sang, "He polished up the handle of the big front door." Despite himself, Sullivan laughed at the idea of the heir to the throne of Germany singing a song from *Pinafore.*

All too soon for Sullivan, it was time to return to England for the opening of the Savoy. Shortly after the English ships got under way, a dense fog blotted out all visibility and half-speed was ordered. The Duke, despite his position as a member of the royal family, took his tour of duty along with the other officers on the bridge of the *Hercules.* For thirty hours, His Royal Highness stood watch and laughed off his guest's compliments by saying, "Well, Arthur, it had to be done. After all, old man, you see I was responsible for a squadron of the fleet, a good many valuable sailors and a musical composer!"

While his partner was associating with nobility, Gilbert had not been idle. In company with his wife, the author had

also been at sea, cruising up and down the southern coast
of England in his small yacht. While sailing, he discussed
dozens of plots with Mrs. Gilbert, who wisely refrained
from expressing any opinion about her husband's writing.
She had learned early in her marriage that William would
not tolerate criticism of his ideas.

The opening of the Savoy Theater was a gala affair.
Everyone of importance who could get a seat was in the
audience. Sullivan conducted *Patience,* took the Prince of
Wales backstage after the performance and presented the
entire company to Victoria's oldest son. Then, excusing
himself, the composer rushed to the railway station to catch
a train which would carry him to Norwich, where the next
morning he conducted *The Martyr.* Nine days after the
Savoy opened its doors, Gilbert called on Sullivan. The
author brought with him the result of his cruise: the outline
of *Patience's* successor. Sullivan thought Gilbert's idea was
excellent, but insisted that there was no hurry. "After all,"
he explained, "why worry about a new opera? The old one
is doing very well. It's playing to capacity houses every
night. Many people are seeing the piece two or three times,
although I don't know if they do so on account of *Patience*
or to enjoy the novel lighting and beautiful decorations of
the Savoy. At any rate, there is no need for us to bother
with a new production at this time."

Sullivan was right. There was no hurry. *Patience* was to
run 408 nights at the Savoy, making a total of 578 performances in all. The composer moved into a luxurious flat in
Victoria Street, left his servants in charge and then set out
for a three months' tour of Europe. In the meanwhile, Gilbert, never one to drop an idea, worked away on the libretto
of the new work. Many a night Mrs. Gilbert would carry
him in a midnight snack as he sat at his desk. "Let Sullivan

have his royalty, dear," he would say, his mouth full, "I have something far better, you." With a cheery wave, his wife would leave the room, knowing that once her husband returned to his writing he would appreciate her more if she were not in sight!

In addition to his creative endeavors, Gilbert was very busy directing revivals of his plays, and frequently checked the performances at the Savoy, finding fault if the players were "stale" and ordering numerous rehearsals. Gilbert's calling of rehearsals was not popular with the cast of *Patience*. The company felt they were presenting the operetta as well as it could be played. Few of the actors dared tell the author of their feelings, for they knew and feared his temper. At last, Grossmith, playing Bunthorne, became so annoyed at being forced to rehearse a bit of "business" he thought he did perfectly, complained, "I've rehearsed this confounded thing until I feel like a perfect fool."

"Good," snapped Gilbert, "now we can talk on equal terms!"

Meanwhile, Carte, trying to salvage something from the raids of the American pirates who were playing *Patience* without payment of royalties, decided to send a company overseas. The clever showman realized that the United States was not going through the same craze for peacock feathers, blue and white china and impossible poetry as was England. As a result, he reasoned, Americans would not really appreciate Gilbert and Sullivan's satire on Wilde and his followers. The manager's problem was to make theater-goers across the Atlantic realize what the operetta was about. Once this was accomplished, Carte was sure Americans would flock to an "authorized production." Suddenly, he had a stroke of genius. He decided to send the "exquisite and professionally super-sensitive Wilde" on a lecture tour to pave the way for *Patience!* It was a brilliant idea—to make the poet a walking advertisement of the opera that poked fun at him and his theories. Only Carte could have thought of it, and only Carte could have persuaded Wilde to agree. Perhaps the lover of "true high art" was swayed by the fact that the manager offered to pay all the expenses of the tour and give Wilde one-third of the receipts.

America had learned that *Patience* had something to do with a poet named Wilde. So the country was prepared for the dreamy youth in knee-breeches, long hair, and flower-filled buttonhole. People had no desire to listen to Wilde. What they wanted was a chance to laugh at him. News-papermen were ready to inform their readers all about the poet when the *Arizona* docked. Paper and pencil were ready in every reporter's hand to write down everything Wilde had to say. First they made notes of his costume—a bottle-green, fur-lined overcoat, with a fur collar, yellow gloves and a round sealskin cap. Wilde answered all the journalists' questions and told them that he had been "disappointed in the Atlantic Ocean." Following the apostle of aestheticism to the customs' shed, the reporters listened carefully while the inspector asked, "Have you anything to declare?" They looked at each other with amazement when Wilde answered, "Nothing, I bring nothing to these shores but my genius."

No sooner did the reporters hear this statement than they made up their minds that every word Wilde said was "good copy." The result was that the poet could not say, "Good morning" without having it recorded in the daily press. By the time Wilde was ready to begin his tour, he was a well-known character to Americans. Everyone was anxious to see and hear him. In most cities, it was impossible to secure a seat for his lectures. Few if any of the audience cared about his views on art, civilization and poetry. What people wanted was to see Wilde, sunflower in hand, and hear him say such things as: "Longfellow is a more beautiful poem than anything he ever wrote," "America's ideas of sculpture have been derived from the wooden Indians outside tobacconist's shops," and "Niagara Falls is not artistically designed. It must be one of the earliest, if not the keenest disappointments in American married life." This last remark was based on the fact that in the Eighties, all newlyweds who could afford it went to Niagara Falls on their honeymoon.

To be sure, there were those among his listeners who understood what Wilde was talking about, but they were few in number. Most of those who heard the poet agreed with the newspaper reporter who wrote, "The only real thing about Wilde is his hair." The small minority who wanted to learn about art and poetry from the bizarre Englishman were greatly annoyed by the actions of some of those who attended his lectures. In Boston, in the old Music Hall, sixty Harvard students marched in just before Wilde was about to speak. They wore long blond wigs, ties of brilliant colors which flowed to their waists, knee-breeches and black silk stockings. Each Harvard man carried in his hand either a lily or a sunflower. As they walked to their seats in the front row, they stopped and posed in imitation of Bunthorne.

Wilde waited for the students to quiet down and then began his lecture. Wisely he laughed with the audience and turned the table on his mimics by saying he was so impressed with Harvard men that he was going to visit their university at Cambridge the next day. He did go to Cambridge and told the reporters who accompanied him that he was "enthralled" with the university's gymnasium and had but one suggestion to improve it. The building should, he explained, have a noble statue of a Greek athlete. Such a statue would inspire youth and—Wilde modestly announced—if it would be accepted, he would be delighted to present such a sculp-

ture to Harvard. . . . It would, of course, he went on to
say, be a statue of himself!

The poet's tour of America was under the direction of
Helen Lenoir, who had been Carte's secretary and was later
to become his wife and continue the production of the Gilbert and Sullivan operas after his death. Miss Lenoir sent
Wilde up and down America. He must have longed for the
comforts of London and his collection of priceless china, as
he sat in stuffy trains and ate his meals from thick plates in
grimy resturants, as he rode across the prairies, journeyed
into the Deep South, and visited the Pacific Coast. Big cities,
small towns, and everything in between heard his voice.
While those who listened did not understand much of what
Wilde was talking about, they learned enough about him to
be able to appreciate the satire of *Patience,* which was, after
all, the main objective of his travels. Carte had not been
the least bit interested in educating Americans, he merely
wanted to advertise Gilbert and Sullivan's operetta. Proof
that the manager had accomplished his purpose was seen in
the fact that when the company playing the "authorized
version" of *Patience* came to any town in which the poet
had lectured, every seat in the theater was sold.

Back in England, there were signs that the run of *Patience*
was coming to a close at the Savoy. Gilbert and Carte agreed
that it was time to start rehearsing the new opera. As usual,
the author had most of the libretto written. Just as usual,
Sullivan had done very little work on the music. The composer was unable to settle down to serious labor and merely
dabbled with his score. What Sullivan needed was inspiration. This time it came as it had before, through sorrow. Arthur Sullivan's mother died.

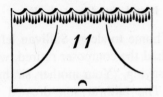

"What Is This Fairy Form
I See Before Me?"

○

—The Sorcerer

PROUD as she had been of her son's success, plain Maria Clementia Sullivan had constantly refused to share his life in London. How could she live in a house in which members of the royal family were constant visitors and great men dined? So, content with frequent visits from her famous son and the letters he wrote describing his activities at home and abroad, Mrs. Sullivan made her home at Fulham, a suburb of London, with the widow of Frederick Sullivan. From time to time she came in town to attend a theatrical performance and have lunch with "my boy, Arthur."

It was just three days after Sullivan's fortieth birthday, May 13, 1882, that Mrs. Sullivan came to London to attend a concert and have tea with the composer in his new apartment in Queen's Mansions. Mother and son were chatting gaily over the teacups when Mrs. Sullivan became ill. Sullivan rushed her home. Her condition grew critical. Then, just as suddenly as the attack appeared, it vanished. By this time the son needed the attention of the doctor far more than the mother. Ordered home to sleep, Sullivan left Fulham in a daze. No sooner had the composer retired, when Louis, his valet, awoke him saying, "Your mother, sir, has taken a turn for the worse." The faithful son dressed hurriedly and rushed to his mother's bedside. He knew at once that there was no hope, although as the hours passed, Mrs. Sullivan would wake and speak to him. Finally, she drifted off to sleep.

"You can't do anything here, Arthur," said the doctor. "I advise you to go home and rest. If you are needed, we'll send for you."

Big Ben had just chimed four when the anxious Louis opened the door at 60 Victoria Street and admitted his master and the yellow fog rolling in off the Thames. In less than four hours, Sullivan was called back to Fulham. As the horses galloped over the cobbled streets of London, the composer knew he would never get there in time. The coachman did his best, but it was not enough. Sullivan rushed upstairs to his mother's bedroom and threw himself on her bed, sobbing. It was hours before he could say a word. For the third time in his life, Arthur Sullivan was stunned with grief.

Only in music could the grief-stricken Sullivan find comfort, and once again the death of a loved one brought him inspiration. The loss of his father had motivated *In Memoriam,* that of his brother Frederick, *The Lost Chord,* both serious compositions. Out of the loss of his mother, however, was to come something vastly different: the gay, entrancing, fairlylike score of *Iolanthe.*

Despite the fact that Gilbert had written much of the book of the new operetta and had plenty of verses waiting for his partner to set to music, the author was having trouble with the opening act of the piece. For the first time since his reign started, the King of Topsy-turvydom could not get his subjects to behave in the manner he desired. Gilbert wrote, rewrote, and wrote again. For days he dug around, as was to be expected, in the rich mine of the *Bab Ballads,* lifting a character here and a line there. While Gilbert worked on his libretto, Sullivan began to compose the music for the second act, which was in its final form. Still grieving over the death of his mother, the composer found it very difficult to settle down to the routine of preparing a score.

While Gilbert was sitting at his desk, with bound volumes of *Fun* spread open before him, looking for ideas, Sullivan went to visit one of his titled friends at a country estate. Unable to work in London, the composer thought he might get inspiration from contact with nature. It was like him to choose the country home of a friend with a title as a place to seek the notes which evaded him—Arthur Sullivan was always happiest when associating with people of rank and title. In Cornwall, where "the famous pirates of Penzance" had their lair, Sullivan found the stimulation he needed. For several days after his arrival, he stayed in his room, not even leaving it for meals. For hours he jotted down the music that had so long eluded him. In fact, during this period, none of the other guests even knew Sullivan was a member of the house party. Not that they cared one way or the other. From early morning until late at night, they spent their time playing cards. Then, suddenly, Sullivan appeared in the card-room, announced he had written several numbers for "our new opera for the Savoy" and declared he was seeking relaxation. A place was made for him at one of the tables and he sat down and had a marvelous run of luck. Refreshed and feeling gay for the first time in weeks, he returned to his room. Again he locked the door and during another period of seclusion wrote more of his score. Proud of his accomplishment, he joined his fellow guests. But on retiring to his room he found that his inspiration had vanished as suddenly as it had appeared and he could not write another note.

Feeling depressed and still grieving over the loss of his mother, he decided to go to the spa at Betrich, Germany, to drink the waters. After a short stay at that famous European health resort, he felt much improved and had a keen desire to get down to work. He set out for home, and when he arrived in London he was met by Gilbert. The partners went to Sullivan's apartment where they stayed up half the night smoothing out the rough spots in the second act of their new opera.

By the time they had finished their conference, all difficulties with *Patience's* successor had been overcome. Now Gilbert and Sullivan could listen to a suggestion of Carte's. While the excellent showmanship of the manager had provided the trio with some of the money Americans were paying to see *Patience,* Gilbert, Sullivan and Carte had lost thousands of dollars through pirated productions. "This is what I want to do," Carte explained. "When the new opera is finished, I want to put two companies into rehearsal; one for the run here at the Savoy, the other for a New York theater. We'll offer the piece simultaneously in England and America, the way we did with *The Pirates.* This will assure the American copyright. I know this will mean more work for you chaps, but it will also mean more money. Are you agreeable?"

Both Gilbert and Sullivan thought Carte's suggestion excellent, and plans were made to rehearse two companies. Then the manager offered his composer and librettist a new business agreement. Carte outlined his plans for sending *The Sorcerer, Pinafore, Patience* and *The Pirates* and all future operettas written for the Savoy on tours of Australia,

Canada, and the other British colonies. The companies playing these countries were to be under Carte's sole direction.
In return for the right to do this, he offered Gilbert and Sullivan a yearly royalty of $8,750 apiece. The offer was ac-
cepted and the contract signed.

Gilbert was as healthy as Sullivan was ill. The author was
never in better form. He bullied the cast at rehearsals, drove
the scene painters and costumers frantic with his insistence
upon perfection. Gilbert's tongue was like a newly sharp-
ened knife. One night, invited to dine at the home of one of
the few actors with whom he was on speaking terms, he was
seated beside an elderly woman who tried to make up for
her lost youth by the use of too much powder and rouge.
Gilbert, who liked women only as long as they were young
and pretty (his scorn of old ladies shows in such characters
as Lady Jane, Ruth and Little Buttercup), was far from
civil to his dinner companion. During the evening, the conversation came around to the Crimean War. The author,
who had tried desperately to serve in that conflict as an officer, talked at great length about the battle in which the
Light Brigade made its famous charge into the Russian guns.
At last, turning her over-made-up face to Gilbert and smiling coyly, the unfortunate woman lisped, "This is all very
interesting, my dear sir, but—you see—I don't recall the
Crimean War."

Gilbert glared at her for a moment and then roared,
"Madame, I'm sure you could if you tried!"

At the Savoy, Gilbert danced from one end of the stage
to the other, showing the ladies of the chorus what he expected of them. Once, in a genial mood, he agreed to give
an actor recommended by Carte a tryout. What the dramatist said to the young man is not known, but it must have

been extremely cutting, for Gilbert reported to the manager, "Your friend has all the faults of being an actor without the excuse of being one!"

One day, while listening to the rehearsal, Gilbert told Sullivan that he was dissatisfied with the words of one of the songs and would rewrite it that evening. The composer, always indolent, suggested that making the change was too much trouble. "After all," Sullivan said, "a bird in the hand is worth two in the bush."

"Indeed," inquired his partner, "but supposing the bird happens to be a vulture?"

The company, hearing this exchange, took no chances. Principals and chorus alike listened carefully to every direction and made sure they knew all their lines. They remembered all too well what had happened when Barrington, weary of being corrected time after time, had lost his temper and yelled across the footlights at Gilbert, "I know my lines!"

"Indeed you do," sneered Gilbert, "but unfortunately you don't know mine!"

Sullivan, on the other hand, had no strength to argue with anyone. The composer's old kidney trouble was causing him terrific pain. It was a chore to write music, and tunes came slowly, while the daily rehearsals took a terrible toll of his vitality. Always at his best when working under pressure, it seemed that for once the pressure was too great. Carte, as active as Gilbert when there were things to do, had made most of the arrangements for the American tour. The manager could not, however, complete his plans until Sullivan finished his music. When the company crossed the Atlantic, they had to have the completed score with them. For a while it looked as if it would never be ready. Then, in less than two weeks after promising Carte (who was greatly worried about Sullivan's health) that he would have everything done in time, the composer finished his work. Now the cast could sail for America with the music of the operetta in a strong box in the ship's safe.

On November 21, 1882, just four days before the opening of the piece at the Savoy, Sullivan decided that the overture would not do. While he had laughed at Gilbert for thinking it was necessary to rewrite a song, he did not hesitate to revamp his own work, but soon found it better to compose an entirely new overture. Sullivan worked far into the early morning hours for three nights in a row before the task was finished. Gilbert, meanwhile, was perfecting the gestures and diction of the principals and chorus. Until one or two o'clock every morning, the cast kept going through the operetta, while the author criticized one and all. Then, after having browbeaten and berated them for hours, Gilbert would give the ladies of the chorus cabfare home—a gesture he always made when he knew the girls were upset by his bullying.

There was just one thing that might cause confusion on the opening night. Carte, taking no chances with theatrical pirates, had given out the word that the new operetta was to be called *Perola*. This title sounded logical enough, as Gilbert and Sullivan's three previous successes had had titles beginning with "P": *Pinafore, Pirates of Penzance* and *Patience*. Thus the name seemed a likely one, and nobody thought of questioning it. Even the company thought it was the name of the piece. It wasn't until the final run-through, when the cast was assembled on the stage for last-minute instructions, that its members were told that the real title of the operetta they were going to present was *Iolanthe, or the Peer and the Peeri*. The Savoy company, superstitious in the fashion of many theatrical folk, appreciated the fact that there were "P's" in the correct title, but raised their voices in loud complaint. "How are we going to remember the change?" they wailed. "We'll make all sorts of mistakes. You can't expect us to say *Iolanthe* when we've been saying *Perola* all these weeks."

Gilbert merely glared at them, and they stopped complaining. The rehearsal got under way. As the finale began, the author left the theater. He would not enter the Savoy again until the next evening, just as the curtain was to ring down, ending the performance. While Sullivan was conducting their joint work, Gilbert, as was his habit, would be walking the streets of London. Just as the finale began, he would rush through the stage door, dash to the wings, remove his hat and coat, and then go in front of the curtain to take the bows or hisses of the audience.

The dress-rehearsal was almost over, the last notes of the finale died away and the curtain rose, showing the last picture. Sullivan called out, "Hold your positions, please. I don't want you to worry about this sudden change of name. Just sing the music and sing it well. Sing any name that comes into your head. The aduience, I am sure, won't know the difference! The only one who would find fault with you for getting mixed up is Mr. Gilbert—and he, as you know, won't be here! Go home now, get as much sleep as you can and come back tonight refreshed. I say tonight, for it is already tomorrow! Good luck to each and every one of you!" The cast, despite its nervousness, laughed and promised to do what the composer suggested.

Perhaps the principals, chorus and stagehands slept, but Gilbert, Sullivan, and Carte did not. The author of *Iolanthe* tossed about while he wondered if the players would speak his lines clearly enough to be heard in the balcony; Sullivan suffered with illness the entire night; while Carte did figures in his head for hours.

At last the evening of Saturday, November 25, 1882, arrived. As the composer entered the stage door, the players were going to their dressing rooms. All of them stopped, formed a circle around Sullivan, and gave him three cheers. He smiled and thanked them. Waving to the cheering cast, he turned and entered the tiny office of the stage-door keeper. The man's wife had been very ill, and Sullivan was anxious to learn if her condition had improved. As he left, stagehands and electricians on ther way to set the stage and train the lights crowded around to shake his hand and wish him luck. He thanked them for their hard work during rehearsals and chattered with them for several minutes. Then he went to get ready for the performance. None of those who had cheered or spoken to him knew that while Sullivan was eating his dinner, a special messenger had brought a note to his apartment stating that the friend to whom the composer had entrusted his life savings had gone bankrupt. Sullivan's entire fortune was gone. He was as poor as the day he had arrived in Leipzig!

Nor did the audience see or feel anything wrong while they watched Sullivan conduct the "Entirely New and Original Fairy Opera." They cheered the cast, called for the author and composer and went out of the theater humming Sullivan's new tunes and chuckling over Gilbert's jibes and jokes. Two hours later, in New York, theatergoers just entering the Standard Theater crowded around a bulletin board in the lobby and read a cablegram describing the wonderful reception given in London to the operetta they were about to see!

The audience in New York was as enthusiastic about the new piece as the one in London had been, and it settled down to a four months' run at the Standard, and then moved to the Fifth Avenue Theater for some weeks before going on a tour of the country.

Two days after the opening of *Iolanthe* at the Savoy, every seat had been sold for the rest of the year! Everyone wanted to see the new work which most critics hailed as the best thing Gilbert and Sullivan had ever written. There were some complaints, of course. *Punch,* always anti-Gilbert, said, "It isn't a patch on *Patience."* And one reviewer ended his criticism of the operetta by asking, "Where is this topsy-turvydom, this musical and dramatic turning of ideas wrong side out, to end?" But very few wanted it to end and thousands proved it by flocking to see performances of *Iolanthe* on both sides of the Atlantic. Those who were fortunate enough to get inside the Savoy saw the first dramatic performance in which electric lights were used as a part of theatrical costume—the fairies' wings were tipped with twinkling bulbs and their wands lit up when they were waved in time to Sullivan's music.

Of all the Gilbert-Sullivan operettas, none is more perfect than *Iolanthe.* Search through the list of the fourteen pieces in the Savoy series and it is impossible to find a more delightful work. In *Iolanthe* the author and composer are at their very best. Gilbert was never so capable as when writing about Fairyland. Despite his church music and classic compositions, Sullivan had a definite flair for light, airy tunes. In *Iolanthe,* these talents are perfectly blended. It seems as if Gilbert's words call forth the best in Sullivan, while the composer's music demanded the best of Gilbert. Full of humor, delightful conversation, gay music and sly jests at the law courts and the haughty House of Peers, it has fascinated nearly everyone who has seen it. Queen Victoria, however, was definitely not amused at the operetta's theme. Her Imperial Majesty made it plain that she failed to understand why William Gladstone, her Prime Minister, thought the piece "admirable." However, Victoria quickly forgave Sullivan for composing the music to *Iolanthe*—people were always forgiving him—and she heaped royal honors on him. Gilbert was another matter; the Queen ignored him completely, waiting to take her revenge on the man who had made fun of England's army, navy, law courts, police force, and House of Peers.

The first act of *Iolanthe* takes place in Fairyland. The sprites are singing and dancing in a ring when the curtain goes up, but it is plain to see that they are not happy. All of them still miss, after twenty-five years, their sister Iolanthe, whom their queen banished to the bottom of a stream in punishment for having married a mortal. The Fairy Queen could have sentenced her to death, but was so fond of her that she allowed Iolanthe to live on condition that she would never see her husband again. The fairies beg their leader to forgive Iolanthe, and after some hesitation the Fairy Queen summons Iolanthe from the bottom of the brook, where she has spent her exile. When Iolanthe appears, her sisters greet her with delight. "Why," they ask, "did you choose such an unattractive spot in which to live? Then, too, you've always had such a delicate chest!"

Iolanthe explains that she wants to be near her son Strephon, an Arcadian shepherd, who is half fairy, half mortal. This conversation is interrupted by the appearance of Strephon himself, who announces to all that he is "going to be married today!" His aunts—for all the fairies are his mother's sisters—flit around with joy at this news (fairies being very romantic). The only difficulty is that Strephon's loved one, Phyllis, is a ward of the Lord Chancellor of England, and that distinguished gentleman is violently opposed to the marriage. His Lordship refuses to let a common shepherd marry one of the girls under his charge. All of his wards must have wealthy husbands. Phyllis, being his favorite, must not even think of marrying someone who sits on a hillside watching sheep and who plays a flute all day. The idea of such an alliance, the Lord Chancellor has made clear, is out of the question.

Phyllis and Strephon have decided to pay no attention to

the wishes of His Lordship and have made plans to elope. The fairies tell Strephon if he needs any help in escaping from the Lord Chancellor to call on them, and dance merrily away. Phyllis, who has been looking for her loved one, rushes in and tells him that they will have to postpone their elopement, for the entire membership of the House of Peers, escorting the Lord Chancellor, is coming to visit her. All of these earls, dukes, barons, viscounts and counts appear, wearing their colorful court robes, with coronets gleaming on their heads. The reason for their costume is simple—they want to make the best possible impression on Phyllis—for all of them are in love with her. Poor girl, she doesn't know what to do! She loves Strephon, but she can have her choice of any title in England! As the peers sing to her, telling of their love, Strephon appears. The Lord Chancellor orders him to leave at once, reminding the young shepherd that there is a court order forbidding him to love Phyllis. "I know no court of law," says the youth, "the only laws I obey are those of Nature." Turning to His Lordship, Strephon cries, "The bees, the breeze, the seas, the rooks, the brooks, the gales, the vales, the fountains and the mountains cry, 'You love this maiden—take her!' Sir, are you Chancellor of the Bees and Birds, King of the Winds and Prince of Thunderclouds?"

The Lord Chancellor is greatly impressed with this speech. He admits that the shepherd has raised a fine point of law. The difficulty is that, as a judge, His Lordship can see no evidence that Nature has allied herself with Strephon. If he could provide an "affidavit from a thundercloud, or a few words on oath from a heavy shower," it would help the young man's case a great deal. As no such evidence is possible, marriage between Phyllis and Strephon is out of the question.

The members of the House of Peers surround the Lord

Chancellor and they all strut off to the stirring strains of one of Sullivan's finest marches, *The March of the Peers,* a favorite of high school orchestras on graduation day. Strephon is heartbroken. He is almost in tears when Iolanthe finds him. She is comforting him, as a good mother should, when Phyllis, escorted by two rivals for her hand, appears. Shocked to find the man she hopes to marry in the arms of a most attractive young lady, she breaks their engagement. In vain, Strephon insists that "the lady is my mother!" Unfortunately, Iolanthe, being a fairy, looks but seventeen years old, and Strephon, Phyllis knows, is twenty-four! She is sure he is lying. The peers, pefect gentlemen, merely remark, "they would not say a word that could be considered as injurious, but to find a mother younger than her son is really very curious." In anger, Phyllis offers her heart and hand to any peer who wants her. The result of this outburst of temper is an engagement to two earls at once!

Suddenly, Strephon remembers the promise of the fairies to help him and he calls for aid. Magically, the Fairy Queen and her band appear. The Lord Chancellor thinks the Queen is the mistress of a boarding school, out for a walk with her charges, and orders her to go away. Furious at this insult, the Queen weaves a spell, making Strephon a member of Parliament, and, with the backing of the fairies, he will be able to pass any law he wishes. To further punish the rudeness of the peers, she decrees that the peerage shall be thrown open to "competitive examination." Stunned, His Lordship realizes that the Queen is "a fairy from Andersen's library." The curtain falls on act one as the peers are begging for mercy, while Phyllis lies in a faint in the arms of the two earls to whom she is engaged.

Weeks have passed when the curtain rises on the second act. The stage is set to represent the yard of the Houses of Parliament, with Big Ben in the background. Everything is flooded with moonlight, and a sentry on duty marches up and down, singing "to chase monotony." Soon the yard is filled with the fairy band that has come to see how their nephew is getting along as a Member of Parliament. The fairies have another reason for visiting London—they want to see the peers; for every one of the sprites, except the Queen, has fallen in love with the lords. When the members of the upper house complain that, because Strephon has brains, he is ruining the peerage, the fairies gleefully explain that they are responsible. Yet they cannot help but feel sorry for the poor mortals who are suffering from their magic—because they love them. There is no time to comfort the peers, for the Fairy Queen enters the yard and wastes no time reminding her band that the penalty for falling in love with a mortal is death. The fairies immediately fly back to Fairyland.

Meanwhile, Phyllis, unable to choose between her two earls because she still loves Strephon, is very unhappy. To make matters worse, the Lord Chancellor has decided he would make her an ideal husband, for he admits, "I'm not so old and I'm not so plain, and I'm quite prepared to marry again." Strephon, meeting Phyllis as he is about to leave the House, asks politely which title she has decided to accept, and the heart-sick girl breaks into tears. The shepherd seizes the opportunity to tell her about his ageless mother, young-looking aunts, and the fact that he is half a fairy. His explanation is more than satisfactory. Phyllis understands perfectly, saying, "Whenever I see you kiss a very young lady, I shall know it's an elderly relative."

Happily reunited, the lovers are met by Iolanthe, who welcomes her new daughter. Everything would be perfect if it were not for the Lord Chancellor. What is Phyllis to say. to him? Will Iolanthe please use her fairy magic and win him over? Iolanthe consents, but knows that it will mean her death—for the Lord Chancellor is the husband she has promised never to see again! Wanting only to make her son happy, she goes to His Lordship, reveals her identity and pleads her boy's case, then awaits the wrath of the Fairy Queen. Just as sentence is to be pronounced upon her, all the fairies admit that they have married members of the House of Peers. If the Queen does her duty, she will wipe out the entire population of Fairyland. No one will be left but herself. The Lord Chancellor comes to the rescue. As a lawyer, he sees a most simple way out of the difficulty. The law, he points out, states that every fairy who marries a mortal must die. All that has to be done is to insert a single word— make the law read that every fairy who *doesn't* marry a mortal must die—and there you are! The Fairy Queen asks the sentry to marry her and that pleasant chap agrees, immediately sprouts wings, and the entire cast gets ready to fly away, "exchanging House of Peers for House of Peris!"

Iolanthe ran for 398 performances. Sullivan needed every cent of his share of the profits to help make up the losses his investments had brought him. One of the composer's chief sources of revenue was the sale of the vocal and piano scores, which was enormous, ten thousand of them being shipped from the music publisher's daily. Despite Sullivan's need of money, he did very little writing during the run of *Iolanthe.* He was too tired and ill. An examination by his doctor made the truth known: Sullivan's condition was so poor that he had to stop and rest before it was too late. A few conducting engagements, two or three religious compositions, the payment from Carte for the productions given in the Colonies, and his weekly portion of the receipts from the Savoy box office gave Sullivan money enough. Always a gambler, he knew that, sooner or later, he would get a chance to regain his fortune. Meanwhile, he was more than willing to wait for Lady Luck to come calling and not to go looking for her.

Gilbert, never happy when idle, began working on an idea for another opera as soon as the Savoy had been transformed into Fairyland. The author was planning to take one of his earlier comedies, *The Wicked World*, rewrite some of the verse, and let Sullivan do the rest. All the old material he had put into new form had done well—why shouldn't this work? When he talked the plan over with Carte, that master showman bluntly told the author that he didn't think much of the idea. The manager pointed out that the proposed operetta, like *Iolanthe*, was full of wand-waving sprites, and it would be "poor theater" to produce such a piece immediately. Gilbert stalked out of the Savoy in a rage. He went to Sullivan's apartment and asked the composer what he thought of the proposition. Sullivan, sick and tired of his partner's upside-down plots, agreed with Carte. Relations between the two men, never too good since the American trip, grew more strained. Gilbert failed to understand why Sullivan would agree with Carte. So, in a fit of temper, he threw the results of his work in a desk drawer—but he would, as usual, use it later. Then the author suggested something complicated called *The Mountebanks*. That, too, was turned down by Carte and Sullivan—and was also put away to be used another time.

As a matter of fact, Gilbert was having difficulty finding suitable ideas to use as the basis of a comic opera. Those newspaper critics who disliked the author (and most people didn't like him) took great delight in informing their readers that Gilbert and Sullivan were not preparing a succesor to *Iolanthe*. The reason for this, the newspapermen explained, was that Gilbert had lost whatever small ability to write he once had. Lovers of music, Glbert's foes pointed out, would in time benefit from the situation, for now Arthur Sullivan could write some worthwhile music, unhampered by Gilbert's stupid plots and silly words. All this newspaper ridicule did not make the author any easier to discuss matters with, when the partners met at the Savoy.

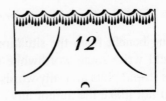

"Nature's Sole Mistake"

—*Princess Ida*

MAJOR-GENERAL STANLEY, in *The Pirates*, was speaking of the average Englishman of Victoria's day when he sang: "With all its faults, we love our House of Peers." Gilbert, as we know, was not typical of his day. The author had little or no respect for a title, or for people in high positions. Therefore, he was not especially flattered at his partner's approval of his new libretto. A lesser man might have been, but not Gilbert. For Sullivan had in May, 1883, gone to Windsor Castle, where he was dubbed a knight by Queen Victoria. Sullivan must have wondered, as he felt the sword strike him lightly on the shoulders, if Her Royal Highness remembered the day, so many years before, when she had sent him ten shillings by the Prince Consort in appreciation of his fine singing at the christening of the Duke of Albany in the Chapel Royal. How much had happened since those days of his youth! Fame and success were Sullivan's—he had everything except health. Only one thing marred his pleasure at receiving the title. If only his father and mother were alive—how proud they would be.

Sullivan's knighthood made it necessary to reprint the Savoy programs. No longer would they read "Composed by

Mr. Arthur Sullivan," but "Composed by Sir Arthur Sullivan." The new title made a difference to everyone except Gilbert. Musical England hailed the granting of the knighthood with delight. Critics who had long wanted the composer to break his partnership with Gilbert reminded their readers that while Mr. Arthur Sullivan could write comic operas, it was not proper for Sir Arthur Sullivan to devote his talents to anything save serious music. One newspaper article dealing with Sullivan's knighthood ended with a punning sentence which would have done credit to Gilbert back in the days when he was writing for *Fun:* "Let our musical daze be broken by our musical knight, and that night be the forerunner of brighter days."

Gilbert, however, was not in the mood for puns, his own or anyone else's. The author and composer, who had not been too friendly for months, were now constantly bickering. They would argue back and forth about the new opera hours on end. For the first time they seemed to be unable to understand each other professionally. Moreover, the dramatist, despite the fact that he snorted "Knighthood is a silly thing," was in reality very jealous of the honor that had come to his associate. He knew that the letter asking if the composer would accept the title had said the honor was being offered ". . . in recognition of your distinguished talents as a composer and of the services which you have rendered to the promotion of the art of music generally in this country." Gilbert, an exceptionally proud individual, could not help but wonder about his own talents as a dramatic author, and how his works had raised the standards of the British stage. Being the sort of person he was, he said nothing of this, but made cutting remarks about the honor of knighthood, and, like a spoiled child, pretended he did not care that he had not been granted a title as well as his partner.

The gossip he overheard being whispered wherever theatrical folk gathered did not help improve Gilbert's attitude toward Sullivan's title. Over the traditional midnight snack, after performances, players were boldly stating that the Queen had knighted Sullivan in order to break up the Savoy combination. During one of these discussions an actor summed up the situation in this manner: "Her Highness has been planning revenge for a long time. The only way she could show her dislike of Gilbert's work was to knight Sullivan and not his librettist. You don't think the Queen was going to let Gilbert get away with those jests in *Pinafore* at the expense of the Navy, the gibes at the police in *The Pirates* and those cutting remarks about the House of Peers which made *Iolanthe* so funny." Gilbert, overhearing this conversation, knew that the speaker was absolutely correct. What the author didn't know was that the head of the British Empire was to show her dislike of him in a much stronger form before she satisfied her desire to punish him for making fun of English traditions.

Always an irritable man, Gilbert was getting more difficult each day. He had not completely forgiven Carte and Sullivan for turning down his two suggestions for a Savoy opera and barely spoke to them. As critical of his own work as he was of a fellow author's, Gilbert realized that *Iolanthe*'s successor was not up to the standard he and Sullivan had set in their previous works and he was annoyed at himself for offering an inferior production to the public. Add to this the feeling he had about his partner's knighthood, and it is easy to see why everyone sighed with relief when Gilbert left the Savoy after one of his meteoric visits.

Sullivan, however, was his usual gracious self so far as Gilbert was concerned. Still smarting from the cutting remarks aimed at him during the American tour, the composer smiled understandingly at his associate's jests at knights and knighthood. He went out of his way to show Gilbert that their relationship was just the same as it had always been. Unfortunately, even when he tried to be pleasant to his partner, Sullivan caused friction between them. Take for example the party he gave celebrating his forty-first birthday and his title. It was a gala affair. The list of guests included members of the royal family; Burnard, the editor of *Punch,* who never would print any of Gilbert's verse; Millais, the famous painter, and other important people. Nothing had been omitted that might make the evening a success. For entertainment, Sullivan had the most famous opera stars of Europe sing, and his guests were thrilled. That is, they were all thrilled but one. The name of the exception was W. S. Gilbert.

Gilbert had no love for music and never enjoyed the words of any writer except himself. As a result, the beautiful voices of the singers bored him. Boredom gave way to annoyance when Sullivan, who delighted in surprising people, told him that he had had a telephone line strung up between his apartment and the stage of the Savoy. Why, Gilbert wondered, had the composer done this? He soon found out. At a quarter past eleven, Sullivan excused himself and telephoned the theater. Waiting on the stage of the Savoy was the entire company, who sang selections from *Iolanthe*—the first broadcast on record! While the other guests sat spellbound, little realizing that another generation would not only hear, but see the Gilbert and Sullivan operettas in the comfort of their living rooms, their author sat, arms folded, his face livid with rage.

"This has been, no doubt, quite interesting, *Mr.* Sullivan," he snarled, "but personally I think the only way our work can be really appreciated is to see it on the stage of the Savoy. Therefore, if you will allow me, may I offer your guests a box at the theater tomorrow evening, so that they can watch the opera, instead of merely hearing it?" Most of the assembled company knew what had prompted the invitation—Gilbert's pride in his stage-direction. They smiled and accepted.

Knight or no knight, Sullivan was committed to *Princess Ida, or Castle Adamant,* so he began to compose the score. It did not take Sir Arthur long to discover that the piece was far inferior to any of the other works Gilbert had given him. Carte set the date for the opening as the first week in January, 1884. As the days went by, Sullivan, as usual, accomplished little. It wasn't laziness that prevented his working. He was ill—far more ill than he had ever been before. Usually the composer took his ailment in stride—for he had learned to live with pain. Now, for the first time, he was really worried about his physical condition. Fred Clay, who had introduced Gilbert to Sullivan, had recently suffered a paralytic stroke while taking a midnight stroll through the streets of London, after conducting the first performance of his play, *The Golden Ring.* Clay's misfortune upset Sullivan terribly and made him extremely nervous about his own health. Despite the fact that the opening of *Princess Ida* was only three weeks away, he was unable to work.

Sullivan steeled himself to his pain and thoughts, and began the task of composing the music for *Princess Ida.* As the days passed, he grew weaker and weaker. He spent all day at the Savoy—and usually most of the night—for things were not going smoothly at rehearsals. When the composer arrived at Queen's Mansions, worn out from his prolonged activities, he still had a great deal to do, and often remained at his desk working until daybreak. The strain was terrific and Sullivan was in agony with pain. Day after day he followed the same routine, dragging himself from theater to home, from home to theater. He lost all track of time. One day was like another. New Year's Eve found him composing. The bells of London chimed out a farewell to 1883 and a greeting to 1884, but Sir Arthur did not hear them. Intent on his music, he was completely lost in a world of his own making. The first the composer knew that another year had arrived was when his door opened, after a soft knock, and Louis, leading the rest of the servants, entered to wish their master a "Happy New Year."

Sir Arthur staggered to his feet and thanked his visitors. Then he went back to work. It was well into the next morning before he completed his score. The rest of New Year's day was spent in rehearsing the company at the Savoy. Exhausted, he drove himself at top speed for the next three days. The day before the opening of *Princess Ida*, Gilbert and Sullivan drilled the cast until nearly three o'clock in the morning. Utterly fatigued, Sir Arthur went home, fell into bed and tried to sleep. Suddenly, a terrible pain swept through his body and he screamed for help. The doctor, who had been summoned by a frightened Louis, minced no words. "Sir Arthur, you are overworked, completely rundown, mentally and physically exhausted. You must make up your mind that you must stay in bed for a long period and rest. Yes, I know your new operetta is being produced tonight for the first time, but you won't be there, for now I'm going to give you an injection of morphine that will bring you the sleep you need so greatly."

Sullivan got the injection, but he did not sleep. The pain grew worse. The afternoon wore on, and the doctor, aware of the suffering of his patient, gave him another jab. It was now almost curtain time. Sullivan called for a cup of black coffee, crept out of bed, fell heavily to the floor, clambered to his feet and rang for Louis. The valet tried to argue with his master, but the composer insisted that Louis help him dress. François Cellier, the old friend of Chapel Royal days, and now assistant conductor at the Savoy, was just about to start the overture when Sir Arthur entered the orchestra pit. A packed house gave him a wonderful reception. The composer raised his baton—it took every bit of strength he had to make the gesture—and the first notes of Gilbert and Sullivan's "respectable perversion of Tennyson's *Princess*" began.

There are several unusual things about *Princess Ida*. It is the only one of the Savoy series in three acts. All of the other Gilbert and Sullivan operettas, excluding *Trail by Jury*, consist of two acts. The entire libretto is written in blank verse. This literary form has confused audiences since the opening night. Few of the players enjoyed their parts, though normally the Savoy company were very happy in the roles Gilbert created for them. Finally, because it makes fun of a situation that does not seem to be the least bit funny today, it is the least interesting of all the operas. In this streamlined age, we see nothing strange in women scientists, doctors, lawyers and professors; the idea was laughable when Victoria ruled, but that was years ago. The Savoy audience found Gilbert and Sullivan's treatment of the woman of the future quite amusing, however, although the operetta only ran from January 5, 1884, to October 9, 1884, for a total of 246 performances. The author and composer had looked forward to a run of at least a year.

When the curtain rises on *Princess Ida,* the pavilion in King Hildebrand's palace is seen. Courtiers throng the stage, looking through spyglasses and telescopes "for a sign of royal Gama, who today should cross the water with his fascinating daughter—Ida is her name." From time to time, the lookouts report to King Hildebrand and his son, Prince Hilarion, that they can see no trace of the ruler of the neighboring country. This is quite serious, for in order to assure peace between the two nations, Hilarion and Ida were married when they were babes in the cradle. The bridesmaids were six weeks old and the wedding feast was "rolls steeped in milk, and other softened food." Now, some twenty years later, Hilarion has claimed his bride. If King Gama does not produce his daughter immediately, the two nations will have to go to war!

At last Gama appears. A misshapened old man, "with an irritating chuckle and a fascinating leer," he brags, "I can tell a woman's age in half a minute and I do!" A most disagreeable person, Gama tells King Hildebrand his favorite sport is finding fault with people. Hildebrand stops his royal cousin's chatter about the joy of annoying people to ask why he has not brought Ida with him. Gama explains that his daughter is a modern maiden and has no respect for her father! Moreover, against his royal wishes, Ida has left the court and gone to the Woman's University at Castle Adamant, where she is lecturing on the stupidity of men and the wisdom of women. No man, Gama tells his listeners, is allowed inside the walls of the castle. In fact, the students sing no music in church, for they dislike "hymns"! Nor will these serious young ladies have any male animals in the university barns, so they are awakened in the morning by crowing "done by an accomplished hen!"

While Hildebrand agrees that all this information about modern education is quite interesting, His Royal Highness points out that the marriage contract has been broken. Ida has not been delivered as specified. Hildebrand orders his men to throw Gama and his three sons into a dungeon. Meanwhile, Prince Hilarion and his friends, Cyril and Florian, decide to go to the castle and see for themselves just what the women are doing there. So, as Gama is marched off to jail, the Prince and his companions set out for Adamant.

The second act shows the garden in Castle Adamant.

There is a river at the back of the stage, crossed by a rustic bridge. Seated on the river bank are all the beautiful students of the university, dressed in cap and gown. They are listening to a lecture by stout Lady Blanche, one of the best loved and most learned professors on the faculty. Her words about men are most important ones, for she alone, of any of the instructors, has been married (poor thing!). It is impossible to secure a place in the lecture hall when she lectures on "The Is, the Might Be, and the Must," so her classes are conducted outdoors, weather permitting. While Lady Blanche is talking to the girls, Hilarion and his friends climb over the castle walls. The young men examine everything they see, and come across some academic robes. They try them on, find they fit perfectly, and dance about the garden, pretending they are young girls. Just then Princess Ida enters.

Startled, Hilarion and his chums immediately stop dancing. Forgetting themselves, they bow deeply to Her Royal Highness. Then, suddenly remembering where they are, and what they are supposed to be, the three make low curtsies. Ida greets the trio warmly and asks, "What would you with us?" Hilarion explains that they are three maids who wish to join the university. The Princess welcomes them as students on condition that they will obey all the rules. The chief rule says:

> *"There are a hundred maids within these walls,*
> *All good, all learned, and all beautiful:*
> *They are prepared to love you: will you swear*
> *To give the fulness of your love to them?"*

With one voice the young men assure her that they will obey *that* rule! Nor do they hesitate to promise "that they will never marry any man," and nod assent when asked if they will "prefer our maids to all mankind." Arrangements are made for Hilarion, Cyril and Florian to join the classes, when Florian discovers that one of the students is his sister, Psyche, who "at school alarmed her mates because she called a buttercup *'ranunculus bulbosus.'*" What shall the Prince and his friends do? Psyche is sure to recognize her brother. The boys decide to explain everything to Psyche. They do so and she promises to keep the identity of the new students to herself. Unfortunately, Melissa, Lady Blanche's daughter, overhears the conversation! Everything seems lost, but Melissa is thrilled. These are the first men she has ever seen! Never would she expose such delightful persons to the wrath of Princess Ida. Psyche takes her brother and his companions to their dormitory as Lady Blanche appears. She asks Melissa questions about the new students. The confused girl tries to answer her mother, but all she can do is murmur something about their fine voices. Lady Blanche agrees that the new students have fine voices, but suggests it is very odd that one should be "a tenor, two baritones!" Melissa explains that they have colds, but her mother makes it plain that she knows they are men. There being no escape, Melissa explains that Prince Hilarion has come to take Princess Ida away—and if he does, Lady Blanche will, as a matter of course, be promoted to head the university. An ambitious woman, Lady Blanche agrees to keep silent.

The silence of Psyche, Melissa and Lady Blanche is in vain. Ida discovers that the new students are men. Angry at the idea of males within the walls of Castle Adamant, she runs to the bridge, calling on all the students to help her throw the intruders over the wall. Blind with rage, she cannot see where she is going, trips and falls into the water. Hilarion saves her from drowning. The Prince's heroism makes no difference, Ida still will have nothing to do with men! In a loud voice she calls her "Daughters of the Plough," who bind Hilarion, Florian and Cyril and march them off to prison. Just then Melissa rushes in and cries that Hildebrand and his army are at the castle gate. Before Ida can organize a defense, her father-in-law and his soldiers rush in. His Royal Highness informs the Princess that she and her father, King Gama, have broken a contract and he demands justice. Hildebrand gives Ida until morning to release the Prince and his two companions and make arrangements to return to court as Hilarion's bride. Ida angrily refuses as the curtain falls because she maintains:

> *"Man is of no kind of use—*
> *Man's a donkey—Man's a goose*
> *Man is coarse and Man is plain—*
> *Man is more or less insane—*
> *Man's a ribald—Man's a rake,*
> *Man is Nature's sole mistake!"*

The third act takes place in the courtyard of the castle. Ida has spent the night rallying her forces. The students of the university are dressed in armor and carry battle-axes. They have left their rifles behind "for fear they might go off." Pysche, who is in charge of the castle's supply of gunpowder, suggests that the girls use their flashing eyes instead of an explosion to blind the invaders. This is too much! Princess Ida is almost ready to give up the struggle when she learns that her father and brothers wish to see her. Gama explains that, as a hostage, he cannot fight for his daughter, but Hildebrand does not want to fight women. Therefore, it has been arranged that Hilarion, Florian and Cyril will fight Ida's brothers. If the Prince and his friends lose the contest, Gama and his sons will be allowed to return to their native land. If Ida's brothers are defeated, the Princess must abide by the marriage contract. At first Ida refuses to become a prize fought over by *men*. Gama begs his daughter to consent, and at last she gives her permission.

After a brief battle, Hilarion and his friends triumph over their rivals. The Princess turns the university over to Lady Blanche, admits she loves Hilarion, Psyche falls into Cyril's arms and Melissa swears undying love to Florian as the curtain falls.

Sullivan did the best he could with his partner's plot. There is much delightful music in the score of *Princess Ida*, and much orchestral humor. Gilbert had tried to overcome the weakness of his story by making the production the most lavish of any of the operettas presented at the Savoy. The costumes of the sweet girl graduates were of the finest materials, rich in coloring and beautifully made. The armor was not fashioned of papier-mâché, which was normally used on the stage. It was made of silver-gilt by a famous French firm, the finest armor that ever appeared in an English theatrical performance. Never had such artistic scenery been built—and never had Gilbert drilled a cast more thoroughly.

However, he had written his operetta with too heavy a hand. Perhaps if Sullivan had taken *The Mountebanks* instead of *Princess Ida*, the partners could have created a more pleasing work. At any rate, *Princess Ida* is definitely not Gilbert at his best. Nor, despite its somewhat brilliant music, does it show the great musical genius of Sir Arthur. The faithful, as usual, came to the Savoy, but newspaper critics, always anxious to belabor Gilbert, wasted no time in pointing out that the plot of the new Savoy production dragged. The worst of all this criticism was the fact that the author knew it was true. Gilbert had no defense. Nor could he talk matters over with Sullivan. The composer was confined to bed, seriously ill.

Meanwhile, there was trouble backstage at the Savoy. Most of the principals were asking for higher wages. A look at Gilbert's face should have warned them it was no time to ask for a raise! The members of the company should have known by the number of vacant seats that faced them at every performance that *Princess Ida* was not making the large sums of money the previous operettas had earned. Nevertheless, they asked for pay increases. Gilbert glared and glowered at the players and grunted "NO!" to every demand for more money. Carte agreed with the author about raising salaries, for the manager was always careful of expenses. As for Sullivan, in his condition, the payroll at the Savoy was the least of his worries.

Jessie Bond, the leading lady at the Savoy, was extremely upset at the refusal of the management to increase her salary. Miss Bond wrote long letters to Gilbert, explaining that *Princess Ida* was a most difficult piece to play. She got short letters back, but no additional money. Charming Jessie Bond was right. *Princess Ida* was a laborious chore for the players. Henry Lytton, who many years later succeeded George Grossmith as the "comic" in the operettas (and who was knighted for his skill), used to spend an hour making up his face for Gama. Then he had to adjust the humpback and twisted leg! Incidentally, Sir Henry tells a delightful story of how a young naval officer who had overstayed his leave came to Lytton's dressing room one night after the show and asked for help. "You see, sir," the sailor explained, "I am due at the Naval College in an hour. It is an impossibility to get there in time—and I will be court-martialed for being late and my career will be ruined."

"I'm very sorry to hear it," replied the actor, "but what can I do about it?"

"Well, Mr. Lytton, you do such a wonderful job making up your face for Gama, I wonder if you would make me up to look like an admiral. Admirals do not have to report at fixed hours! I'm sure you could make me look like an admiral, Mr. Lytton. Please, sir, will you try?"

Lytton was delighted with the idea and set to work immediately. Two hours later, the young officer, wearing a false beard, not only walked through the gates of the Naval College unchallenged, but was saluted by the guards. They knew an admiral when they saw one! The best part of the story is that, years later, the young man really became an admiral—and he owed it all to Gilbert and Sullivan!

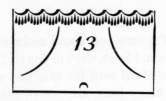

13

"Here's a Pretty Mess"

—*The Mikado*

RICHARD D'OYLY CARTE, seated in his office at the Savoy, was looking through his mail. The manager recognized Sullivan's writing on one of the envelopes and tore it open. What, he wondered as he unfolded the single sheet of paper inside, did the composer want? Carte soon found out. Sir Arthur was resigning from the partnership! At first Carte was dumbfounded; then, remembering Sullivan's illness, was not too concerned. As soon as the musician felt better, he would change his mind. There was no need to worry. It might be well, however, Carte reasoned, to have dinner with Sir Arthur and talk things over with him. So the manager took Helen Lenoir, his secretary, who had "booked" Oscar Wilde's tour in America and who was soon to become Carte's second wife, to see the composer. The manager felt that with a lady along, his call would appear to be merely a friendly visit. Sir Arthur, still weak but feeling much better, was delighted to see Carte and Miss Lenoir. After an hour of general conversation, Carte brought up the note he had received that morning. Sullivan insisted, "The letter means just what it says. I am not going to write the music for any more comic operas!" Carte went home upset and worried.

The manager of the Savoy had good reason to be worried. Carte had created the combination of Gilbert and Sullivan and now it looked as if it were going to fall apart. He was determined to do everything in his power to prevent this happening. A friendly letter went from the Savoy to Sir Arthur, asking if the composer had changed his mind. The answer came back, "No more comic operas."

"Let us talk this matter over," requested Carte in another letter. Sullivan and Carte discussed the composer's attitude and the result of their conversation was—"no more comic operas!" By this time it was mid-March and *Princess Ida* was playing to poor houses. Not only was it Lent (always a difficult time of year for theaters), but Gilbert's blank verse was proving rather unpopular with audiences. The combination hurt the box office. Something must be prepared to take *Princess Ida's* place. Carte put more pressure on Sir Arthur—and in the midst of a series of very heated discussions, the composer packed his bags and took a boat for Brussels.

Sir Arthur's departure for Belgium brought about a change in Carte's attitude toward the composer's resignation from the Savoy combination. A close friend of both Gilbert and Sullivan, he had, up to now, discussed the proposed break-up with Sullivan in an amicable fashion. However, his harmonious relations with Gilbert and Sullivan had not prevented Carte from securing a legal claim on their services. He had, a year before, drawn up an agreement in which he legally bound the author and composer to write, score, and have ready for production an operetta at six months' notice. Realizing that nothing would move Sullivan save this legal claim, Carte sent the composer a formal request for a new work. Carte has never received the full

credit due him for his part in the Gilbert-Sullivan partnership. High upon the list of brilliant things he did in managing the two men must go the contract which gave him the
right to demand a new operetta at six months' notice. For
if this agreement had not been signed, the most delightful,
famous and colorful of all the Savoy series never would
have been written. Victoria and the music critics would have
rejoiced, but how theatrical history would have suffered!

Gilbert, of course, had a plot ready for Sullivan. Finding
a theme for an opera was a simple task for the author of
the *Bab Ballads*. All Gilbert had to do was to study his
bound volumes of *Fun*. The only problem was, would the
idea be worth while? Carte told Gilbert of Sullivan's desire to resign, and the news shocked him. Like Carte, Gilbert failed to understand the composer's attitude. Gilbert
and Sullivan were making money and were famous. Why
should Sir Arthur want to resign? Gilbert promised Carte
he would try to make Sullivan change his mind. The author
wrote to Brussels and tactfully (a major accomplishment
for him), reminded Sullivan of the partners' legal responsi-
bilities to Carte. In his letter, Gilbert also mentioned his
new libretto and stressed the point that he had borne in
mind all the composer's objections to previous works and
had governed himself accordingly.

Sir Arthur had, meanwhile, written to Carte and definitely stated that he could not, and would not, write another
work of the type he had been doing with Gilbert. When the
letter arrived, Carte and Gilbert sat in the office of the
Savoy, planning an attack. The one thing the pair was afraid
of was that Sullivan was taking his knighthood too seriously.
Perhaps he was, after all, going to devote himself to classical
music!

"I just can't understand Sullivan," sighed Gilbert. "I just
can't. Look here, Carte. I've got a perfectfully wonderful

idea for a new opera. Listen. A man swallows a lozenge and by means of its magical powers becomes the person he would like to be. For example, an elderly gentleman turns into a young, handsome lad; a thief into a judge and a . . ."

"Yes, I know, Gilbert," interrupted Carte, "that's the plot you've been forcing on Sullivan for a year. That's one reason why he doesn't want to work with you any more. He thinks your plots are too outlandish. There's nothing real about the themes of your librettos. Besides, as your manager, I tell you frankly, I don't think much of that lozenge idea either. It's too much like Wells' potion in *The Sorcerer* —a charm that would change people's characters. However, right now that's not the main issue. It is more important to decide what we are going to say to Sullivan to make him change his mind about composing music for comic operas."

There was nothing that Carte and Gilbert could say to Sir Arthur, for Sullivan, in a blistering letter to Gilbert, made it very plain that he had no desire to be associated with him. The composer bluntly said that he was sick and tired of upside-down plots and he had, in *Princess Ida,* drawn upon his last bit of originality. Sir Arthur went on to say that if he continued to write music for comic opera, he would have to present the same tunes, slightly disguised, over and over again. Then came the statement that made Gilbert's blood boil. "The music is never allowed to rise and speak for itself," Sullivan wrote. Always, complained the composer, his music had to give way to Gilbert's words.

Gilbert pounded on Carte's desk. "What is the matter with the man?" he shouted. "Anyone with common sense knows that Sullivan's music has always drowned out my words!" Reading the next paragraph in Sir Arthur's letter, the author's blood pressure reached new heights, since the composer made it very clear that Gilbert's plots were the main reason why he wanted to break off his relations with the Savoy. On the other hand, Sullivan wrote, he would welcome a story that was better written, and one in which humor did not spoil serious situations. In other words, Gilbert was to forget his twisting of fact into fancy and write more seriously. If, however, the author could offer nothing but his usual comic opera plot, much as Sullivan regretted it, their joint workmanship was at an end.

Gilbert was almost frothing at the mouth when he reached the end of Sullivan's letter! Choking with rage, the author sputtered, "How dare he tell me how to write!" Within an hour of reading Sir Arthur's criticism of his work, Gilbert had replied to his composer in an extremely nasty note. On receiving Gilbert's reply, Sullivan decided that he had better return to London and discuss matters with Gilbert and Carte. At the conference which followed Sir Arthur's return, Carte did nothing but insist that Gilbert and Sullivan fulfill the requirements of their signed agreement. The manager let the composer and author do most of the talking. At last, after several hours of argument, Sir Arthur declared, "There is no need of any more discussion. I will have nothing to do with the lozenge plot."

Gilbert, despite his temper, was an extremely just person and he suggested a way out of the difficulty. "I say, Carte," the author proposed, "what do you think of this idea—let me drop out of our arrangement for one work and let Sullivan set someone else's plot? Perhaps the trouble lies in the fact that Sullivan has worked with me for such a long time that my words fail to give him any inspiration." Turning to Sir Arthur, Gilbert continued, "I can't figure out what you want for a comic opera plot. There's a very great possibility that someone else can. So why not work with another librettist for one piece?"

"I wouldn't think of doing any such thing," Sir Arthur quickly replied. "There is no one in the world who can write comic operas as well as you do. Bret Harte, the American author, has asked me to set a musical piece about the California gold rush, but I am not interested in working with any other writer. If I am to compose music for light opera, it will be for a work written by you, Gilbert, and no one else. But I repeat, I will not accept the lozenge plot!"

For hours the two men argued back and forth. Gilbert finally took his plot home, rewrote it and called on Sullivan, accompanied by Miss Lenoir and Carte. For hours Gilbert, Sullivan and Carte discussed the rewritten opera, while Miss Lenoir took notes. Finally it was decided that Gilbert should go ahead, submit his finished work to Sullivan, and if the composer approved, it would be set to music. In a few days Gilbert had the manuscript ready for Sir Arthur to read. Sullivan did not like what Gilbert had written and told the author so in a diplomatic note. If only Gilbert would write an opera that did not depend on the supernatural or improbable, sighed Sullivan as he signed the letter!

Sullivan was, of course, expecting far too much!

When Sir Arthur's refusal to score the final version of the lozenge plot arrived, Gilbert's temper exploded. Now it was the author who refused to consider working with Sullivan! Gilbert and Sullivan exchanged another series of bitter letters, with the result that both men were convinced that the partnership was ended. Carte went from the composer's apartment to the author's house, begging his associates to reconsider their decision to sever relations. There was absolutely no hope that Gilbert and Sullivan would ever pool their talents again, when something "supernatural" actually did happen. The Japanese sword that hung on the wall of Gilbert's study fell to the floor—and *The Mikado* resulted!

Anyone else but Gilbert would have merely picked up the weapon and rehung in on the wall. But as the author held the sword in his hands, he thought of what was happening in the Knightsbridge section of London. There, for the amusement and instruction of sightseers, several Japanese families, dressed in their national costumes, went through their daily activities as if they were in their homeland. In fact, an entire village—inhabitants, shops, tea-houses, theater, temple and homes—had been brought directly from Japan. Even the planks on which the toymaker, potter and letter-writer squatted as they worked had been imported. Visiting this panorama of Oriental life was one of the popular amusements of the day. It was considered stylish to go to Knightsbridge for tea, served Japanese fashion—and everyone wanted to be considered stylish.

Always quick to use a current fad as material in his librettos, Gilbert had an inspiration. "I wonder," the author muttered as he placed the sword on his desk, "if I can use this interest in the Japanese village. There ought to be some way of treating it. Such a plot would overcome Sullivan's silly objections to what he calls my constant use of supernatural and improbable plots. Now, let me see . . ."

It was only a matter of an hour or two before Gilbert had a definite plan. The author then wrote a letter to Sir Arthur, informing the composer that in a day or two he would call, bringing a rough outline of a new operetta. Gilbert made it clear that there was no magic lozenge, no love philtre, no exchanging of babes in the cradle in his proposed plot. Sullivan answered immediately. He promised that he would compose the music to such a piece without waiting to hear more about it. Carte, who was informed of the contents of these letters, sighed with relief. The partnership was saved!

Gilbert set to work immediately. Sir Arthur decided to take a vacation. The composer announced that he did not intend to write a single note until Gilbert's libretto was in its final form. Neither Gilbert nor Carte argued with Sullivan. Both the manager and author were content that Sir Arthur had returned to the Savoy. While Gilbert devoted all of his time to the new opera, Sullivan joined his society friends and made the rounds of all the race tracks. There was nothing the composer liked as much as watching a horse race—especially if he were backing one of the entries. Sir Arthur's skill in musical composition was great, but it did not equal his ability to pick "also rans"—horses which never won! The reason for his constant failure to pick winners was the fact that the composer, being a reckless gambler, always bet on "long shots"—horses which had little chance to win, but if they did, paid tremendous sums to those who had backed them. Only once did Sir Arthur win a huge bet. This was when he backed Throstle in the Derby, one of the most famous of English races. For the $150 Sullivan wagered that the horse would win, the composer collected $5000. Even this large sum failed to make up for his losses, for he, like all gamblers, lost far more than he won.

Meanwhile, not wishing to close the Savoy until the new opera was ready for production, Carte decided to revive *The Sorcerer* and *Trial by Jury*. It was a brilliant idea. The operettas were received with great enthusiasm. In fact, the revivals were greater successes than the original productions! The reason for this hearty welcome to Gilbert and Sullivan's earlier work lay in the fact that over the years the partners had created, along with their operas, an appreciative audience. When their comic operas first appeared, they were so totally different from the usual theatrical offerings that many theatergoers didn't understand them. Now, seven years later, English audiences knew the folk and countryside of Gilbert and Sullivan's magic land as well as they knew their local neighborhoods. For 150 performances, packed houses roared at John Wellington Wells and the learned judge. Sullivan had stopped long enough in his round of social engagements to rewrite some of the music. Busy with *The Mikado,* Gilbert had done nothing to his original librettos. He had, of course, supervised rehearsals of the revivals, but that was all.

Once he had completed the new music, Sullivan went to Switzerland. Gilbert returned to his desk after the opening nights and worked on the new operetta. Carte, delighted with the long lines outside the Savoy box office, decided to try another attraction. Recalling the tremendous success of the children's performance of *H. M. S. Pinafore,* Carte instructed his stage manager, Richard Barker, to prepare a juvenile production of *The Pirates of Penzance,* to be shown at matinees during the Christmas season. Barker enjoyed working with youngsters and was delighted with the assignment. As soon as the announcement went out that young singers and actors were wanted at the Savoy, applicants swarmed to the theater. Although Barker had ruled that no child above the age of sixteen could apply—400 adolescents within the age limit appeared at the audition! Carte and Barker spent two weeks listening to tryouts. Finally they picked the principals and chorus of twenty boys and twenty-five girls. François Cellier then set to work teaching the juvenile company the music of *The Pirates.* Barker took charge of the stage direction.

No sooner had the children settled down to the routine of rehearsing than the busybodies became active. Hands were raised in horror at the idea of youngsters appearing on the stage. The proposed juvenile version of *The Pirates* caused so much discussion that the London Board of Education conducted an investigation of the Savoy and its management. In its report, the Board of Education stated that the young actors were well taken care of at the Savoy and would, beyond all doubt, gain much from association with such upstanding gentlemen and artists as Barker and Cellier. Once the opposition to the venture was removed, the young folk were free to be drilled in their parts. Gilbert would not have worked an adult company any harder than Barker did his juvenile troupe. The results of hours of rehearsal was a production perfect in every respect. After the Christmas holidays, the juvenile company was sent on a tour of the larger cities of Great Britain and played to capacity houses at every stop.

Meanwhile, Gilbert was rehearsing *The Mikado* with the regular Savoy company. As usual, the author nearly drove the players into nervous breakdowns with his insistence on perfection. It was no easy task to change Savoyards into Japanese. Even Gilbert admitted the chore was too much for him, despite the fact that he had spent long hours in the library reading everything he could find about things Japanese. Then he thought once more of Knightsbridge. Quickly he made arrangements with the management of the Japanese village for a native couple to attend rehearsals at the Savoy and assist him.

One flaw marred this arrangement. The Japanese girl who was assigned to teach the ladies of the Savoy chorus how to walk, sit, dance, open, close and wave a fan could say but two words in English! In Knightsbridge, the Oriental miss had worked in the tea-house, and all she had to say when serving her customers was, "Sixpence, please." Despite this language handicap, however, she managed to instruct the ladies of the company in Japanese gestures. Soon the cast was as Oriental as one could wish. Even Gilbert was satisfied.

Whenever Gilbert produced a play he made it a rule to use the best possible scenery and costumes. For *The Mikado* the author insisted that the chorus girls' robes be made from the best Japanese silk. The men's costumes were copies from real Japanese designs, prepared by an expert in Oriental art. Dresses for the women principals were, for the most part, genuine antique robes—one of them being over two hundred years old. Remembering the attention the beautiful armor in *Princess Ida* had attracted, Gilbert had imported from Japan some very old suits of mail. When the armor arrived at the Savoy, it was found that not only was every suit too small for any member of the cast to wear—it was also so heavy that not one actor, even if he had been able to get into it, would have been capable of taking a step!

Thanks to the aid of the Japanese couple from Knightsbridge, Gilbert was ready long before the opening night. Sullivan was not ready. Nor did it look as if he ever would be. Sir Arthur was devoting every waking minute to his task —one night he composed sixty-three pieces of music! It was not until a week before the first performance that the composer finished his score. Then a final mad round of dress rehearsals began. At last, on Saturday, March 15, 1885, before an audience which filled the Savoy, the first performance of *The Mikado, or the Town of Titipu* took place.

The courtyard of the official residence of the Lord High Executioner of Titipu is seen when the curtain rises on the first act of *The Mikado*. A large throng of singing and fan-waving Japanese are interrupted by Nanki-Poo, a wandering minstrel, "a thing of shreds and patches," who asks where he can find the beautiful maid, Yum-Yum. "Young man, I'm sorry for you," says a haughty noble, "but Yum-Yum is engaged to Ko-Ko." Pish-Tush, for that is the noble's name, goes on to explain that although Ko-Ko was formerly a tailor, he is now, as Lord High Executioner, the most important person in Titipu.

Nanki-Poo is dumbfounded. How, he asks, did a person of such lowly birth as Ko-Ko reach so high a position? Pish-

Tush tells the minstrel that when the Mikado passed a law against flirting, in which the penalty for one "who flirted, leered or winked" at a girl was beheading, the decree "caused great dismay throughout the land." So:

> "... *we straight let out on bail*
> *A convict from the county jail*
> *Whose head was next*
> *On some pretext*
> *Condemned to be mown off*
> *And made* him *Headsman, for we said*
> *'Who's next to be decapited*
> *Cannot cut off another's head*
> *Until he's cut his own off.'* "

Pish-Tush tells Nanki-Poo that all the high ranking officials of the town resigned rather than serve under Ko-Ko. That is, all of them resigned except Poo-Bah, who willingly took over the offices of First Lord of the Treasury, Lord Chief Justice, Commander-in-Chief, Lord High Admiral, Master of the Buckhounds, Groom of the Back Stairs, Archbishop of Titipu and Lord Mayor (both acting and elect). Incidentally, Poo-Bah also took over the salaries attached to these positions!

The entrance of Ko-Ko makes further conversation impossible. The Lord High Executioner introduces himself and promises to be an outstanding Headsman. As a matter of fact, Ko-Ko informs his fellow-townsmen, he has been thinking about his duties and "has a little list" of people "who never would be missed" and soon will start beheading these unfortunates with his snickersnee. Poo-Bah and Ko-Ko then discuss the Lord High Executioner's approaching wedding, and as they are talking Yum-Yum and her two chums, Peep-Bo and Pitti-Sing, the "three little maids from school," enter, see Nanki-Poo and rush to greet him.

Ko-Ko is extremely angry with the girls and order Nanki-Poo to leave Titipu at once. The minstrel pretend to do so, but comes back to talk to Yum-Yum. Nanki-Poo tells the maid how much he loves her. Yum-Yum is thrilled but says she is promised to Ko-Ko. Moreover, she point out, "a wandering minstrel who plays a wind instrumen outside tea-houses is hardly a fitting husband for the ward of a Lord High Executioner." Nanki-Poo asks his loved on if she can keep a secret. She assures him that any secret i safe with her. Nanki-Poo then asks whether it would make any difference in Yum-Yum's attitude toward his proposa of marriage if he could prove he was no musician. Laugh ingly, Yum-Yum says that she was sure Nanki-Poo wasn' a musician the minute she heard him play! Slightly annoyed because he is proud of his musical ability, Nanki-Poo draw himself up proudly and tells the astonished girl that he i really the son of His Imperial Majesty, the Mikado, in dis guise! Nanki-Poo explains that he has fled his father's cour in fear of Katisha, a homely and elderly lady. "All I did wa act pleasant and smile at her," he moans, "but she, unde the flirting law has claimed me for her husband. I mus marry Katisha or be put to death!"

Just then the entire population of Titipu comes rushing into the courtyard. A message has been received from the Mikado, stating that unless the town of Titipu has an exe cution within a month, the office of Lord High Executione will be abolished and the city reduced to the rank of a vil lage. What is to be done? Everyone will be punished fo making a tailor Lord High Executioner. Of course, Ko-Ko *could* execute himself—for he is the first one on the lis to be beheaded, but as suicide is punishable by death, he refuses to commit the act! In the middle of the discussion Nanki-Poo appears, rope in hand. Broken-hearted because he cannot marry Yum-Yum, the young man has decided to hang himself. Ko-Ko tells the Mikado's son he is foolish to commit suicide. It would be far better to be beheaded at the hands of the Lord High Executioner. Ko-Ko lists the advantages for Nanki-Poo. There will be, he states "a procession—bands, death march—bell tolling—all the girls in tears—then, when it's all over, general rejoicings and a display of fireworks in the evening. *You* won't see them, but they'll be there just the same."

Nanki-Poo consents to Ko-Ko's proposition. There is, however, one condition. Yum-Yum must marry him immediately. Then, at the end of the month, when she is a widow, Ko-Ko can marry her. Worried about the message from the Mikado, Ko-Ko agrees to this arrangement and all are rejoicing that the city is saved when Katisha enters. She is a most ugly and disagreeable woman. Her demands that Nanki-Poo come with her are drowned out by the chorus as the curtain falls.

Night has fallen when the second act begins. The soft Japanese moonlight falls on Ko-Ko's garden, which is lit by beautiful lanterns. Yum-Yum is braiding her raven hair and making up for her wedding. Everything is as perfect as it can be. Then Ko-Ko dashes in and makes the startling announcement that he has just discovered that when a man is beheaded, his wife is buried alive! Yum-Yum bursts into tears. Suffocation is such a stuffy death! All seems lost! There is no time to figure a way out of this difficulty, for a blare of trumpets announcing the arrival of the Mikado is heard. With no time to make plans, Ko-Ko, shaking with fear, says he will bribe Poo-Bah to sign an affidavit that an execution has taken place. Ko-Ko rushes Yum-Yum and Nanki-Poo out of the garden and prepares to greet the Mikado.

"A more humane Mikado never did in Japan exist" than this one. His Imperial Majesty's "object all sublime" is a most simple one. He wants to make "the punishment fit the crime." Ko-Ko informs the Mikado that he is very sorry that His Highness has arrived too late to see the execution. What a wonderful sight it was! With the help of Poo-Bah and Pitti-Sing, Ko-Ko describes how the victim died. His Royal Highness regrets that he missed the show, but states that the execution isn't important. The reason why he has come to Titipu has nothing to do with executions. Has anyone, asks the Mikado, seen his son, who, disguised as a Second Trombone, has fled the Imperial court? Of course, no one has seen him!

Meanwhile, Katisha has been reading Poo-Bah's affidavit —signed, as is to be expected, by all the title-holders in Titipu. The signatures were easy to get. After all, Poo-Bah signed them in his official capacities! Suddenly, Katisha screams! She has discovered the name of the executed man —Nanki-Poo! Most fathers would be upset at this news. Not so the Mikado. His Majesty is very understanding. To be sure, he is quite distressed, for in order to carry out the imperial demand for an execution, Ko-Ko has beheaded the heir to the throne of Japan! However, the Mikado makes it clear, it was a natural mistake. If Nanki-Poo went about disguised, he must take the consequences. Everyone is relieved. "What," mumbles the Mikado, "is that law? Oh, I remember: 'Anyone who puts the Heir Apparent to death is boiled in oil.' However, as this has been a mistake, I won't want to put anyone to death—until after lunch. That is, providing you folk are willing to wait till then?" All are willing to wait except Ko-Ko—he doesn't want any lunch!

What are Pish-Tush, Poo-Bah, Ko-Ko and Pitti-Sing to do? There is only one way out of their difficulty, Nanki-Poo must come back to life! That young man, about to start on his honeymoon, refuses. If Nanki-Poo admits he isn't dead, Katisha will claim him. If Ko-Ko really wants to save his life and the lives of all his fellow plotters, Nanki-Poo has a suggestion: Let Ko-Ko propose to Katisha and the existence for all will be "as welcome as flowers that bloom in the spring." Ko-Ko forces himself to make love to Katisha and wins her heart by telling her the sad story of "Tit Willow." The entire company begs forgiveness from the Mikado who, happy that his son is unharmed, declares himself perfectly satisfied as the curtain falls, with everyone singing, "For he has gone and married Yum-Yum."

When the last notes of the finale of *The Mikado* had died away on the opening night, the audience rose, cheered and called for Gilbert and Sullivan. The partners took their bows, shook hands—and Carte was content. The combination he had created was never on a firmer basis. There was no chance that Sullivan would want to break away from comic opera after this great success!

Not since *Pinafore* had Gilbert and Sullivan written anything so popular as *The Mikado*. The piece was to run for 672 performances. There were only two people in the whole of England who were not satisfied with the production. One was the dramatic critic of *Punch,* who, as usual, found fault with Gilbert's work. The other was the author himself, who, hearing from Sullivan that Grossmith had given a poor performance as Ko-Ko, immediately called more rehearsals! Poor Grossmith! Gilbert's constant prodding had made him so nervous that he had had a bad attack of stage fright the opening night. Now Grossmith was to be bullied some more. It was the "business" with the fans that confused the company's comic. Gilbert lost his temper repeatedly and at last screamed, "My good fellow, if you don't know your right, ask the gentleman on your left!" This made Grossmith more confused than ever. At last, everything was smoothed out, however, and the operetta continued on its tuneful way. But Grossmith never recovered from the strain of playing Ko-Ko.

Not only was England delighted with *The Mikado,* but it played to capacity audiences all over the world. The opera became the rage in Holland and Germany. Like *Pinafore,* it furnished many a catch-word: Poo-Bah took his place in the English language, his name becoming a term for men who were capable of holding down several positions at once. Everyone had "an object all sublime," greeted visitors by telling them they were "as welcome as flowers that bloom in the spring" and referred to the things they had to do by saying, "I've got a little list." Dance bands, concert orchestras and pianos by the thousands played Sullivan's wonderful music. *The Mikado* was the latest rage, and its popularity has lasted for nearly seventy years.

There was only one thing that spoiled the triumph of *The Mikado* for Gilbert, Sullivan and Carte. The trio kept receiving reports from America of unauthorized versions of their latest work. John Duff, a leading theatrical producer and one of the most daring pirates, was playing *The Mikado* despite an injunction against his doing so, secured by Carte's American lawyers. Other managers in the United States were rehearsing the piece and announcing the dates of their openings. All this was annoying, but the worst of it was that Stetson, manager of the Fifth Avenue Theater, had offered a fat royalty for the exclusive American rights to *The Mikado.* Unless this honest American was assured a clear title, he would not, naturally enough, sign an agreement. What should be done?

The situation in America was Carte's problem. A man of action, he wasted no time in finding a solution. Secretly he gathered together a troupe of actors. Not a soul in theatrical London knew what he was doing except those he hired, and they were sworn to silence. As a matter of fact, none of the regular Savoy company knew what was happening. Once he had assembled his actors, Carte herded them on a special train which carried them to Liverpool. On the way, Carte told the group that he was taking them to the United States and not until the boat was under way were they to speak to anyone. Nor were they to admit to being actors during the voyage. The cast, ordered Carte, was not to assemble on the boat as a group, but to go aboard singly, so that newspapermen would not discover the plot. Although Carte himself would be along, he was not to be "recognized" by any of the troupe. On the passenger list Carte would appear as "Mr. Henry Chapman," and if introduced to him during the voyage, members of the company must be careful not to call him by his correct name. Once in New York, Carte continued, everyone was to report immediately to the Fifth Avenue Theater. All went as planned. Carte and his cast landed in America on August 18, 1885, and two days later an authorized production of *The Mikado* was presented by Stetson's theater. Duff and the rest of the American pirates were stunned! Nevertheless, aided by the decision of a judge who refused to grant Carte an injunction, Duff continued with his production, but despite the flaws in the Carte presentation, could not compete and failed.

Ever since Carte showed Americans how *The Mikado* should be acted and sung, the piece has been a great favorite in this country. Easily the most popular work in the Savoy series, *The Mikado* has been produced in theaters in the United States countless times. Not only has the opera been played in regulation fashion, but in many other ways. There have been "Hot Mikado" companies, starring Negro jazz experts; "Swing Mikado" productions, presented by an agency of the United States Government; and dozens of other variations. "Bojangles" Bill Robinson, the famous tap dancer, scored one of the biggest hits of his career in a jitterbug version of the work. All the liberties taken with

Pinafore have been taken with *The Mikado*. The opera has been burlesqued, played in modern dress, offered with Charleston dancing girls in the chorus, and in many other ways. Yet, as written by Gilbert and Sullivan, *The Mikado* still retains a hold on the theater-going public of this country unequaled by any other Savoy piece, not excluding *Pinafore*.

The Mikado, incidentally, is the only one of the operas in which Gilbert made complete changes in his text. Ko-Ko's list of people "who never would be missed" was changed by the author with the passing of the years. This action by Gilbert has set a pattern, and each revival finds new "social offenders" mentioned. Another change, approved of by Gilbert, was varying Nanki-Poo's address. During the original production, when the Mikado asked where his son might be found and was told he had gone abroad, His Imperial Majesty's request for Nanki-Poo's new address was answered, to the delight of the audience, by Ko-Ko, who said it was Knightsbridge. Such an allusion meant nothing after the closing of the Japanese village, nor in America. So Gilbert gave directions to choose the suburb of the city in which the performance was being given. These changes were the only ones he approved—how he would roar if he saw a swing version of his "entirely new and original Japanese opera!"

It seems strange, but to *The Mikado* must go much of the credit for the establishment of the Statler Hotel chain. E. M. Statler was running a restaurant in Buffalo, New York, and business was slow. Looking for a way to attract more customers, Statler decided to serve his ice cream in the form of a Japanese lady, with a paper parasol stuck in her frozen hand, and list it on the menu as "Yum-Yum Ice Cream." The dish became a very popular dessert—and no wonder, for in order to get customers to order this specialty,

Statler put five-dollar gold pieces into some of the figures. If the diner found one in his "Yum-Yum," he could keep the coin. Everyone, of course, ordered the dish, hoping to find one of the gold pieces. So great was the demand for "Yum-Yums" that it became necessary for Statler to hire several people to do nothing but open the tiny, colorful parasols and put them in place. Business at the restaurant boomed, and soon its owner was in a position to expand. Thus Statler entered the hotel business . . . thanks to Gilbert and Sullivan.

The Mikado has other unusual distinctions. It was the first of the Gilbert and Sullivan series to be offered on a radio broadcast from the stage of the Savoy, and it is also the only one of the operettas to be made into a motion picture. When the Crown Prince of Japan visited England in 1907, the English government suppressed a revival of *The Mikado* because the officials feared the work would offend their Pacific ally. Gilbert, always a grumbler, immediately blamed King Edward for the ban and was furious because he was forced to lose royalties. When the author found out that the King had nothing to do with the suppression, he apologized, but still was annoyed about the loss of money. Angrily, Gilbert demanded of the Lord Chamberlain, who was responsible for the action, "Why should a play about an imaginary happening be banned and take twenty-five thousand dollars out of my pocket?"

Gilbert would have been delighted to hear that shortly after the occupation of Japan by American troops at the close of World War II, a performance of *The Mikado* was given by a GI troupe. It was a most elaborate production and, according to newspaper reports, a great success. The Japanese who attended the operetta showed no signs of being offended—although few of them understood a single word!

Always quarreling with adults, be they his partners, government officials, or fellow workers in the theater, Gilbert never had a cross word for young people. Nothing gave him so much pleasure as rewriting some of the Savoy operas for his juvenile friends. His last bit of writing was to revamp *The Mikado* for youngsters. No one could make children laugh like this unpleasant man could. Look what he did to Ko-Ko's famous "I've Got A Little List":

"As some day it may happen that a victim must be found,
I've made a little list—I've made a little list
Of inconvenient people who might well be underground,
For they never would be missed—they never would be missed.
The donkey who of nine-times six and eight-times seven prates
And stumps you with inquiries on geography and dates,
And asks for your ideas on spelling 'parallelegram'—
All narrow-minded people who are stingy with their jam,
And the torture dealing dentist, with the forceps in his fist—
They'd none of them be missed—they'd none of them be missed.

"Then the teacher who for hours keeps you practicing your scales
With an ever-aching wrist—she never would be missed.
And children, too, who out of school are fond of telling tales.
They never would be missed—I'm sure they'd not be missed.
All people who maintain (in solemn earnest not in joke)
That quantities of sugar-plums are bad for little folk,
And those who hold the principle, unalterably fixed,

*That instruction with amusement should most carefully be
    mixed:*
All these (and many others) I have placed upon my list,
*For they never would be missed—never, never would be
    missed."*

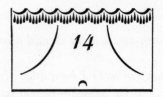

"Placed by the Moralists Under a Ban"

◉

—Ruddigore

CARTE watched the long lines form in front of the box office of the Savoy with smiling satisfaction. *The Mikado* was playing to full houses at every performance. "You won't," he laughingly told Gilbert and Sullivan, "have to supply me with another piece at the end of the next six months! All you chaps will have to do for the next year or two, so far as comic opera is concerned, is collect royalties."

"Speaking of royalties," replied Gilbert, "I've been thinking that my habit of calling you on the telephone every night to learn the receipts is a risky business. Someone might cut in on the line and hear us. Suppose we use a code. As *The Mikado* is the favorite attraction of London right now, let us take the word 'favourites' and use that as our code word. It has ten letters, repeats none of them. We'll let the F stand for one, A for two, and so on. Suppose the ticket sales amount to $1,725 this evening. When I ask you for the night's returns, you'll merely say FTAR."

"That's an excellent idea, Gilbert," approved Carte. "What do you think, Sullivan?"

Sir Arthur didn't care one way or another. The composer was too busy making arrangements for his trip to America. Sullivan left England, sailing on June 20, 1885, leaving to his partners the task of organizing the company for the production of the authorized version of *The Mikado* in the United States. When he arrived in New York City, he was swarmed upon by reporters who asked him if it was true that he had come overseas to put on "an English version of *The Mikado*." Despite the fact that Sullivan knew it would be two months before Carte and his troupe would sail for America, the composer wisely let the newspapermen think this was the reason for his visit. If the theatrical pirates believed the story, perhaps they would refrain from stealing the operetta. As a matter of fact, Sir Arthur had no intention of staying in New York City a moment longer than necessary. All he wanted to do was to get to Los Angeles as quickly as possible and visit his brother's children, whom he imagined were living in poverty. There were, of course, some things Sullivan wanted to do in America's largest city—visit important people, dine at famous restaurants and see some plays. Sir Arthur soon found out that he was not going to be allowed to follow this routine. From the time that he cleared customs, he was always surrounded by reporters. Journalists followed him everywhere, demanding interviews. Annoyed because he never was allowed a moment's privacy, Sullivan did everything in his power to avoid newspapermen, but they never let him out of their sight. Meanwhile, New York grew hotter and hotter. Summer came early and soon it was over one hundred degrees in the shade. The composer found the combination of heat and reporters too much. Quickly he made up his mind. Despite fine friends, excellent food and interesting theatrical performances, Sullivan decided to leave New York—and he hoped the besieging journalists would roast in the heat!

Crossing the breadth of America in 1885 was not a simple matter. There were no air-conditioned, streamlined trains running from coast to coast in those days. The only way the trip could be made without completely exhausting the traveler was to make frequent stops. Sullivan's first stop was Chicago, where he planned to rest from the hot, dusty trip in a slow-moving train. The composer got no rest. Reporters surrounded him in Chicago, just as their fellow newspapermen had in New York. There was, if possible, even less privacy in Chicago than there had been in New York. Once, on entering his hotel room and finding a couple of journalists waiting for him, Sir Arthur decided to get rid of them by saying he was about to retire. The reporters did not move. Sullivan took off his coat. Still the interviewers did not leave the room. In desperation he began to undress, but it made no difference. His visitors fired questions at him as he removed his clothes! This was too much for the composer. He left Chicago for Denver the next day. In the capitol of Colorado, he managed to avoid the newspapermen and get some rest. Refreshed, he then set out for Salt Lake City, Utah. The journey was made exciting by the collapse of a bridge. The train on which Sir Arthur was riding could not proceed until the structure was repaired, and as there were no dining cars attached to trains in those days, he had to go without food for twenty-four hours.

Weary, Sir Arthur finally arrived in Salt Lake City. A curious man, he inspected every phase of the Mormon settlement. A friend introduced the composer to Brigham Young, president of the Mormon Church and founder of Salt Lake City, who invited Sullivan to play the famous organ at the great Tabernacle. On Sunday, he attended divine service with some Mormon acquaintances and was extremely flattered to hear one of his own hymn-tunes played. The next day Sullivan took another train and at last reached San Francisco.

The city by the Golden Gate fascinated him. He had a wonderful time and would have enjoyed himself even more, if it had not been for the everlasting reporters. Compared with the journalists of San Francisco, the newspapermen back in Chicago and New York had been pleasant fellows. The only time Sir Arthur escaped from the journalists who followed him day and night was the evening when he accompanied a San Francisco police detective on a tour of the city's world-famous Chinatown. Sullivan went into all sorts of queer places and enjoyed himself immensely. The evening was spoiled, however, on Sir Arthur's arrival at his hotel. In the lobby was a throng of people waiting to see, shake hands with, or interview him. Once again the composer had had enough. He packed his bags and took the next train for Los Angeles.

To Sir Arthur's great satisfaction, he found Frederick Sullivan's children well, and as happy as they could be without parents. While they did not have a great deal of money, they were not in dire need—a situation which relieved their uncle of one of his greatest worries. No sooner had the excitement of Sir Arthur's arrival died down than the reporters appeared. Once again the composer decided to run away from the men who were noting his every mood. In the wild and deserted country of the Yosemite Valley, he was sure he would not meet any newspapermen. So Sullivan, accompanied by his nephews and nieces, set off for the Sierra Nevada Mountains. He had been correct in thinking there were no reporters so far from a big city. Not once during the entire trip was he bothered and as a result enjoyed every minute of the jaunt.

Upon his return to the "City of the Angels," the composer received unpleasant news. A letter from Carte informed him that the Savoy management had lost the case against the pirates who were stealing *The Mikado*. The only satisfaction the partners had in the whole affair was the knowledge that the company they had brought over from England was playing to capacity houses. When Sir Arthur heard that it had been legally decided that anyone could print his music, sell it, and not pay a cent in royalties, he lost his temper in a fashion that would have done Gilbert credit!

At length the pleasure of being with his young nephews and nieces palled. Always happiest when traveling, Sullivan decided it was time to leave. He planned to make the trip back to New York City in short hops, stopping for days in some towns where he was unknown, hurrying out of those cities where reporters besieged him. Sometimes Sir Arthur traveled by train, sometimes by stagecoach. One day as the horses clattered up to the Wells Fargo Office in a Midwestern town, the driver, climbing down from the "boot," drawled, "Guess the folks were expecting you, Mr. Sullivan." The composer looked at the crowd gathered on the board sidewalk, wondering who could possibly know anything about him in this out-of-the-way place. The mystery was soon solved.

"How much do you weigh, Sully?" yelled one of the crowd.

Sir Arthur, astonished at the question and the manner in which it was asked, stammered, "One hundred and sixty-two pounds. Why?"

"What, you only weigh one hundred and sixty-two pounds? Then how were you able to lick Sheehan down in Pittsburgh?"

"I never licked Sheehan in Pittsburgh or anywhere else," came the amazed reply.

"Aren't you 'Slogger' Sullivan, the famous prize fighter?"

"No, I'm not. I'm Arthur Sullivan!"

At this point a lean cowboy with a weather-beaten face pushed his way to the front of the crowd. With thumbs hooked in his gun-belt, the puncher drawled, "Say, you aren't the author fellow who wrote that funny *Pinafore* piece that played in the Opera House, are you?"

"As a matter of fact, I am."

"Well, me and the boys are just as glad to see you as if you were the champ himself. Come on and meet the gang!"

It was late in September before Sullivan arrived in New York City. Sir Arthur went to the Fifth Avenue Theater and saw *The Mikado* and made a few suggestions for improvements. One was that D'Oyly Carte arrange a special performance of the operetta, which the composer would personally conduct. The manager planned a festive affair. Every lady in the audience was to receive a bouquet, programs like those given out at the Savoy were ordered, and the entire theater was decorated with flowers. All of fashionable New York turned out to see the performance at the Fifth Avenue Theater on the evening of September 24, 1885, and the audience gave the piece and its composer a tremendous reception.

When the applause died down, Sullivan was called upon to make a speech and he responded. Sir Arthur graciously acknowledged the kindness of the audience, but he seized the opportunity to tell his listeners exactly what he thought of the lack of copyright laws in America. He brought out the fact that the audience had just witnessed a performance of *The Mikado* presented exactly as the author and composer of the operetta had intended it should be presented. No pirated version could do this. Sir Arthur closed his talk by hoping that the day was not far distant when a man "who employed his brains in Literature and Art would receive as much protection as the inventor of a new type of nail." Incidentally, this speech did more to bring about a revision of the copyright law in America than any other factor.

A round of social engagements followed the gala performance of *The Mikado,* and then Carte and Sullivan went on to Philadelphia, where they offered another production of the operetta at McCaull's Opera House. After this chore had been accomplished, there was nothing for Sir Arthur to do. Restless, the composer decided to return to England, arriving home at the end of October. He immediately went to the Savoy and learned that every seat for *The Mikado* was sold out for weeks. "London is *Mikado*-mad, Sir Arthur," the clerk in the box office informed him. "Everyone is singing and whistling your tunes. They say that the Queen herself, God bless her, plays your score on the piano at the castle. We've got three companies playing the piece in the provincial towns, and, as you know, Alfred Cellier is going to take a troupe to Australia. If you want my opinion, sir, this opera is going to run for years!"

Gilbert had been enjoying a vacation while his manager and partner were in America. The author had seen every theatrical performance in London, taken several trips on his yacht, gone swimming, and played a great deal of tennis. All of this had been great fun, but the dramatist had enjoyed most the parties he gave the youngsters in his neighborhood. He would write humorous verses for his young guests, dance the Highland Fling, invent guessing games to keep them amused and fill everyone present full of candy. When it came time to go home, each child received a wonderful present. Let Sullivan enjoy the company of royalty. Gilbert preferred the delightful friendship of youth. Perhaps that is why his work never grows old!

Nor had he been idle. While playing tennis and entertaining his young friends, the author had been thinking about preparing a successor to *The Mikado*. The fact that it would be months before a new piece was needed at the Savoy didn't make any difference to him. Unlike Sullivan, he was not lazy and enjoyed work. The partners would have to prepare an operetta for Carte at some future date, so why not get it ready at once? For hours Gilbert pored over his files of *Fun,* but nothing in his earlier work appealed to him as a theme for a comic opera as much as the idea Sir Arthur had rejected before they produced *The Mikado*. The composer had not been in England a week before he was writing to convince Sullivan that "the admirable plot I proposed last year" should be used as the plot of the next Savoy presentation.

Sullivan showed the letter to Carte. "Admirable!" snorted the composer. "Admirable indeed! Maybe Gilbert thinks it's admirable, but I don't, nor do you. I'm telling you that I won't have anything to do with that lozenge of his. It's a fantastic idea and I want no part of it. I've told him so a dozen times. You'll have to convince him, Carte. I can't go through all that argument again. Remember, no lozenge!"

"I'll do my best," sighed the manager, "but I really think you can handle the matter better than I. Since *The Mikado,* you two have never been so friendly, and I don't think Gilbert will lose his temper if you explain about the lozenge. Before I speak to him, why don't you write him a letter, tactfully giving your objections to the plot?"

"Gilbert's heard all my objections, Carte, so what good will a letter do? However, I'll send him a note, as you suggest."

Sir Arthur's note to his partner was a masterpiece. The composer, a genius at the art of flattery, told his associate that he was sure so capable an author could think of something better than the lozenge plot. Sullivan also made it clear that he could not swallow Gilbert's pill. Sir Arthur was so diplomatic that Gilbert reluctantly dropped the idea. That is, he dropped it for the time being—he was to offer it again at a later date. So there the matter rested until the middle of January, 1886. The new year had blown itself in with a terrific storm. London's streets were piled high with drifts, and still it snowed. One morning, while the roaring blizzard halted wagons, trains and hansom cabs and blanketed the Thames, the door chimes at Sullivan's apartment announced the presence of a visitor. Wondering who could be out on such a day, the composer opened the door himself. There on the steps, covered with snow and sleet, was the burly figure of Gilbert.

Sullivan threw open the door and let his partner and an icy blast into the hall. "Here, let me take some of that snow from your coat, Gilbert. Why, you must be half-frozen. Whatever brings you out on such a day as this? Nothing wrong at the Savoy, is there?"

"Thanks," grunted Gilbert as he handed the composer his greatcoat and stamped his feet to warm them. "No, there's nothing wrong at the theater. I've just had a wonderful idea for our new piece and rushed over here to tell you all about it."

"Come and sit by the fire. Warm yourself first and then we'll talk. I say, doesn't your coming here in a snowstorm to outline a plot remind you of the time you called with the libretto of *Trial by Jury?* How much has happened since then! Are you comfortable? Warm enough? Now, tell me about the new opera."

Reaching into his pocket, Gilbert brought out a sheaf of notes. He moved his chair closer to Sullivan and began to outline his plot. Sir Arthur listened carefully. There was no mention of a lozenge! As the author talked, the composer interrupted to offer a suggestion or two. Before Gilbert and Sullivan realized it, it was time for lunch. Louis told them everything was ready. Still discussing the proposed operetta, they sat down, but hardly touched their food. When the meal was over, the partners were in complete agreement about *The Mikado*'s successor. It was to be called *Ruddygore, or The Witch's Curse; A New and Original Supernatural Opera.*

However, Sullivan could not immediately begin work on the new piece. Sir Arthur had promised to write a cantata for the Leeds Festival. As usual, the composer had no idea as to what he was going to use for a theme. Weeks slipped by and still he did nothing about the composition. Then Joseph Bennett asked him to read a libretto he had written, based on Longfellow's *Golden Legend.* Sir Arthur was delighted with the treatment given the medieval romance and bought Bennett's manuscript. Now that he had the words for his cantata, he should have settled down to writing the music. Being Sullivan, he didn't. There were more horse races to attend, and he guided Liszt, the Hungarian composer (and one of the greatest of pianists) on a tour of London. Always looking for an excuse to avoid working, Sullivan convinced himself that he could not leave the distinguished visitor from Hungary without an escort and devoted all his time to him.

He had far too much to do to play the part of a gracious host. Not only did the composer have *The Golden Legend* to write and a new operetta for the Savoy to score, but, in addition, the Prince of Wales had asked him to set to music an ode which Tennyson had written for the opening of the Colonial and Indian Exposition. The result was that Sullivan did nothing—and enjoyed himself immensely. Meanwhile, Gilbert and Carte were asking when he was going to begin work on the music for *Ruddygore*. Feeling guilty, the composer took refuge in calling attention to the fact that he had said that he could not start a new operetta until he had finished his assignment for the Leeds Festival. The argument became heated, but Carte finally settled the matter by saying that the music for *The Mikado*'s successor would not be needed until late fall.

Forced to get to work, Sullivan took a cottage in the country and sat down to his desk to write the music for Bennett's libretto. From April until August he did nothing but work on *The Golden Legend*, composing all day and half the night. Visitors were not welcome nor did he leave his summer retreat for the attractions of social life. At last, on the twenty-fifth of August, 1886, his Festival score was finished. Now there were weeks of rehearsal ahead with the singers and the orchestra. There was absolutely no chance of working on the Savoy music for several months.

Gilbert was furious. Carte was worried. The summer had been very hot and theatergoers had not rushed to fill the Savoy. The theater had electric lights, but no air-conditioning! The manager made plans to start another series of revivals, but with the coming of September, the weather turned cool and *The Mikado* again attracted full houses. At a conference Gilbert and Carte decided that cherry blossoms and fans could hold the stage until the first of the year.

Sir Arthur was too busy at Leeds to pay any attention to what his associates were doing at the Savoy. In mid-October, *The Golden Legend* was presented. The cantata was a huge success. At the conclusion of the work, hats and programs were hurled into the air and the audience stood on its seats and shouted, "Bravo!" at the top of its lungs. Never in the history of the Leeds Festival had a composer received such a tribute. The newspapers the next day were unanimous in their praise of the cantata. Sir Arthur Sullivan, the critics said with one voice, had written the finest piece of serious music ever composed by an Englishman. Even Gilbert sent congratulations to Sullivan. The author tempered his message by stating that the complete libretto of *Ruddygore* was awaiting his partner and it might be well for Sir Arthur to plan to devote some time to the preparation of the score for *The Mikado*'s successor.

Although he was worn out from the strain of writing, rehearsing and conducting *The Golden Legend,* Sullivan agreed that Gilbert's suggestion had merit. The Savoy combination set the date for the production of the new piece at the end of January. It was now November. Once again Sir Arthur had to work under pressure. It was difficult enough to write the music for Gilbert's libretto and help supervise rehearsals at the Savoy, but he had other commitments as well. The composer had accepted engagements to conduct *The Golden Legend* at many places in and about London. After a rehearsal, Sullivan would leave the Savoy, rush to a concert hall, supervise a last-minute practice by the orchestra, nibble at a bite to eat, change his clothes, conduct *The Golden Legend* and then go home and work on the score of *Ruddygore*. It was a mad whirl. Sir Arthur was soon completely exhausted, and Gilbert gave him no comfort. "If you didn't put things off until the last minute, Sullivan, you wouldn't be in this fix," the author growled as he watched his partner drag himself into the orchestra pit.

Not only did Gilbert refuse to give his partner any sympathy, but he made the composer's task more difficult by making continual changes in the libretto. A perfectionist, the author kept altering his text and Sir Arthur was forced to rewrite many tunes. Rarely did he get to bed before five in the morning. On January 13th, after writing until dawn, he finished the last bit of music for *Ruddygore*. Rehearsals were in full swing at the Savoy, and everything but this music was ready by the time the final performance of *The Mikado* took place on January 10th, when the curtain fell on the residents of Titipu for the last time. Sullivan wasn't at the theater to hear the cheers of the audience; the composer was across the city, conducting a performance of *The Golden Legend* for a throng of 10,000 listeners.

A few last-minute changes—Gilbert was busy checking scenery, costumes, lights and properties. Then, on the night of January 22, 1887, the curtain rose on *Ruddygore, or the Witch's Curse*.

The village of Redeering, in which the action of *Ruddygore* takes place, is like every other fishing port in Cornwall, except for one thing: it boasts an "endowed corps of professional bridesmaids who are bound to be on duty every day from ten to four." As the opera begins, these bridesmaids are bewailing the fact that for six months their services have not been required. Beautiful Rose Maybud is the reason. Every youth in Redeering is in love with her, and until she accepts one of them, no other girl can hope for a proposal. In fear of losing their jobs, the bridesmaids ask old, fat and ugly Dame Hannah please to marry someone so they can go to work. There is no chance—for Dame Hannah explains that, years ago, she became engaged to a young man who, just before the wedding, revealed himself to be Sir Roderick Murgatroyd, "one of the bad baronets of Ruddygore." Such a creature, despite his manly beauty and personal charm, was "no husband for an honest girl." So, madly as she loved Roderick, Dame Hannah cancelled their wedding plans. For who wants a husband who is the victim of a witch's curse?

The bridesmaids, of course, want to know why the Baronets of Ruddygore were cursed. It began, explains Dame Hannah, with the first baronet who "his leisure and his riches, ruthlessly employed in persecuting witches." One of these evil creatures, while being tortured, cried out:

> *"Each Lord of Ruddygore,*
> *Despite his best endeavor,*
> *Shall do one crime or more,*
> *Once every day for ever!*
> *This doom he can't defy,*
> *However he may try,*
> *For should he stay*
> *His hand, that day*
> *In torture he shall die."*

Dame Hannah tells her listeners that the baronets, hoping to stay alive, have done horrible things daily through the years. Finally, however, there came a time when each refused to commit a daily crime and died before midnight! Rupert, Jasper, Lionel, Conrad, Desmond, Gilbert, Mervyn and fourteen others have perished in agony, relates the talkative old woman—and she leaves no doubt that so will all the heirs to the title who refuse to meet the demands of the witch's curse!

At this point Rose Maybud enters. As usual, she is going about the village doing good deeds. Rose is taking rock-candy to an old man, a set of false teeth to a little girl, and a pound of snuff to an orphan child! Everyone is delighted with such kindness and tells her how happy she would make some village youth. Just then, the one man in whom the maiden is interested appears. He is Robin Oakapple, who is so shy and modest that he cannot bring himself to tell Rose how much he loves her. He tries, but fails, and Rose goes about her charitable duties, leaving him desolate.

It is strange that Oakapple should be timid and reserved,

for he is no ordinary village lad. He is actually the rightful heir to the baronetcy of Ruddygore, but no one knows it except his faithful servant, Old Adam. In horror of committing a daily crime, he had run away twenty years previously and let his younger brother, Despard, succeed to the title—and the curse! Robin is about to follow Rose when Old Adam brings him word that his foster-brother, Richard Dauntless, a hearty sailor, has just arrived in port. Oakapple is delighted. He has not seen Dick for ten years and rushes to meet him. The sailor, a plainspoken man, soon finds out about his foster-brother's difficulty in telling Rose of his love. Dauntless reminds the shy youth of their boyhood oath, that they would "always act upon our heart's dictates." Robin admits that he recalls the oath, but claims that he has not the courage to propose to his loved one. Everytime he sees Rose he tries to express his feelings, but finds it impossible. He realizes that his modesty is a terrible handicap, for:

> *"If you wish in the world to advance*
> *Your merits you're bound to enhance,*
> *You must stir it and stump it,*
> *And blow your own trumpet,*
> *Or trust me, you haven't a chance!"*

Dick tells Robin not to worry. The sailor explains that he is not modest and will gladly propose to Rose for his foster-brother. Unfortunately, in performing this friendly service, Dauntless, "always acting as his heart dictates," finds himself asking the girl to marry *him*. She agrees, after consulting the etiquette book she always carries with her wherever she goes. On hearing that Rose has accepted Dick's proposal, Robin is at first overjoyed, but soon is brokenhearted when he learns that his foster-brother has spoken for himself. Yet, because he is a fair man, Oakapple understands that Dick had to listen to the dictates of his heart, and he wishes Rose well. Dick, he tells her, is a good man. He may be tattooed to the shoulders, but he dances a hornpipe well; he may have a girl in every port, but he is as nimble as a pony. By now Rose sees that she has made a mistake in accepting Dauntless and decides to marry Robin instead, remarking that her decision is not an easy one, because:

> *"In sailing o'er life's ocean wide*
> *No doubt the heart should be your guide;*
> *But it is awkward when you find*
> *A heart that does not know its mind!"*

When Dick learns that Rose has changed her mind about marrying him, he is furious. The sailor rushes to tell Sir Respard, Robin's younger brother, that he is not really the Baronet of Ruddygore. His Lordship is delighted. No more daily crimes! Sir Despard breaks up the procession by denouncing Robin as Sir Ruthven Murgatroyd. Rose, in horror, flies to Dick's arms, as the curtain falls on act one.

We see the picture gallery of Ruddygore Castle in the second act. Gilbert's stage directions describe the setting: "The walls are covered with full-length portraits of the Baronets of Ruddygore from the time of James I—the first being Sir Rupert alluded to in the legend; the last, that of the last deceased Baronet, Sir Roderic."

As the curtain rises, Robin (now Sir Ruthven) and Old Adam, no longer a valet but steward of the castle, are discussing their next crime. None of his faithful servant's suggestions please the Baronet. At last, sick of his "accursed doom," Sir Ruthven turns to the portraits of his ancestors and begs them to help him. Suddenly the lights go out—and when they come on again, the Baronets have come to life; all the people in the portraits have stepped out of their frames and surrounded the last of their line. Sir Ruthven gets no comfort from his kin. The idea of a Baronet of Ruddygore wanting to live and *not* commit a daily crime causes the ghosts to howl in rage:

> *"Coward, poltroon, shaker, squeamer,*
> *Blockhead, sluggard, dullard, dreamer,*
> *Smirker, shuffler, crawler, creeper,*
> *Sniffler, snuffler, wailer, weeper,*
> *Earthworm, maggot, tadpole, weevil!*
> *Set upon thy course of evil*
> *Lest the King of Specter-Land*
> *Set on thee his grisly hand!"*

Sir Ruthven is terrified. His ancestors demand that the new Baronet perform his daily crime "in a conscientious and workmanlike fashion." Sir Ruthven claims that he has done so, and his ancestors demand that he list his evil deeds. The frightened Baronet explains that he has forged a will —but admits that it was his own! Moreover, he cheated on his income tax, but the ghosts tell him that almost everyone does that, even though it isn't good citizenship. Anxious to please the specters, Sir Ruthven tells how he forged a check —it was Old Adam's so he gets no credit for this deed, for the servant hasn't a checking account! Desperate, he announces that he has acted in an atrocious fashion and disinherited his only son. His ancestors point out that he hasn't got a son, but Sir Ruthven tries to explain that his deed will save bother when the child is born, for he will be cast off without a penny. However, his forefathers rule that they cannot accept this action as a suitable crime. In fact, the wraiths are dissatisfied with the Baronet's attitude toward his duty—he must do something really criminal. After a conference they decide that their descendant must kidnap a lady.

Scandalized at his ancestors' demand, Sir Ruthven refuses to commit the crime they suggest. The ghosts then turn their magic powers on the rebellious Baronet. Unable to stand the pain inflicted upon him, he consents to kidnap a lady. Satisfied that they have accomplished their purpose, the spirits return to their frames. Faithful Old Adam then kidnaps Dame Hannah for his master. Outraged at the treatment she is receiving, she is about to stab Sir Ruthven with a dagger when Sir Roderic steps down from his place on the wall and saves his son. Dame Hannah is overjoyed to see her old lover. While they are talking about the days when they were engaged to be married, Sir Ruthven interrupts them. He has found a way to overcome the witch's curse! "A Baronet of Ruddygore," he explains, "can only die through refusing to commit his daily crime. Then refusing to commit a daily crime is the same thing as suicide. But suicide is itself, a crime—so you should not have died at all!"

Sir Roderick can find no flaw in this typical bit of Gilbertian logic and decides to stay alive. His Lordship and Dame Hannah plan to be married at once. Robin, no longer a baronet, pairs off with Rose. Dick, still following "the dictates of his heart," proposes to one of the bridesmaids and all embrace as the curtain falls.

Sullivan brought his baton down—and the last note of *Ruddygore*'s finale died away. Then, for the first time in the history of the Gilbert and Sullivan partnership, loud boos were heard, mingled with the applause. Sullivan and Carte were not surprised. The composer and manager had both noticed that the operetta was failing to hold the audience's attention in the closing scenes of the first act. Gilbert, who of course had arrived at the theater only in time to hear the finale, was forcibly restrained from locating the booers and throwing them out of the Savoy. When he finally calmed down, he called a conference in Carte's office. "We'll have to rewrite part of the piece. Let's meet at Sullivan's place in the morning. Carte, I know you've made a list of suggestions as usual. Sullivan, if you think the music is at fault, it's up to you to rewrite your tunes. I'll be prepared to make any cuts and changes in the libretto that Carte suggests. Now, let's go home."

The trio met early at the composer's apartment. All day long, until it was time to go to the theater for the performance, they went over *Ruddygore*. Carte, who was one of the finest theatrical managers of his time, had, as Gilbert supposed, taken careful notes of what the audience did not like on the opening night. Gilbert, without a grumble, accepted Carte's suggestions and revamped his lines. It was agreed that the finale was the weakest part of the operetta, and the author concentrated on changing it. By the time he had finished, little of his original work remained. This meant that Sullivan had to write entirely new music! The composer set to work immediately. In thirty-six hours, with pauses only for meals, Sir Arthur had finished his task. Rehearsals were called and the clever cast soon knew the new words and music—but it mattered little. It was evident to all concerned that *Ruddygore* was not going to be any more popular with the theatergoing public than *Princess Ida* had been.

The title of the new Savoy offering was most unfortunate. Englishmen of all classes avoid using the word "bloody," and Gilbert's "ruddy" was a near thing. Many people who had attended all the previous Gilbert and Sullivan productions refused to go and see their latest work because of its name. For once, the newspaper critics had something tangible to find fault with in Gilbert's work, and they filled columns with articles against the "not happily selected title." As can be imagined, Gilbert was extremely angry. To one young lady who called his attention to the fact that the opera's title almost contained a word no nice girl would think of using, he bellowed, "Oh, is that so? They are nothing alike. Ruddy, my dear young lady, does not mean bloody. Let me give you a lesson in English. When I say, 'I like your ruddy cheek,' I do not, I assure you, make any reference to your bloody cheek!"

This typical Gilbertian answer did nothing to overcome the public's dislike of the title. The press continued to berate Gilbert—always Gilbert, but never Sullivan! Finally, the author, goaded into a fit of temper, exploded, "Very well, we'll change the name of the piece to *Kensington Gore, or Robin and Richard Were Two Pretty Men!* No one thought this was funny, however, and Gilbert was accused of trying to be humorous about a matter of public morals. This charge, of course, angered him even more.

Nor was the dislike of *Ruddygore* confined to England. Anglo-French relations became strained as a result of the piece. This was due to Richard Dauntless' song in which that hearty, bragging sailor told how he and his crew, sailing in a sloop, defeated a French frigate of thirty-two guns! The London correspondent of the Paris *Figaro* sent a story to his editor, complaining about this song which poked fun at a "miserable Parley-Voo." Several hotheaded Frenchmen immediately challenged Gilbert to duels. The government of France took official notice of the song. At this point, the situation became even more involved; some Englishmen claimed that Dick's song did not insult the French, but the British Navy!

Gilbert and Sullivan wrote an apologetic letter to the editor of *Figaro* in their best French. The partners made it clear that they had no intention of insulting the great and glorious land across the Channel. Nothing had been intended but fun! In the letter, the partners claimed that they never could, nor would, cast slurs on a country *"aussi brave que chevalersque."* The statement from the collaborators cleared the matter up and officially the *Ruddygore* incident was closed.

Meanwhile, the English dislike of the title had its effect. The "y" was dropped and "i" substituted and the work became *Ruddigore.* The cuts and changes made by Gilbert helped somewhat, but it was plain that other alterations were needed to make the operetta a success. Gilbert was willing to revamp more of the piece, but his associates decided that the story of the witch's curse would have to succeed or fail as it stood. So nothing more was done.

Anxious to avoid blame for the failure at the Savoy, Gilbert confided in a friend that the main reason for the unpopularity of the piece was the music, claiming that it was not suitable for comic opera. Sir Arthur, just as anxious to shift the blame to Gilbert, told the same person that Gilbert's words were at fault! Yet, despite the fact that *Ruddigore* was not receiving an enthusiastic reception in the press, it was doing good business. The operetta ran 288 nights—even longer than *Princess Ida.* Smarting from the jibes of the critics who found nothing to praise in the piece, Gilbert took delight in announcing that the eight months' run had brought him $35,000 as his share of the profits. This was a high return, for the work had been mounted expensively. The pictures of the Baronets had been painted to represent those members of the cast who stepped from them when the portraits came to life. No less a personage than the Quartermaster-General of Her Imperial Majesty's Army had supervised the costumes worn by the men's chorus in the first act —they were authentic reproductions of the full-dress regalia of twenty famous British regiments.

Once his share of patching up *Ruddigore* was completed, Sir Arthur set out to enjoy the sun at Monte Carlo, and the society life he loved so well. There was plenty of social activity, but no sun. It rained every day during his stay! As if this were not enough, Sullivan was thrown out of bed early one morning by an earthquake! Asked to conduct a command performance of *The Golden Legend* in Berlin, Sir Arthur left the shores of the Mediterranean and went to the German city. On his way the composer suffered another attack and almost died. Yet he forced himself to continue the journey. The planned gala performance of the cantata was a miserable failure, due to Pattini, who sang the role of Elsie. A world-famous opera star, Pattini thought it beneath her to learn songs for a single performance, and had to be prompted all during the evening.

Sullivan almost cried. Not only had his greatest work been poorly presented, but the performance, which was given in honor of the ninetieth birthday of Emperor William I, had been attended by an audience composed, for the most part, of royalty. He was deeply humiliated to disappoint these illustrious holders of titles. Proud of his composition and determined to please the rulers of the land in which he had received his musical education, he asked permission to give a repeat performance of *The Golden Legend*. Permission was granted. Sir Arthur wired his old friend, Madame Albani, who was in Antwerp, and the diva rushed to Berlin to help him. Albani sang Elsie without a rehearsal and received a tremendous ovation. Sullivan's pride and reputation were saved.

Following his triumph in Berlin, there was little for Sir Arthur to do save enjoy the company of royalty and dine with his many German friends. His last day in Berlin was spent in the company of the royal family, attending Princess Victoria's birthday party. Since the wife of the German Crown Prince was an English girl—the youngest daughter of Queen Victoria—the composer chose for his birthday gift a basket of roses, Great Britain's national flower. While chatting with the Princess, the band of the Kaiser Franz Regiment marched up and began playing selections from *The Mikado* as its contribution to the birthday celebration. No sooner had the last note died away than the band of the Cuirassiers wheeled into position and offered their musical birthday gift—the same selections from *The Mikado!*

On arriving in England, Sullivan found that both Carte and Gilbert had been anxiously waiting for his return. A new work was needed for the Savoy. *Ruddigore* was attracting very few customers and was being played on a week-to-week basis. Gilbert, of course, had an idea for the opera's successor. It was the famous lozenge plot. Sir Arthur agreed to let his partner go ahead on condition that if the finished product did not appeal to the composer, the lozenge would be thrown away forever. Gilbert rushed back to Uxbridge and began his libretto. Sullivan nervously awaited the results of his associate's labors. Nothing, he was sure, could be done with the lozenge that would make it easy to swallow. Carte, meanwhile keeping a watchful eye on the nightly returns at the Savoy, decided it was too dangerous to take a chance on Gilbert and Sullivan having a new opera ready when *Ruddigore* began to lose money. So the manager ordered that a series of revivals be prepared. It was well he did.

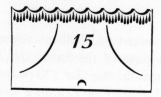

15

". . . The True Embodiment of Everything That's Excellent"

—*Iolanthe*

GILBERT spent the entire summer sugar-coating his lozenge. Sullivan's musical taste would not allow him to swallow the finished product. One night, while visiting Gilbert at Uxbridge, Sir Arthur told his partner that he would not and could not write the score for the libretto offered him. There was no heated argument. Gilbert merely insisted that the lozenge plot was an excellent device for use in a comic opera and he was determined to use it. Just as firmly, Sullivan insisted that the plot was full of flaws. Neither partner would give in to the other and nothing had been decided when Sullivan returned to London. If it hadn't been for Carte's foresight in ordering rehearsals in preparation for the revivals, the Savoy would have closed its doors when *Ruddigore* came to an abrupt end, November 5, 1887. As a matter of fact, even if Gilbert and Sullivan had had a work prepared, it never would have been ready for immediate production. Sir Arthur was not feeling well, and it would have been a physical impossibility for the composer to conduct rehearsals.

While Gilbert sulked and Sullivan rested, old favorites appeared on the stage of the Savoy. *H. M. S. Pinafore* proudly sailed across the stage for 120 performances; eighty times the wicked *Pirates of Penzance* battled the brave policemen, and the residents of Titipu welcomed (as did packed houses) *The Mikado* on 116 occasions. Never were the operettas more popular. Carte had only one worry: would his associates have a work ready when the revivals ended?

It didn't look as if Gilbert and Sullivan would have a new opera prepared. Gilbert had spent too much time compounding the magic drugs in his lozenge to throw away the prescription. Moreover, he had been responsible for another theatrical failure and was still smarting from the abuse he had received from the newspaper critics, so he had no desire to write anything else for the theater. Gilbert's latest failure had resulted from his ambitions to be a serious dramatist. A friend of Rutland Barrington promised that if the actor would leave the Savoy, he would back him in a legitimate play. Barrington asked Gilbert to write him a drama. Since it looked as if Barrington's services at the Savoy would never be needed in a new work, and writing drama always appealed to Gilbert, he consented. The result of the commission was *Brantinghame Hall,* one of the worst things the author ever wrote. The play put Barrington into bankruptcy, for his backer did not have funds enough to cover the cost of the production. Gilbert generously refused any payment for his work in order to help the actor, but everyone else connected with the ill-fated venture sued Barrington for his money.

Moreover, during the legal difficulties which followed the failure of *Brantinghame Hall,* Gilbert aided Barrington in every possible way. The author's attitude both astonished and pleased the unfortunate actor. Well did he remember the rehearsal of *Ruddigore* to which Gilbert had invited a few friends in order to get their reactions to the piece. Every member of the Savoy company was annoyed at being corrected, yelled at, berated and shouted at before outsiders. During one of the rest periods the cast decided that someone should express their feelings to Gilbert. There was just one trouble. Who was brave enough "to bell the cat?" At last Barrington, with his heart pounding, leaned across the footlights and stated in a firm voice, "Sir, I will not rehearse before an audience composed of strangers."

Gilbert gulped in amazement at Barrington's daring. It took him only a minute to regain control of himself—then he lost it! For five minutes he roared, screamed and jeered at the actor. Finally he calmed down. After several minutes of deadly silence, during which he glared at the members of the cast, the author turned to the audience and said, "Gentlemen, I must ask you to leave. I feel that Mr. Barrington has a reasonable complaint." The entire company sighed with relief. Barrington, ears still pounding from Gilbert's rebukes, felt like a hero. In a few minutes everyone except Gilbert had forgotten the matter. As the rehearsal dragged on, one of the theater staff wandered into the auditorium and sat down to watch the action on the stage. Gilbert stopped the company and, turning to the poor chap, bellowed, "Get out, you! Don't you know better than to sit down? Mr. Barrington doesn't like it." Poor Gilbert, he never could forget or forgive anyone who crossed him. Yet he was the only one to offer help to Barrington when the actor needed it!

Sir Arthur was not thinking of a production for the Savoy. The composer's old ambition to write grand opera was dominating his thoughts. The first thing he had done after his strength returned was to conduct a command performance of *The Golden Legend* for Queen Victoria. Her Majesty called Sir Arthur to the royal box and graciously thanked him for the pleasure his music had given her. Then she confirmed something Sullivan had been sure about for years. "You should write a grand opera, Sir Arthur," said the ruler of the British Empire. "We are convinced that no one could do it as well as you." This encouragement to leave the field of comic opera had one drawback for Sullivan. Although the composer was a generous person and quite able to appreciate another musician's success, he now found himself a victim of a common failing—jealousy. Sir Arthur's old chum at the Chapel Royal, Alfred Cellier, brother of the orchestra leader at the Savoy and the man who had taken *The Mikado* to Australia, had written a smash hit in *Dorothy*. While *Ruddigore* was playing to half-filled houses, Cellier's comic opera was turning away would-be buyers of tickets at every performance. Sullivan's pride suffered greatly as he compared the poor reception of his latest work with that given the production of his old classmate. To add to his annoyance, Gilbert was still insisting on using the lozenge plot. Sir Arthur made up his mind. He would quit the Savoy and take his Queen's advice.

One day, while waiting for a train at the Uxbridge Railway Station, the observant Gilbert noticed an advertisement of the Tower Furnishing Company. The poster was a colorful affair and featured the picture of one of the Yeomen of the Guard. The Yeomen are members of the oldest English military corps, established in 1485. Originally the Yeomen were the king's personal attendants day and night, accompanying him everywhere. The safety of the king was the Yeomen's main duty, and they even used to make the royal bed in order to be sure there was no one hiding in His Majesty's bedchamber. The last time the corps surrounded an English king on the battlefield was in 1743.

Despite this, every yeoman, non-commissioned officer, and every officer except the captain (how Gilbertian) must have served in the armed forces. The Yeomen are selected for bravery on the field of battle and their pay is considered a pension.

Through the years, however, the assignments of the Yeomen have become merely ceremonial. Today they have two main assignments: to act as a Royal Guard on state occasions and to guard the Tower of London. Dressed in their original fifteenth-century costumes—red and purple tunics decorated with gold, red breeches and stockings, a ruff, flat-plummed hat and black rosetted shoes—and carrying steel-gilt halberds with a tassel of red and gold, or an ornamental sword, the Yeomen are one of the most colorful sights in the English capitol. The corps is popularly known to Englishmen as "Beefeaters." This nickname was given them in 1699, when Count Cosimo, Grand Duke of Tuscany, while visiting London, wrote a letter home describing these royal guards. In it he reported that "they receive a large daily ration of beef, and as a result, might be called Beefeaters."

Just as the Japanese sword falling to the floor had given Gilbert inspiration to write *The Mikado,* a railway station poster was to provide the spark to ignite his genius. While riding to London, Gilbert kept thinking of the picture of the yeoman he had seen. By the time the author had reached his destination, he had an idea for a new operetta. He went to the Savoy to help supervise a rehearsal of *The Mikado* which was being revived. Sir Arthur greeted him warmly and was delighted to hear that his partner had a suggestion for a new opera. "You'll be interested to hear, Sullivan," said Gilbert, "that there isn't any lozenge concerned and I think that, at long last, I've a comic opera that's serious!" The composer and author talked for some time in a friendly manner and Sir Arthur expressed great interest in Gilbert's rough outline.

A series of conferences followed the meeting of the partners at the Savoy. As Gilbert read what he had written, Sullivan became even more enthusiastic than his associate over the new work. Of all Gilbert's librettos, the composer found this one the most appealing. He could hardly wait to begin work on the music. At first, the partners planned to call their new opera *The Tower of London,* then changed their minds and entitled it *The Beefeaters*—changed their minds once more and labeled their work *The Yeomen of the Guard.*

Gilbert was having a wonderful time gathering material for his plot. The author delighted in historic facts as much as he did in creating fancies. *The Yeomen of the Guard* gave him plenty of opportunity to dip deep into the past. For days on end he visited the Tower of London, examining the instruments of torture; the rooms in which Sir Walter Raleigh was imprisoned; the dungeons in the Beauchamp Tower where high-ranking captives were kept; the Wakefield Tower where the crown jewels are stored; and the Traitor's Gate. Gilbert also spent hours reading books about the Tower—originally built as a fortress on the north bank of the Thames River by Julius Caesar, and enlarged through the centuries by the kings of England. By the time the author had finished his research, he was steeped in all the Tower's tradition and able to transfer the best of them to the new Savoy opera.

Everything was proceeding smoothly when Sir Arthur decided that he had made a mistake. Sullivan felt that he should have stuck to his decision and left the comic opera field! Gilbert was far more worried than angry. The author knew that the libretto on which he was working was the best thing he had ever done, and that Sullivan would do wonders with it musically. So he sat down and wrote his partner a letter. Never a modest man, Gilbert bluntly stated that he was the best librettist in England, Sullivan the best composer, Carte the best manager, the Savoy and its company the best theater. Why, asked Gilbert, did Sullivan want to throw such an organization into the ash-heap? Sir Arthur could not but agree and once more decided to forget his ambitions to compose grand opera. This change of heart was, however, only for the time being. Sullivan would, before long, feel the same compulsions to break away from the Savoy.

Satisfied with Sir Arthur's attitude, Gilbert returned to his writing. As the author finished a number, he sent it to the composer. Before long, act one was in rehearsal, and by mid-August the entire work began to take shape. Then more trouble. Sullivan became dissatisfied with portions of the last act and told the author so. By now Gilbert was his usual self. He would not listen to his partner's complaints, based on what Gilbert considered the foolish requirements of his associate's music. The pair argued back and forth. Finally Gilbert gave in to Sir Arthur. The changes were made and peace returned to the Savoy.

Gilbert was experiencing other difficulties as well. Barrington had failed to return to the Savoy, so it was necessary to train a new star to take his place. The author drilled and drilled the cast until they were ready to drop from exhaustion. Gilbert's temper was never so evident. Grossmith, for whom Gilbert had written a special part, felt the full effect of the author's ire the day he reported that a certain actor was most anxious to join the ranks of the Savoyards. "All the chap wants is assurance that you will give him the first refusal of the part," the great comedian told Gilbert.

"Why, of course I will," said Gilbert in a most charming manner, "why of course."

Grossmith, who had expected a tirade, was overjoyed. "Thank you very much. He'll be most grateful."

"Will he?" snarled Gilbert. "I doubt it. You see, Grossmith, I refuse him at once!"

Part of the action of the opera called for Grossmith to kiss two ladies in the cast. The actor was thoroughly enjoying himself when Gilbert stopped him by remarking, "You are showing too much enthusiasm, Grossmith. Less tenderness, please."

Grossmith, a most capable player, who always tried to follow directions, called across the footlights, "Oh, I see. You would not kiss them more than once."

"Indeed *I* would," roared Gilbert, "but I must ask *you* not to!"

Once Sir Arthur had made up his mind to stay at the Savoy, he devoted all his time to the new opera. Throughout the month of September, he worked night after night until six in the morning. As he composed his tunes, he experimented with various pens, writing and suggesting to their manufacturers additions and improvements. Sullivan was seeking a perfect tool to make the creation of his music a simpler task. While he composed, his amber cigarette holder was always in his mouth, and the ashes piled high on his desk as the hours passed. The higher the pile of ashes in the morning, the more difficulty he had had with his music during the night.

Most of the music for *The Yeomen* came easily to the composer. There was only one song that really bothered him. This was Grossmith's big number. Try as he would, he could not set Gilbert's verses. At last he went to the author and admitted he was having trouble. Gilbert humorously asked if Sir Arthur wanted him to write the music as well as the words of the new operetta, reminding his associate, "I know two tunes. One is *God Save the Queen*, the other isn't."

"That may be true, Gilbert, for it is a brave man who will even ask you to hum," laughingly retorted Sullivan, "but I've noticed that despite the fact that you claim to know nothing of music, you sometimes have, in the back of your mind, an old tune which influences the meter of your verse. Maybe this is what has happened in this case. Normally, I don't want to know what you had in mind, for it makes it impossible for me to get the original theme out of my own work. This time, however, I'm desperate. If you did have anything in mind when you wrote this number, please—and see how brave I am—hum it to me."

"Very well, Sullivan, if you can stand it, I will. For, as a matter of fact, I did have a song in mind when I wrote that bit. It's an old chantey I used to hear the sailors sing on my yacht. You're sure you're prepared? Well then, it goes like this. . . ."

"That's enough!"cried Sir Arthur. "I don't mean your humming, Gilbert. Really, it was excellent. Not enough in tune to get you a position in the Savoy chorus, but quite well done. That bit of humming was just what I wanted. I've got my idea." Pulling out the pad of note paper he always carried, he jotted down a few notes of music as he walked away. An hour later he had completed the song—one of the most beautiful in any of the operas. What had made the composer's task so difficult in writing the music for *I Have a Song to Sing, O* was that Gilbert had taken the old nursery rhyme, *The House That Jack Built*, as a model. The result was that the first verse consisted of seven lines and the last of thirteen! No wonder Sullivan spent two weeks trying to accomplish his task!

Carte, meanwhile, had announced in the newspapers that

the new piece would be produced on October 3, 1888. Sir Arthur looked at the calendar. He still had plenty to do. Only taking a few hours off to conduct performances of his serious compositions at various concert halls, he slaved away, cutting, changing, scoring and rehearsing. Gilbert did not look at the calendar. All days were the same to him—he spent them drilling the company. There was never a last-minute rush for Gilbert—but always a continual grind. As Gilbert worked with the cast, he became nervous about the seriousness of the new work. *The Yeomen* was not comic opera—would the audience, accustomed to gay humor at the Savoy, dislike it? The nearer the opening, the more upset the author became and, as was to be expected, he took his feeling of insecurity out on the company, which now revealed many new faces, including that of Geraldine Ulmar, whom Sullivan had met in New York. The librettist's state of nerves was contagious and the entire cast was jittery when the opening night finally arrived.

Normally Gilbert would have left the Savoy just before the first-act curtain and set out for his traditional stroll along the Thames Embankment while the performance was being given. Tonight was different. The author was in a terrible state. The more he thought about this work, the harder it was for him to leave the theater. In the first place, there would be no hearty chorus to greet the audience when the curtain went up. Alone on the stage would be Jessie Bond, charming leading lady of the Savoy, who would open the operetta with a solo. Gilbert was sure the audience would never stand for a comic opera opening in such fashion. "Poor Jessie," Gilbert kept saying, "she'll be hissed off the stage."

Unable to leave the theater, he rushed to Miss Bond. The actress was sitting beside a spinning wheel, waiting for the curtain to rise.

"Are you all right, Jessie?" demanded the maddening author.

"Certainly. You had better get off the stage. They are starting the end of the overture."

Gilbert ran to the wings. A second later he was back, pushed the spinning wheel to one side and begged, "Tell me honestly, Jessie, are you absolutely *sure* you are all right?"

"Yes, yes, of course, everything is fine. Please go away and leave me alone!"

The dramatist threw one last look at the scenery, though it is doubtful if he could have told a tower turret from a moat, he was so excited. Then, just as the curtain rose, he rushed off the stage and out of the theater. The applause of the audience as Jessie Bond started to sing could be heard by the upset author as he hurried away as fast as possible from the first production of *The Yeomen of the Guard, or The Merryman and His Maid.*

Phoebe Meryll, the beautiful daughter of Sergeant Meryll of the Yeomen of the Guard, is discovered spinning on Tower Green, as the curtain rises. Work and song are interrupted by the appearance of Wilfred Shadbolt, the chief jailor of the Tower—a repulsive man and a genius with racks, pincers, and thumbscrews. Wilfred is madly in love with Phoebe, who will have nothing to do with him . . . first, because she cannot stand his ugly face, and secondly, because she dislikes his "professional duties." Phoebe is in no mood to listen to his love-making, for on this day, brave, handsome Colonel Fairfax is to be executed for being a sorcerer. The Colonel's kinsman, Sir Clarence Poltwhistle, an evil statesman, has brought the charges against Fairfax. Sir Clarence hopes to inherit the Fairfax estate and will do so if the soldier dies unmarried. All that Fairfax is guilty of is doing chemical experiments.

Both Phoebe and her father, who had served under Fairfax, know he is innocent of the crime with which he is charged. They can, however, do nothing to help him. The Merylls' inability to aid the Colonel is most trying, for on two occasions Fairfax had saved the Sergeant's life on the battlefield. However, unless a reprieve comes within a few hours, the gallant soldier must die. As father and daughter are discussing Fairfax's fate, Leonard, Sergeant Meryll's son, arrives at the Tower. Leonard has been made a yeoman for gallantry in battle—and his family forgets its sorrow in the joy of the young man's appointment. Suddenly the Sergeant has an inspiration. No one has seen his son arrive. Will Leonard, out of respect for the debt the family owes the Colonel, remain hidden and give his yeoman uniform to Fairfax, who can then join the Tower warders in disguise, and thus escape death?

A loyal son of a loyal father, Leonard consents. There is only one problem. How will the Merylls secure the key to Fairfax's cell? It hangs on the jailer's waist. Phoebe demurely says that she thinks "you may leave that to me." Father and sister say farewell to Leonard, who departs just in time. The Colonel, under a strong guard of Yeomen, marches across Tower Green on his way to the death cell. He recognizes his old companion-at-arms, and greets the Sergeant warmly. Fairfax is prepared to face death bravely, singing:

> *"What kind of plaint have I*
> *Who perish in July?*
> *I might have had to die*
> *Perchance, in June."*

The Colonel asks Sir Richard Cholmondeley, the Lieutenant in charge of the Tower, if he will grant him a boon. He explains that if he is allowed to be married before his execution, his cousin, Poltwhistle, will be defeated in his attempt to inherit the family fortune. Will the Lieutenant "serve a poor soldier who has but an hour to live," and find him a bride? It will be a marriage in name only, Fairfax's wife will be a widow within sixty minutes and will receive as a dowry a "dishonored name and a hundred crowns to boot," but Sir Clarence's designs will be defeated. Lieutenant Cholmondeley, who feels that Fairfax is being shamefully treated by his evil relation, agrees and sets out to find someone who is willing to be wooed, married and widowed within an hour. The Yeomen then march the Colonel to the death cell in Cold Harbour Tower.

At this moment Jack Point, the jester, and Elsie Maynard, his partner, reach Tower Green, surrounded by an excited throng. The crowd is teasing Jack and Elsie, demanding that they "jibe, joke, jollify." The pair are terrified, and in order to avoid bodily harm Jack Point offers to make a "cuplet, triolet, quatrain, sonnet, rondolet, ballade or what you will. Or we can dance you saraband, gondolet, carole, pimpernal or Jumping Joan." None of these suggestions appeal to the crowd and Elsie proposes that she and Jack sing the song of *The Merryman and His Maid:*

> *"A song of a merryman, moping mum,*
> *Whose soul was sad, and whose glance was glum,*
> *Who sipped no cup, and who craved no crum,*
> *As he sighed for the love of a ladye."*

When the song is finished Lieutenant Cholmondeley pushes his way through the spectators and tells Elsie of Colonel Fairfax's offer. Naturally enough, she hesitates, but finally consents, for her mother is ill and a hundred crowns will buy the medicines needed by the old lady. Jack Point is very much against the idea, for he is in love with Elsie. However, as it is only for an hour, he consents that his partner wed.

"A man about to lose his head
   For half an hour
   You'll be a wife
   And then the dower
   Is yours for life.
A headless bridegroom why refuse?
If truth the poets tell,
Most bridegrooms, ere they marry, lose
   Both head and heart as well."

Elsie is blindfolded and led to Fairfax's cell, is married
and returns immediately with the hundred crowns. Meanwhile, the Lieutenant has hired Jack Point as his official
jester. The strolling players go off as Phoebe and Shadbolt
enter. Slyly she steals the keys from the jailer and hands
them to her father. The Sergeant frees the Colonel, who,
dressed in Meryll's uniform, appears as a Yeoman of the
Guard. Just then the bell of St. Peter's begins to toll. Slowly
the lights dim and the Yeomen, flanking the headsman and
his assistants who are carrying the block, line up for the execution. Sir Richard sends a detail to conduct the prisoner to
the Green and they return crying:

"No prisoner at all we found!
We hunted high, we hunted low,
   We hunted here, we hunted there—
The man we sought, as truth will show,
   Had vanished into empty air!"

Everyone rushes about, looking for Fairfax. Only two
people stand motionless. They are Jack Point and Elsie, who
are stunned with the knowledge that, instead of being a
widow, Elsie is going to be a bride "that's husbandless." As
the finale to the first act reaches its climax, Elsie faints in
Fairfax's arms: all the Yeomen and villagers dash off the

stage in different directions to hunt for the fugitive, leaving only the headsman, standing with his axe in his hands, and Elsie, supported by the Colonel, on stage as the curtain falls.

Two days have passed when the second act begins. The Tower warders report that they have looked:

> "*Up and down, and in and out.*
> *Here and there and round about,*
> *Every chamber, every house,*
> *Every chink that holds a mouse,*
> *Every crevice in the keep,*
> *Where a beetle black could creep,*
> *Every outlet, every drain,*
> *Have we searched, but all in vain!*"

The situation could not be worse. Sir Richard is furious that his men allowed Fairfax to escape. Elsie is married to someone she has never seen and, moreover, she doesn't know who her husband is. Jack Point is most upset, for while Elsie is married, she can never be his wife. Wilfred Shadbolt is being accused of having given his keys (Phoebe had carefully hung them back on his belt) to a friend of the Colonel's, thus aiding in the escape. Shadbolt, however, is not too concerned with the prisoner's disappearance. He is too busy trying to find a reason why Phoebe should act so affectionately toward her brother Leonard.

Told by the angry commander of the Yeomen that he is going to lose his post in the Tower, Shadbolt turns to Jack Point for comfort. The jailer explains that losing his job wouldn't be too bad if he were a jester, for then he would have another trade by which he could earn money to support Phoebe. Jack Point sees a way of making everybody happy. All Wilfred has to do is to swear that he shot Fairfax while the Colonel was swimming across the Thames. The jester promises to confirm this lie, which will make Elsie a widow, Shadbolt a hero, Sir Richard happy and Jack Point an engaged man! Not only will Jack support this story, but he will, in addition, teach the jailer to be a jester. Jesting, the merryman explains, is a wonderful job:

> *"Oh! a private buffoon is a lighthearted loon,*
>   *If you listen to popular rumor;*
> *From morning to night he's so joyous and bright,*
>   *And he bubbles with wit and good humor!"*

Shadbolt agrees to Jack's proposition and the pair prepare "a tale of cock and bull, of convincing detail full." Fairfax, meanwhile is quite disturbed. He has fallen in love with Elsie, but cannot say anything, for he is still bound by his marriage to the unknown, blindfolded girl who wed him in his cell. Elsie has been ill ever since the supposed escape of the Colonel. Dame Carruthers, the maid's nurse, informs Fairfax that in fever the girl has mumbled something about being married to a man about to die. He is overjoyed. Fairfax decides to test Elsie by asking her to flee with him and forget her husband, "the greatest villain unhung." She is shocked that "Leonard Meryll" should make such a suggestion and says so just as a shot rings out.

Everyone rushes on stage, Jack Point and Shadbolt appear and tell their "cock and bull" story of how Wilfred shot the escaping Fairfax, "through the head, and he's very, very, very dead." With the Colonel dead, Elsie consents to become the bride of the man she thinks is Leonard Meryll. Phoebe, heartbroken, lets slip the secret of the plot to save Fairfax's life to Shadbolt, who declares he will tell the authorities unless she marries him. Out of loyalty to her father, Phoebe consents. At this point the real Leonard appears, bearing a reprieve for the Colonel. The paper had been delayed by Fairfax's evil kinsman, in hopes that it would arrive after the execution. Leonard's conversation with his father is overheard by Dame Carruthers, who promises not to tell of the Meryll family's help to Fairfax if the Sergeant, whom she has loved for years, will marry her. Sergeant Meryll has to agree.

Restored to his former rank, Colonel Fairfax demands that his bride be brought to him. Poor Elsie! With head cast down, she falls at Fairfax's feet, begging for mercy. When she discovers that her husband is the man she loved as "Leonard Meryll," she is overjoyed. Jack Point's eyes fill with tears as he kneels and kisses the hem of Elsie's bridal gown and sings:

> *"Oh thoughtless crew!*
> *Ye know not what ye do!"*

He falls down in a faint—or as some Savoyards would have it—dead, at the feet of the happy pair as the opera ends.

The Yeomen of the Guard was a tremendous success on the opening night. Both Gilbert and Sullivan thought the work was going to be the greatest triumph of their career. Even the press found no fault with the author's work. That is, none of the journals except *Punch*. As usual, that magazine pointed out that there was very little originality in the new Savoy production. Technically speaking, *Punch* was correct; Gilbert had stolen much of the opera from the gifted author of the *Bab Ballads*. The interested critic could have found much of *The Mikado* in the operetta. Take, for example, the similarity of the marriage of Nanki-Poo and Yum-Yum to that of Fairfax and Elsie. Theatergoers paid no attention to such similarities, however, and the long lines at the Savoy box office delighted Carte.

Yet, as the months wore on, the piece failed to attract full houses. The operetta was making money for the Savoy combination, but it was plain that *The Yeomen* was no *Pinafore* or *Mikado*. Neither Gilbert nor Sullivan could understand why the public did not consider the piece the finest thing the partnership had produced. Perhaps the reason why *The Yeoman* was the favorite among their operas with the author and composer lies in the fact that Sir Arthur found in its songs an opportunity to advance in the direction of grand opera; while Gilbert expressed his personal feelings toward the world when he had Jack Point sing:

> "I can set a braggart quailing with a quip,
>   The upstart I can wither with a whim;
> He may wear a merry laugh upon his lip,
>   But his laughter has an echo that is grim!
> When they're offered to the world in merry guise,
>   Unpleasant truths are swallowed with a will—
> For he who'd make his fellow creatures wise
>   Should always gild the philosophic pill!"

Although the full audiences for which the partners had hoped did not fill the Savoy, *The Yeomen* held the stage for 423 performances. During the opera's run, it looked as if there was never going to be another work by Gilbert and Sullivan. The men were no longer friendly, nor was the author on speaking terms with Carte. This dissension was felt by the company and, to make matters worse, George Grossmith left the Savoy and returned to his old profession of entertaining at parties and banquets. In addition, Jessie Bond was refusing to renew her contract at her old salary. Richard Temple was talking about leaving the company, and Geraldine Ulmar had already given notice. Carte, Gilbert and Sullivan did not realize it, but the Savoy was soon to become the scene of as violent a battle as took place when the directors of the Comedy Opera Company's hired thugs caused "The Pinafore Riot."

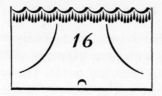

16

"Our Attitude's Queer and Quaint"

○

—The Mikado

O N   T H E surface all was peaceful at the Savoy. Sir Arthur was actively engaged in writing incidental music for Henry Irving's production of *Macbeth*. Gilbert was looking through the pages of *Fun* for an idea that could be turned into an operetta. Carte was busy with his managerial duties. While members of the company knew of the strained relations among the three men, an outsider could not have detected anything amiss.

A month of constant composition and Sullivan had completed the music for Irving's Shakespearean revival. The famous actor-manager was delighted with the composer's work, as was the audience. Sir Arthur noted in his diary that on the opening night there were calls for the author, star and composer, but "only the latter two responded!" Gilbert, meanwhile, had taken upon himself the task of convincing Jessie Bond that she should reconsider her demands for a higher salary. The author was genuinely fond of the charming Jessie, but business was business. Gilbert pointed out to his leading lady that she was an extremely lucky actress, for long engagements with parts expressly written for one are not common in the theatrical world. The two exchanged a long series of letters and at last—as he knew he would—Gilbert gave in and raised Miss Bond's salary fifty per cent.

Yet despite the seeming calm, undercurrents were developing. The first sign of the approaching storm came from Sir Arthur. The success of his music for Irving's *Macbeth* awoke the composer's old ambitions. Nor had he ever forgotten what Queen Victoria had said to him after the command performance of *The Golden Legend*. Instead of going to Gilbert and frankly stating that until he had tried his hand at grand opera he would never be happy, Sullivan wrote Carte to say that he was sick and tired of being a slave to Gilbert's words. Writing such a letter was an extremely foolish and tactless thing for Sir Arthur to do. But such an action was natural enough for Sullivan, who was always looking for the easiest way out of a difficulty. By writing his complaints to Carte, he thought he would avoid a clash with Gilbert. His plan backfired, however. Carte and Gilbert had had words about the management of the Savoy, and in relaying Sir Arthur's message, Carte made it sound worse than it really was. Complaints passed on by a second party are always added to and changed in meaning. The author, who did not know that Carte had added to the composer's list of grievances, was quite upset. Gilbert was perfectly willing that Sullivan should try his hand at grand opera, but he did not want the Savoy combination destroyed. Before he could contact Sir Arthur and ask for a conference, a letter arrived from his partner.

It was a most friendly note. Evidently Sullivan had been doing some thinking since passing his dissatisfaction on to Carte. He informed Gilbert that he had decided to write a grand opera before he composed anything else. Would Gilbert be willing to write the libretto? The letter made it clear that Sir Arthur felt his associate at the Savoy could create a better plot than anyone else in England.

Upon receiving Sullivan's letter, Gilbert realized that Carte had exaggerated the composer's demands. He did not explode. That was to come later. Instead, he sat down and wrote Sir Arthur a long letter, full of good advice. Among other things, he called his partner's attention to the fact that *The Yeomen* was a more serious than comic opera and it was not, unfortunately, attracting large audiences. Gilbert frankly discussed his ability as an author and explained that neither the press nor the public would ever stand for a grand opera libretto from his pen. If Sullivan were determined to try grand opera, there were others far more fitted than Gilbert for the task of writing a suitable "book." He made it clear that he understood perfectly the composer's desire to write an important work, explaining that it was only natural for a man of Sir Arthur's genius to have such an ambition. There was, however, Gilbert went on, no need for Sullivan to devote his entire time to grand opera. Why not write the proposed composition while working on a piece for the Savoy? Tactfully, the author recalled that Sir Arthur had proved he could do two things at once—and do them well. Take *The Martyr of Antioch,* for example. *Both* Gilbert and Sullivan produced that work while engaged in polishing *The Pirates of Penzance.* Incidentally, asked Gilbert, where was Sir Arthur going to find singers who could act? Look at the trouble the Savoy combination had had before securing a suitable company for *light* opera. Finally, Gilbert expressed the hope that his association with Sullivan would go on for many more years.

Without realizing it, Gilbert had found the key to the situation. The author was content with writing for the Savoy, Sullivan was not. Sir Arthur said so in his next letter to Gilbert. If the composer had merely stated that his ambitions went beyond light opera, all would have been well. Instead, he went on to say that he could not stand another of the typical Gilbertian plots: the comic "middle-aged woman with the fading charms" and all the rest. He called Gilbert's attention to the fact that the author had often told him that his music sounded as though it were written for a church rather than for a theater, so perhaps they should part. Then came the composer's constant complaint. At the Savoy, Gilbert's words were always given more importance than Sullivan's music. Sir Arthur firmly stated that he would engage in no more work in which his music was secondary.

Gilbert's patience vanished. He felt that Carte, who was building the Royal English Opera House, to be used for nothing but grand opera, was encouraging Sullivan to break his agreement with Gilbert. The manager wanted a work by Sir Arthur to open his new theater. The author was sure that Carte's new venture was more important to him than the Savoy. In a temper, Gilbert refused even to consider a joint work with Sir Arthur in which the music would have more prominence. More letters were exchanged between the author and composer. Charges flew back and forth: Gilbert wasted time on petty details at rehearsals and deliberately ruined Sullivan's music; Sir Arthur, maintained Gilbert, was not man enough to bring his complaints directly to his partner, but had to hide behind Carte. As the flood of letters streamed into the apartment at Queen's Mansions and the cosy house at Uxbridge, the tide of resentment slowly ebbed. Sullivan became convinced that he could write both grand and light opera at the same time. Gilbert admitted that some of the composer's requirements were reasonable. Little by little, tempers died down—and then Mrs. Ronalds invited both Gilbert and Sullivan to her studio in Cadogan Place.

This was no open house for Bohemian London. The beautiful lady from Boston took care that the servants admitted no one but Gilbert and Sullivan that evening. With diplomacy and tact, plus a sound knowledge of the personalities of the two men, their hostess soon had the partners in a cheerful mood. She stressed the fact that Carte was in no hurry for Sullivan's *Ivanhoe,* with which the manager planned to open his new theater, and pointed out that it was Gilbert who had suggested that Julian Sturgis write the libretto. Surely Sir Arthur must realize that the author wished him success in his new venture. As for Gilbert, Mrs. Ronalds declared, "You should think twice and speak once, and above all, tear up most of your letters before posting them!" For over two hours the two men listened to a chiding lecture. "The time has come," insisted Mrs. Ronalds, "when you two should stop arguing and decide the best means of continuing your collaboration. This fault-finding and name-calling is just ridiculous on the part of two such brilliant artists. Come now, shake hands, talk things over like grown-ups, not children!"

Gilbert and Sullivan looked sheepishly at each other. They smiled, shook hands and ironed out their difficulties in a matter of minutes. Still Mrs. Ronalds was not satisfied. She took Gilbert to one side. "Now that you've straightened out matters with Sir Arthur," she said, "come here tomorrow afternoon. You and Carte have got to settle your differences." Gilbert started to growl, thought better of it, and agreed. The next day the author and the manager were reconcilled, thanks to "the permanent ambassadress of the United States at the Court of St. James" . . . and thanks to her, one of the most charming, delightful and musically perfect of the Gilbert and Sullivan series was written.

Now that he was on friendly terms with Sir Arthur and

Carte, Gilbert immediately set to work on a new opera for the Savoy. Some time previously the author had decided to use Venice as the setting for his next work. All he had to do was to construct a plot whose action would seem logical enough in that ancient Italian city. Seeking suitable material, he turned, as was his custom, to the *Bab Ballads*. As usual, he found a usable idea or two. Always stealing from his own work, Gilbert lifted almost word for word, from his successful play *Engaged*, one of the operetta's funniest speeches. For once he worked slowly. With the utmost care, he consulted Sir Arthur frequently. The two had to confer by mail because Sullivan was enjoying the company of society and royalty on the Continent.

Sir Arthur's travels took him to Venice. In the city of the Doges he wandered up and down, or drifted idly in a gondola. At last, full of the atmosphere of Venice, he returned to London. Gilbert was waiting for his partner with a rough outline of the new piece. Sullivan thought Gilbert's work was excellent and told him so.

"I'm glad you like it," returned the author. "If the verses won't do, don't hesitate to tell me. Let me have them back and I'll rewrite them. Anything you don't like, tear up. If the meter form is too difficult to set to music, I'll do my best to try another form."

What, wondered Sir Arthur, had happened to Gilbert's temper? The composer did not know that the author was determined to avoid offending his partner. Always thinking of Sullivan's complaints about the previous Savoy operettas, Gilbert forced himself to write slowly. As a result, it took him five months to put his libretto into its final form. Sullivan was in no hurry to start composition. He did write a few songs for the new piece and then laid his work aside. Of far more interest to the composer was the libretto of *Ivanhoe*, which Julian Sturgis had completed. To Sullivan, there was no question as to which was the more important. The comic opera for the Savoy would have to wait while Sir Arthur labored with grand opera.

If Gilbert was considering Sir Arthur's demands as he worked on the new production for the Savoy, he also bore in mind those of Jessie Bond. He had not forgotten (he never forgot anything) the actress' request for a salary rise, based on the fact that she was a star. The glamorous Jessie had won her point, but Gilbert was going to make sure that there would be no more personal successes as the result of his writings. "Carte," thundered the author, "I'll never help another player become a star. They get strange ideas about their importance. I'm starting my new system in this piece. There isn't going to be a starring part in it. In fact, there's not going to be any principal part. No character is going to be more important than any other. No singer will have more songs—and I'm even going to count the lines each one has. If I could do more, I would . . . say I can! Carte, even the leading roles will be shared by two people! That will fix these artists who think they are important!"

Meanwhile, business at the Savoy, which had held up excellently during the early weeks of the summer, started to drop. It was obvious to all that a new opera would be needed before the end of the year. Moreover, due to unforeseen difficulties, Carte's proposed theater would not be ready for the public for many months. So Sullivan laid aside his work on *Ivanhoe* and concentrated on Gilbert's plot. From early August to late October, he spent several hours daily at his desk, writing music. Although Gilbert had tried to meet all of his partner's demands in writing the libretto, the scoring gave Sir Arthur more trouble than any of the other operas. The only time that Sullivan took off from his labors was to conduct the Leeds Festival. On October 12, 1889, the last day of the Festival, *The Golden Legend* was presented. Albani,

Damian, Mills and Brereton gave wonderful performances,
the orchestra was superb and the audience cheered the
composer and artists for five minutes. It was the finest production of the cantata ever given.

Once this triumph was over, Sir Arthur gave his full time
to Gilbert's libretto. By mid-November he was working until
four or five o'clock every morning. The operetta, advertised
to open on Saturday, December 7, 1889, did not have a
complete musical rehearsal until five days before that date.
After the rehearsal, Sir Arthur went home and worked on
the overture. It was three o'clock in the morning when he
finished. He had been interrupted about midnight by the
ringing of his doorbell. On the steps was Gilbert.

"Sorry to bother you, Sullivan, but there's a matter that
demands attention. All Carte has done is to advertise 'An
entirely original opera in two acts'—he couldn't do otherwise. For if you stop to think, we haven't given the piece a
name!" announced Gilbert.

"Well, I should think it is about time we did," laughingly
replied Sir Arthur. "Come in and let's choose a name."

Naming the opera didn't take the partners very long.
When Gilbert left a short time later, the work bore the title
The Gondoliers, or The King of Barataria. The sub-title was
a typical Gilbertian touch. If you remember your *Don Quix-
ote*, you'll recall Barataria was the name of the island that
the famous knight deeded to his faithful squire, Sancho, long
before the pair reached it.

The seventh of December came at last. Sullivan was so
weary he could hardly make his way to his dressing room.
Gilbert was tired, too, as he wandered aimlessly up and
down the Thames Embankment. Never had the author rehearsed an opera as he had *The Gondoliers*. No detail had
been too small to receive attention. Take, for example, the
game of blindman's buff in the first act—a very short scene,

lasting less than a minute. For three whole days Gilbert had drilled the cast in this bit of stage action! Every seat in the Savoy was filled by eight o'clock. As was the custom, a half hour was devoted to "community singing." Faithful Savoyards in the balcony sang songs from all the Gilbert and Sullivan operas, to the intense enjoyment of those in the higher-priced seats. Just as these amateur choristers finished, Sir Arthur entered the pit, tapped his baton, the lights dimmed and the curtain rose on Venice.

A singing and dancing group of Venetian maidens, known as *contadine,* are seen outside the ducal palace. They are awaiting the famous gondoliers, Marco and Giuseppe Palmeri. Every maid in Venice is in love with these handsome foster-brothers. There is only one trouble, the *contadine* explain:

> *"We have hearts for them in plenty*
> *We alas, are four-and-twenty!*
> *They have hearts, but all too few.*
> *They alas, are only two!"*

When the gondoliers arrive, the girls crowd around them anxiously. Which of them will be chosen as brides by the Palmeri? Giuseppe and Marco "really do not care a preference to declare," so they decide "to let impartial Fate select for them a mate." The gondoliers blindfold themselves, promising to marry whomsoever they catch. The game of blindman's buff ends with Marco catching Gianetta, while Giuseppe captures Tessa. The happy couples leave the stage, followed by their friends. Suddenly a flourish of drums is heard and a gondola arrives at the Pizazetta steps.

From the craft steps the Duke of Plaza-Toro, his Duchess, their daughter Casilda, and the royal "suite," consisting of one man, Luiz the drummer! His Grace, "a Castilian hidalgo of ninety-five quarterings," is disappointed that no one is on hand to greet that "celebrated under-rated nobleman, the Duke of Plaza-Toro." The truth is, the Duke isn't really important except for one reason. He is the father of a queen!

For Casilda is a queen. When a babe in arms, she was married to the infant prince of Barataria. Of course, Casilda hasn't seen her husband since her wedding day. The poor girl couldn't, even if she wanted to—for Don Alhambra del Bolero, the Grand Inquisitor, has hidden the Prince for safety's sake. As a matter of fact, Casilda doesn't care if the Prince is ever found. She is in love with Luiz. Naturally enough, the Duke and Duchess know nothing of their daughter's love for a drummer boy. All they are interested in is that Don Alhambra produce their son-in-law so that Casilda can be crowned.

The Grand Inquisitor is delighted to bring Casilda and the Prince together. He explains how, during a revolution, he gave the royal infant to a gondolier to raise:

> *"But owning, I'm much disposed to fear*
> *To his terrible taste for tippling,*
> *That highly respectable gondolier*
> *Could never declare with a mind sincere*
> *Which of the two was his offspring dear,*
> *And which was the royal stripling."*

The two youngsters brought up by the gondolier are, of course, Marco and Giuseppe. Only one person can tell which of them is the Prince of Barataria. This is Inez, their old nurse. Don Alhambra regrets that Inez isn't available to identify His Royal Highness, having moved to Cordova, where she is happily married to a most respectable highwayman. The Grand Inquisitor promises to send for Inez so that she can supply the information needed by the Duke and Duchess. Meanwhile, Casilda is married to either Marco or

Giuseppe—"of that there is no matter of doubt—no prob-able, possible shadow of doubt—no possible doubt what-ever!"

Just as arrangements have been made to send for Inez, the gondoliers and the *contadine* dance across the stage. Marco and Giuseppe have just married the girls they tagged in the game of blindman's buff and all are rejoicing when the Grand Inquisitor stops the celebration. Don Alhambra announces that one of the foster-brothers is the Prince of Barataria. At first, Marco and Giuseppe don't think much of the idea, for they dislike kings. On thinking over what they have been told, however, they decide that there could be an ideal king, one "who would abolish taxes and make everything cheap except gondolas." Such a king would also give free entertainments on the canals and scramble money for the gondoliers on the Rialto. Marco and Giuseppe are sure they would be that sort of a king! The foster-brothers joyfully get ready to go to Barataria, to rule jointly until it is decided which one is really heir to the throne.

Then comes the news that dampens their enthusiasm. Marco and Giuseppe, declares the Grand Inquisitor, cannot take their wives with them. The gondoliers may take their friends, give them positions in the court, but they cannot take Gianetta and Tessa! Neither Marco or Giuseppe knows that the reason why they cannot take their new brides to Barataria is because one of them is already married. Wise Don Alhambra says nothing about this matter! Naturally enough, Gianetta and Tessa do not want their husbands of a half hour to leave them, but both girls consent when it is brought to their attention that soon one of them will be "a Queen and sit on a golden throne, with a crown in-stead of a hat on her head, and diamonds all her own!" Marco and Giuseppe, listening to the warning of their wives:

"And O my darling, O my pet,
Whatever else you may forget,
In yonder isle beyond the sea,
Do not forget you've married me!"

embark on the *Xebeque* for the island of Barataria and wave
farewell as the curtain falls.

When act two begins, Marco and Giuseppe are seen polishing the royal plate, while seated on thrones, dressed in
magnificent robes. Poor chaps, they have no time to act
kingly! They are too busy. Their subjects make them do all
the work. Such treatment is annoying, but the worst of it
is, they are allowed only one serving of meals between them!
Suddenly a loud noise is heard and in rush Gianetta and
Tessa and all the other girls. The maids have come to visit
their husbands. In the midst of the celebration, Don Alhambra arrives and is shocked to find that the two kings
have given everyone a title. The gondoliers have forgotten
that "when everyone is somebodee, then no one's anybody."

However, the Grand Inquisitor has not come to find fault.
He is there to inform the two kings that one of them is married to Casilda. How this news stuns everyone! Before they
have a chance to recover, the Duke, Duchess, and Casilda
arrive, accompanied by Luiz. Once again the Duke is annoyed because he is not royally greeted. His Grace addresses
himself to the young man who has married his daughter
and hopes, as he does not know which one it is, that the
other young man will not be impolite and listen to the conversation. "Take her," says the Duke, "and may she make
you happier than her mother has made me."

"Sir!" interrupts the Duchess.

"If possible," finishes the clever courtier.

Just then Inez enters. The Grand Inquisitor demands that
she tell which gondolier is the Prince.

"Neither," says the old woman.—"When traitors came to steal the Prince, I deftly substituted my own son, while I hid the heir to Barataria. See, here he comes now. His name, Luiz!"

The former drummer enters, robed as a king. Luiz offers Casilda his arm and they ascend the thrones. Everyone is delighted with the way matters have turned out and goes into a wild dance, singing:

> *"Once more gondoleri*
> *Both skillful and wary,*
> *Free from this quandary*
> *Contented are we."*

And the curtain falls on *The Gondoliers, or The Prince of Barataria.*

There were no boos when Sullivan brought his baton down at the final note of *The Gondoliers*. The audience rose and cheered—it was the most brilliant first night in the history of the Gilbert and Sullivan partnership. For 554 nights audiences would throng to hear Gilbert's words and Sullivan's tunes. Even the author felt enthusiastic about the operetta. He wrote to Sir Arthur the morning after the opening, thanking him for the excellent music and long hours of work he had given to *The Gondoliers*. Sullivan promptly answered his partner in a letter which gave Gilbert all the credit for the success of the new Savoy piece. More than that, Sir Arthur praised his librettist's good nature and willingness to accept suggestions!

The two men never seemed more in accord. They were like Marco and Giuseppe on the throne of Barataria, agreeing in all things. When the exhausted Sullivan went to the dock to board the vessel that was to take him to Monte Carlo and the rest he so greatly needed, Gilbert was waiting for him. The author had come up from Uxbridge to see his partner off and wish him a pleasant voyage! This action of Gilbert's was positive proof that the breach between the composer and the author was completely healed.

Gilbert then set out on a tour of India. On his return he went to the Savoy and asked to see a list of the expenses connected with the producing of *The Gondoliers*. Always interested in the returns brought in from his writing (Gilbert, Sullivan and Carte each had a third share in the profits of each opera), the author examined the expense account carefully. Quickly he ran his eyes down the column of figures and gasped when he saw the total, $22,500. He immediately demanded a more itemized accounting. Carte prepared it and the author was furious when he saw that included in the expenses was seven hundred dollars for new carpets for the front lobby of the Savoy.

When Gilbert received the manager's figures he wrote at once to Sir Arthur. Sullivan had, by this time, returned from his vacation and was working on his grand opera. In his letter, the author called the composer's attention to the fact that they were, by contract, only responsible for "repairs incidental to the performance." How, demanded Gilbert, could new carpets on the stairways and in the lobby be considered in that classification? Before receiving a reply from Sir Arthur, Gilbert went to see Carte. The manager, who had almost as violent a temper as the author, answered every yell with a shout.

Sullivan, standing on the sidelines, tried to make peace. Sir Arthur suggested that the three of them hold a conference. "In order to give our tempers a chance to cool," said the composer, "I suggest that we wait a week before we get together." Both Carte and Gilbert agreed. During the week before the proposed meeting, Sullivan examined the Savoy accounts. When he had finished, he wrote to Gilbert, suggesting that the partners draw up a new agreement relative to their Savoy productions so that a situation like the carpeting could not arise again. Gilbert had regained control of his temper and was willing to talk the matter over calmly. He welcomed Sullivan's suggestion. However, when the three men met in the manager's office at the Savoy, Gilbert insisted that Sir Arthur side either with him or with Carte. The composer, weary and sick of his associate's bullying manner, defended Carte.

Immediately Gilbert's temper burst into flame. "You are both nothing but a pair of blackguards!" shouted the author, and he stamped out of the office, slamming the door so hard behind him that it shattered. News of what had happened was soon common gossip in theatrical circles. The general public, its curiosity whetted by newspaper stories, wanted to learn more about the disagreement. As a result, Carte found it necessary to call a press conference and give a prepared statement to the reporters. Naturally enough, he painted Gilbert in the blackest possible colors.

Gilbert, insanely furious, sat down and wrote letters to both Sir Arthur and Carte. The author informed his associates at the Savoy that he was withdrawing from the partnership and forbade Carte to produce any of his libretti after Christmas, 1890. *The Gondoliers,* Gilbert told Sullivan, was "our last work together." Gilbert, who had made fun of the law in *Trial by Jury* and *Iolanthe,* now turned to it for help and made legally sure that Carte and Sullivan would not profit by any of his writings in the future. Sir Arthur was greatly shocked at Gilbert's attitude and by the cutting remarks the author had written in his letter. The composer was having a most difficult time with his grand opera, and his task was made no easier by the carpet controversy. Nor did the curt letters that Sullivan received daily from Gilbert bring him any comfort.

Then, as usual, Gilbert had a change of heart. Regretting his outburst and slanderous statements, the hot-headed author admitted he had been wrong. Sullivan, although still smarting from the treatment he had received, realized how much such a statement had cost his former partner, and sent Gilbert tickets for the opening night of his grand opera, *Ivanhoe*. The mercurial Gilbert, after holding out his hand to be shaken, withdrew it. He returned Sir Arthur's tickets with an extremely nasty note—and Sullivan read it just as he was about to leave his apartment to go to the opening at the Royal English Opera House. Gilbert's statements sent him on his way with a heavy heart.

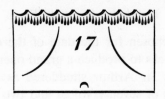

17

"*My Cup Is Not of Nectar*"

—The Sorcerer

SULLIVAN had worked long and hard on *Ivanhoe*. Sir Arthur had begun to compose the music for Julian Sturgis' libretto on May 17, 1890, and did not finish it until December of that year. There were 117 pages in the score, representing seven months of creative effort. Most of the time the composer had worked twelve hours a day. Often he stayed at his desk until three or four o'clock in the morning. Between the battle with Gilbert, arising from the situation at the Savoy, and the demands of his grand opera, he was exhausted when he set down the last note of the finale. At no other time in his long career did Sir Arthur rewrite as much as he did in scoring *Ivanhoe*. He would spend half a day composing and then, after a walk, come home, play it and decide his composition would not do.

Writing the music for *Ivanhoe* had made great demands on Sullivan's strength. He was weary and emotionally upset constantly, thanks to Gilbert. True to form, the changeable author kept writing insulting letters, making his former partner so mentally tired that he doubted he could face the deadly routine of rehearsing *Ivanhoe*. Since January 31,

1891 had been chosen for the date of the opening night, there were six weeks to produce a grand opera in three acts and nine scenes! Sir Arthur shuddered as he thought of training a chorus of seventy voices and two sets of principals (since *Ivanhoe* was grand opera, no singer could be expected to perform two nights in succession). Now that the composer was about to achieve his life ambition, he was in no condition, either mentally or physically, to enjoy reaching his goal. Then, to add to his depression, his constant companion, Tommy, his dog, suddenly died. The animal had come to him from the firm which had failed on the night that *Iolanthe* was produced. Sir Arthur had taken the dog in payment of the $35,000 he had lost at that time!

Exhausted, dreading the daily arrival of the mail (because it was sure to contain another nasty letter from Gilbert) and mourning the death of his faithful pet, Sullivan began the rehearsals of *Ivanhoe* in Prince's Hall. The composer, having learned his lesson at the Savoy, personally collected the music after each rehearsal and locked it up in his safe at Queen's Mansions. Meanwhile, D'Oyly Carte was overseeing the final touches of the Royal English Opera House. The manager had spared no expenses in building his new theater—and its furnishings put the Savoy to shame. This adventure into grand opera was, of course, the big mistake of Carte's theatrical career. No single composer, not even a genius like Sullivan, could continually provide such an institution as the Royal English Opera House with a series of grand opera—and there was no other musician in England capable of writing even one such work.

Gilbert had told Carte all this and much more before their separation. "I'm warning you, Carte," the author had said, "the location of your new theater is poor. People will have to go out of their way to reach it. While I know if anyone can write a grand opera, Sullivan can, I don't know how you are going to get a company to sing it. English Opera, bah! There's no such thing as an Englishman who can sing grand opera successfully. Moreover, what are you going to do if, at the end of the run of this piece of Sullivan's, you find that he hasn't got another opera ready? If you ask me —or even if you don't—I'd say you're risking too much on one man's ability."

Carte paid no attention to Gilbert's predictions. Always a gambler in things theatrical, the manager continued to lay out lavish sums on his new enterprise. Nor did he spare any expense in mounting *Ivanhoe*. The cost of the scenery and costumes was tremendous. Carte had announced that everything connected with the Royal English Opera House would be of the best—and he well knew the publicity value of spending money. All the time Sir Arthur was rehearsing his company, Carte was watching painters, carpenters and electricians, checking their work. At last the new theater was completed.

It was all too soon for Sullivan when the opening night arrived. Perhaps if he had not received the note from Gilbert and the rejected tickets just before he left for the performance, he would have been in a better mood. For the audience which greeted him was composed of the people with whom he delighted to be associated. Never in London theatrical history had an opening night drawn so many distinguished men and women. With the exception of a very few real lovers of music who managed to squeeze in, everyone in the theater was a member of royalty or a society figure. Sullivan entered the pit not too confident of success. The composer was bothered with the knowledge that Gilbert would not be there. Despite the nagging letters and bitter words, Sir Arthur sincerely regretted that his former partner was not in the audience. Sullivan had missed Gilbert often during the trying days of rehearsals—longing for the author's skill in stagecraft as *Ivanhoe* was being whipped into shape.

Once Sir Arthur appeared in the orchestra pit, he was given no time to brood over Gilbert's absence. The audience gave him a wonderful reception. Finally, the applause and cheers died down and the composer began the performance. There was no time to think of Gilbert as the first act began —Sullivan had to watch the singers and the members of the orchestra. Nor did he have a minute to himself between the first two acts, for he was invited by the Prince of Wales to his box to smoke a cigarette; then between the second and third acts, the Prince and his brother, the Duke of Edinburgh, returned the visit by joining Sir Arthur in his dressing room. When the final curtain came down, the composer was loudly cheered. He had achieved a triumph—at long last, his great ambition had been consummated! Flushed with excitement, he tipped the stagehands, thanked them for their many kindnesses and went out into the London night. It was four o'clock in the morning before Sir Arthur got to bed—then he could not sleep—the applause of the admiring audience kept ringing in his ears.

Newspaper critics were loud in their praise of *Ivanhoe*. As was to be expected, most of the journalists called attention to the really fine work Sir Arthur could do without Gilbert. From cities on the Continent, cables arrived asking for permission to produce the work. Sullivan was extremely happy when he opened his mail and read compliments from so many sources. Even Queen Victoria found time in her round of duties to send the composer best wishes. Her Imperial Majesty pointed out that Sir Arthur's success was of particular interest to her because she had suggested that he desert comic for grand opera some time ago. Indeed, Victoria had—and Sullivan had dedicated the music of *Ivanhoe* to her. It was the least he could do for a Queen who had rewarded him with a gold piece when he sang as a child in the Chapel Royal, had made him a knight as a young man, and now, in his middle years, was congratulating him on what the composer considered his major work.

Carte and Sullivan were both sure that they had a greater success in *Ivanhoe* than in anything that had ever played at the Savoy. Sir Arthur sincerely felt that the opera contained his finest composition. However, the public knew better. For 160 performances they came to hear a grand opera written by an Englishman, produced by an Englishman, and sung by Englishmen. Then they lost interest. Everyone who saw the piece agreed that it was splendidly sung and that the costumes were gorgeous, but there was definitely something wrong with the opera. It hadn't been written by Gilbert and Sullivan!

About a month after the opening of *Ivanhoe,* Gilbert went to the Royal English Opera House to see the opera. By this time the author was regretting his outburst of temper and decided he should accept Sullivan's invitation. Despite the fact that Gilbert bragged that he didn't understand grand opera, he enjoyed it. His masterly eye for stage management detected several flaws in the production, and he wrote *Mrs. Carte* a letter full of suggestions: this actor overplayed his part, that one moved around too much, and the stage groupings were poor in certain scenes, but could be corrected by moving a few of the players either to the left or right. The placing of the scenery did not meet with Gilbert's approval either, and he gave some excellent advice about changes which were gratefully received, although his suggestions came too late. However, it is doubtful that even Gilbert's flair for stage direction would have made *Ivanhoe* popular with the theater-going public. The professional musicians approved of the work, Victoria considered it a masterpiece —but the box-office sales showed a noticeable lack of enthusiasm on the part of those who had to buy their tickets.

Slowly the truth dawned on Sullivan. *Ivanhoe* was a success artistically, but that was all. Gilbert had been correct in his statements about grand opera—and all the time Carte had said that the author was just jealous! Sir Arthur was frank in admitting that he had made a mistake in leaving the comic opera field. Take, for example, the time Reginald De Koven, the brilliant young composer of *Robin Hood,* turned to Sullivan, who was watching a performance of *Ivanhoe* with him, and said, "I like your piece very much, Sir Arthur."

"That's more than I do," came the bitter reply. "A cobbler should stick to his last."

While Carte and Sullivan were busy producing *Ivanhoe,* Gilbert was not idle. Despite the fact that the author had gone on record as being against his former associate's venture into grand opera, he did not gloat when it was announced that Carte had been forced to sell his beautiful theater to a vaudeville circuit. In fact, Gilbert told several of his friends he was sorry Sullivan had not achieved a greater success with *Ivanhoe.* "It's a shame," he confided to a member of his club, "that Sullivan hasn't a hit. For years he has been talking about a grand opera, and now that he has done so, it seems that it wasn't worth the effort."

By this time Gilbert's temper had run its course. Quick to anger, he was just as quick to desire peace. The author's lawsuit against Carte had been successful and this put him in an excellent mood. Incidentally, the evidence presented in court showed that Gilbert's share of the profits from the partnership had been $350,000 for the London rights alone (payments for performances in America, Australia and by touring companies totaled another $100,000). Sir Arthur had received an equal share and when the composer recalled the nightly returns from *Ivanhoe,* he could not but agree

hat Gilbert had been right in stating that comic opera was
ar more profitable than grand opera.

While Sullivan was slowly recovering from the nervous
exhaustion brought about by the months of work on *Ivan-
oe,* Gilbert was dashing from one end of London to the
other. Never a man to waste time, the author was planning
a new comic opera. He had his plot ready—it was, of course,
the one Sir Arthur had refused so many times—the lozenge
theme. The only difficulty was, whom should he choose to
write the music? Dozens of composers, anxious to be associated with Gilbert, asked for the assignment. One of
those who applied was no other than Sullivan's friend, Reginald De Koven. The American composer was in London,
supervising the production of his famous *Robin Hood.*
There was nothing De Koven would have liked better than
to work with Gilbert. The visitor from overseas had admired
the clever author's work even since the start of his own
theatrical career—a performance of *Iolanthe* in Minneapo-
lis, Minnesota! Thrilled with the opportunity of being considered for the job of scoring Gilbert's latest work, De
Koven called at Uxbridge.

De Koven entered Gilbert's study. The author waved him
to a chair and for what seemed hours to the American, did
nothing but stare at him. Just when De Koven felt he could
not bear the silence any longer, Gilbert observed, "You're
very young, Mr. De Koven."

"That," calmly retorted the quick-thinking De Koven, "is
a matter time will cure." So saying, he reached for his hat
and walked slowly out of the room!

After interviewing dozens of other applicants, Gilbert
chose Alfred Cellier to write his score. The next problem
was to secure a cast. Naturally enough, Gilbert thought of
the company at the Savoy. He had trained them and knew
what they could do. There were no better singers, dancers

and actors in England. Why look elsewhere? Moreover, they
would be willing to come. After the end of the run of *The
Gondoliers,* the company would be without engagements.
Gilbert wrote letters, stating his proposition. Several of the
Savoy troupe agreed to join forces with him. When Sir Arthur heard that Jessie Bond was thinking of leaving the
Savoy and working for Gilbert, the composer begged her to
stay. Sullivan's request had very little effect on the charming actress. For Jessie Bond, like all the other members of
the Savoy troupe, considered that Gilbert had been unfairly
treated by Carte and Sullivan. None of the players knew
the full facts in the case. It was just that all of them were
fonder of Gilbert than of Sullivan, for strangely enough,
despite Gilbert's bullying at rehearsals, his cutting remarks
and hot temper, the company had a deep affection for their
director. Another salary increase, however, persuaded Jessie
to stay at the Savoy.

Once Gilbert had made arrangements for his new work,
he was willing to make a few apologies. The author called
on the Cartes and ruefully admitted that he had said things
that he shouldn't. His excuse was that his gout was bother-
ing him and the pain had been so terrific that he had been
unable to discuss the matter of the carpet in a calm fashion.
As a rule Gilbert usually made fun of his gout. He called
one of his feet "Labouchere," and the other, "Clement
Scott," after two dramatic critics who took great delight in
finding fault with his work. He got a strange pleasure out
of jamming his swollen feet into shoes too small for him,
remarking as he did so, "How do you like that, you dramatic
critics, you!"

Shortly after his reconciliation with the Cartes, Gilbert
was approached by Thomas Chappell, the music publisher
who printed all the Gilbert and Sullivan music. Chappell
had known the author, composer and manager for years

In fact, he had been one of the original backers of the Comedy Opera Company. The music publisher was anxious to bring Gilbert and Sullivan together again for two reasons. First, as a lover of the theater, he regretted the rupture which meant there would be no more light operas written by the pair. Secondly, as a businessman, he hated to lose the revenue which came to him every time a new piece was produced by the partners.

"I say, Gilbert," inquired Chappell, "do you think there is any chance of your working with Sullivan again?"

By this time Gilbert had forgotten his actions, letters and slanderous statements, and he replied, "If Sullivan wants to work with me, all he has to do is say so. Why don't you ask him?"

Chappell immediately called at Queen's Mansions. He told Sir Arthur of his conversation with Gilbert. What, asked the music publisher, was the composer's reaction?

"I really don't know, Tom," came the serious reply. "I can never forget Gilbert's mean actions and his nasty remarks. Oh yes, I know it is all due to his temper—but why should I open the way for another outburst? He'll fly off the handle again just as soon as something occurs that he doesn't like. You tell me that he should submit our disagreement to a third party. What good would that do? It would only stir matters up all over again. However, I'll do this: tell Gilbert that while I can't forget what he has done, I'll forgive. There's just one condition attached, however— never again is the carpet to be referred to in any way."

Chappell reported to Gilbert. The author sat down at once and wrote Sir Arthur a letter. Sullivan answered immediately and Gilbert wrote another note. The composer then invited Gilbert "to meet and shake hands." The pair met in Sullivan's rooms, chatted in a most friendly fashion for two hours and then parted on excellent terms.

Meanwhile, Cellier was writing the music for Gilbert's lozenge plot. On January 4, 1892, the piece was produced at the Lyric Theater. It was an immediate success. Gilbert's libretto was equally as good as any of the work he had done for the Savoy, and Cellier's music for *The Mountebanks* was very well done. Strangely enough, the lozenge did not dominate the operetta's plot! There is no doubt that Sullivan would have found Gilbert's "book" acceptable in its final form. It is interesting to wonder what would have happened if Sir Arthur had written the score. Would *The Mountebanks* have been an even greater success than it was?

Sullivan was also busy. Lord Tennyson, who had forgiven him for the publication of *The Wrens,* had requested that the composer write incidental music to his play, *The Foresters*. This work, the poet laureate's adaptation of the story of Robin Hood and Maid Marion, was going to be produced in America by Augustine Daly, with the famous Ada Rehan in the leading role. The play did not appeal to Sir Arthur. He did not like the title and suggested it be changed to *Maid Marion*. The aging poet refused. Sullivan's dislike of the piece showed in his work. He found writing the few songs required a most difficult task. *The Foresters* was never produced in England and was a failure in the United States. Today, it is as unknown as most of the sick-sweet love ballads Sir Arthur wrote to make rent money in his struggling days following his return from Leipzig.

While Gilbert and Sullivan were busy, Carte was not idle. The manager realized that *The Mountebanks* was proof that Gilbert could get along without Sullivan—his next task was to prove that Sir Arthur could get along without Gilbert. Carte had read dozens of manuscripts, looking for one suitable for use at the Savoy. One of them had been submitted by J. M. Barrie, the author of *Peter Pan*. The manager liked

Barrie's libretto and sent it to Sullivan. Carefully the composer read the work, *Jane Annie,* but found it did not appeal to him and refused to set it. Carte then turned the libretto over to one of his former associates at the Royal English Opera House. So Ernest Ford composed a score for the piece, but *Jane Annie* turned out to be a failure—running for only fifty performances.

Meanwhile, Sir Arthur had left for Monte Carlo, in hopes of regaining his health. The composer was a very sick man. His old physical ailment was never more active. He tried to rest while awaiting the arrival of Sydney Grundy's libretto, *Haddon Hall,* which he and Carte had agreed had great possibilities. By the time Grundy's words reached Sir Arthur, the composer was comfortably established in a villa. Feeling better, he began to compose. Then, without warning, he suffered a severe attack. He fought it with all the courage at his command. It seemed as if he would never find relief from suffering. The agony was continual. Still he worked doggedly on *Haddon Hall.* The weeks passed in a fog of pain, and then, at the end of February, Sullivan collapsed.

Louis, the faithful valet, called a doctor. The physician shot his patient full of morphine and gave strict orders that he was to be watched carefully. The composer's servants took turns watching at their sick employer's bedside. Sir Arthur lay in a coma, and it was feared he was dying. From time to time Sullivan would have a minute of consciousness, during which he carefully made arrangements for his funeral. Reports of the composer's condition reached England, and Queen Victoria sent a telegram inquiring about Sir Arthur's condition. The Prince of Wales was far more practical. His Royal Highness sent the Surgeon Royal, but that dignitary decided that Sullivan, nearly fifty years of age and almost consumed with pain, could never stand the shock of an operation. The only thing to be done was to keep him under drugs—for the pain was unbearable.

One morning Sullivan was seized with a series of chills. Unable to warm his master, Louis decided to give him a hot bath. He did, and almost immediately the pain vanished. Inside of a week Sullivan was almost completely cured. The doctors were amazed, being unable to find any reason for the composer's recovery.

"Let's not look for reasons, gentlemen," said Sir Arthur. "Let's just be thankful for the miracle."

Now able to read the thousands of letters and telegrams that had been sent, inquiring as to his condition, Sullivan took a new interest in life. He received visitors and daily grew stronger. By the end of April he felt well enough to return to London. He made the trip to Calais in easy stages and was carried aboard the steamer on a litter borne by four husky sailors. By June the composer was riding about the parks of London in his carriage, soaking up the warm sunshine. With the return of his strength, Sullivan went to watch a few cricket matches and accepted an invitation of the Prince and Princess of Wales to stay at Sandringham Palace.

Tempted to try to work, he sat down to write some music. For once, the composer found it impossible to think of a single bar. It was mid-July before he was able to resume work on *Haddon Hall*. Recalling the terror of the past few months, he did not work at night. As a result, the composition went very slowly, for Sir Arthur had long found working at night far easier than working days. The *première* of *Haddon Hall* had been set for Saturday, September 24, 1892, and it was not until September 11th that Sullivan finished his scoring.

What a task writing this score had been! Almost every note had been written with death seated on the other side of the desk. Worn out, Sir Arthur went to the Savoy for the opening. As usual, the composer was warmly greeted. The performance went smoothly, and both Grundy and Sullivan were called at the end of the finale. Sir Arthur was extremely happy at the result of his labor. What made the opening night even more delightful to him was the fact that Gilbert came to the performance and spent the intermission in Sullivan's dressing room, talking pleasantly to the composer.

The next day the critics had their say about *Haddon Hall*. With one voice they praised Sullivan's music—and with the same unity they found fault with Grundy's libretto. Strangely enough, most of the journalists blamed Grundy for not being another Gilbert! Grundy, who had a wonderful sense of humor, did not let the criticism annoy him. To the staid London *Times* he wrote a letter proposing that, if anyone else except Gilbert wrote a libretto for a comic opera produced at the Savoy, that foolish person should be punished in a fashion approved by His Imperial Majesty, The Mikado. He suggested that the punishment should include "something with boiling oil in it." While very few people went to the Savoy to see *Haddon Hall,* thousands whistled its tunes, military bands played its airs, and classical orchestras presented selections from its score. The music of the piece was definitely popular—just as definitely, Grundy was no Gilbert.

By now Carte was worried. His venture into grand opera had failed. The choice of Grundy as a partner for Sullivan had proven unwise. *The Mountebanks* had shown that Gilbert did not need Sullivan. *Ivanhoe's* failure had shown that the English people would not support grand opera, and *Haddon Hall* had furnished proof that Sir Arthur needed Gilbert. What was more important to Carte, he needed them both. He had not had a single success since *The Gondoliers.* Grundy had shown himself to be inadequate, Sullivan had not approved of Barrie, none of the manuscripts written by unknowns had had any value. There was only one way in which Carte could recoup his fortunes—bring Gilbert and Sullivan together again.

So the manager went to Gilbert and asked him to collaborate with Sullivan once more. The author consented without hesitation, and by the end of 1892 the turbulent trio were reunited.

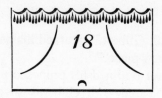

"*Woe Is Me! Alack a Day!*"

—*Patience*

G ILBERT was taking no chances. Before the author
agreed to write another work with Sullivan for production at the Savoy, he insisted that a new agreement be
drawn up with Carte. "There isn't," he told Mrs. Ronalds,
"going to be any more paying for carpets out of my profits!"
Wise Mrs. Ronalds merely smiled and warned, "Now, be
careful! You and Sir Arthur are reunited after a separation
of four years. Don't start anything that will cause trouble.
Everyone is delighted that you are going to work together
again. Why, if the pair of you ever write half the operas
the newspapers say you have planned, Gilbert and Sullivan
are going to be turning out a work every month! If you go
around looking for trouble, you'll never write even one with
Sir Arthur. Stop grumbling, and you'll find everything will
work out all right."

Everything did work out all right. Gilbert saw to that.
With extreme caution he read every word in the new agreement and then signed it with a flourish. Turning to Sullivan,
he announced, "I've got an idea for our next work. There's
no lozenge in it and I think you'll find the plot quite interesting."

"I am sure I will, Gilbert," returned his partner. "What's your idea for our new piece?"

Briefly the author outlined his proposed plot. Sir Arthur was very much pleased with Gilbert's suggestion. In his pleasure at working again with his brilliant associate, Sullivan failed to notice that Gilbert was going to poke fun at everything English in the new opera. The author had never forgotten any slur upon him and had long planned revenge for the slight Queen Victoria had given him during the run of *The Gondoliers*. When a command performance of that opera was presented at Windsor Castle on Friday, March 6, 1891 (the first entertainment at the Castle following the death of the Prince Consort), the opera was announced as having been written by Sir Arthur Sullivan. Gilbert was furious. Nor was Victoria content with deliberately neglecting to give credit to the man who had made fun of her army, navy, police and law courts; Her Majesty had ordered the name of the wigmaker to be printed in big, bold type, while failing to mention Gilbert at all in the program! Livid with rage, the author could do nothing about Her Imperial Majesty's action. Injury to his pocketbook was added to the insult to his pride by the fact that his share of the cost of sending the company down to Windsor was $457, and moreover he lost a night's profits at the Savoy! His new operetta was going to pay off this old score and collect long-due interest.

Once again Sir Arthur set out for Monte Carlo while his partner began to work on his libretto. In Gilbert's spacious study in the new home he had bought in Harrow Weald, the author wrote and rewrote. The house had originally belonged to Frederick Goodall, the famous Victorian painter. It was a very large mansion, with many beautiful rooms, among them a drawing room containing a fireplace over fifteen feet high, carved in Cornish alabaster. Rare art ob-

jects were displayed everywhere, including unusual paint-
ings and carvings. Scattered among these curios were many
souvenirs of Gilbert's dramatic successes. The block and
axe used in *The Yeomen of the Guard* was in the billiard
room, and on the walls there were 250 framed original
drawings from the *Bab Ballads*. In fact, Grim's Dyke, as
Gilbert's home was called, was one of the showplaces of
England. There was only one plain room in the entire building. This was the author's bedroom. In it there was nothing
but a narrow iron bed and a bookcase! Gilbert's love of
beauty expressed itself in the gardens of Grim's Dyke, which
were famous for their exotic blooms and formal pattern of
the flower beds.

The author didn't stay at his desk too long. An attack
of gout made it impossible for him to work. "Labouchere"
and "Clement Scott" rebelled at being forced into too tight
shoes and nearly drove the dramatist out of his mind with
pain. At last, unable to stand the torment, he went to Germany to drink mineral waters at Homburg. As he began
to feel better, he worked on the new operetta. It was tedious
going and he made slow progress. Anxious to avoid difficulties with Sir Arthur, he kept in touch with the composer
by mail. In his letters, he discussed his writing and made it
plain that so far everything was tentative, and if Sullivan
found any of the material too difficult to set to music, the
composer was to throw it away. Relations between the two
men were very cordial. In fact, when Sir Arthur complained
that one verse was absolutely impossible, Gilbert suggested
that the composer write a tune and he would then fit words
to it! For once Gilbert allowed the music to come before
his words! Of course, the author claimed that such verses
were "mere doggerel"—and couldn't be otherwise, written
under such conditions.

By the end of January, 1893, Gilbert had the plot of the

new opera fairly well outlined. He went to the Riviera and held long conferences with Sullivan. The men did not talk in the stuffy confines of a theater office or in a study; they took long walks together, talking over past successes and plans for the future. When Gilbert left, after a three-day visit, the partners were in accord not only about the coming attraction at the Savoy, but in personal matters.

Home in London, Gilbert wrote immediately to Sullivan. It was a friendly letter, summing up all the work on the new operetta to date. The author suggested that he had enough material to send to Sir Arthur, if the composer wanted it— but Sullivan quickly refused the offer. Since his illness, he had found that he was unable to work away from his desk in Queen's Mansions. The composer did nothing these days in the line of composition, except to jot down themes which came to him as he walked along the blue Mediterranean. There were other reasons, too, why Sullivan did not want Gilbert's libretto. The social life of the Riviera was far too attractive to Sir Arthur to give up for work. So he told Gilbert to hold all his verse until he returned to London.

Once in the English capital, Sullivan did not immediately begin composing music for the new opera. Commissioned by Her Majesty to write a march for the state opening of the Imperial Institute, he set to work on that chore. It took him only three days to complete an "Imperial March," and the work was an outstanding success when played by an orchestra of ninety-eight performers, conducted by Sir Arthur himself.

Carte was terribly impatient. The failure of Barrie's *Jane Annie* had made it necessary to close the Savoy for the first time since its opening. The manager hounded Gilbert and Sullivan, begging them to prepare their proposed piece for immediate production. Despite Carte's demands, it was mid-June before Sullivan felt like starting to score. He soon found that the tunes for this, the first work since the reconciliation of the partners, were not going to come easily. As if this were not enough, Sullivan quickly realized that Gilbert had not changed a bit during their years of separation. During one of the conferences between the author and composer, Sullivan objected to Gilbert's treatment of one of the characters. At first, Sullivan tried to reason with his associate. It was no use. Gilbert flew into a rage. When the smoke of the battle had blown away, the differences between the two were settled. Sullivan now knew that Gilbert would forever be Gilbert, and never change!

Sir Arthur worked slowly on his score. It was hot during the summer of 1893, and he decided to do all his work at night and enjoy life during the day. So he went boating, attended race track meetings, and rode a tricycle for exercise. Slowly the operetta began to take shape. Then the composer was distracted by the vanishing of his pet parrot. For several days he and his servants searched the countryside for Polly. From time to time his pet was seen flying around, and at last a quick youngster climbed a roof and snatched the bird before it could take flight.

Overjoyed at regaining his lost companion, Sir Arthur gave the lad a reward of two pounds, and went back to his composing. The heat was unbearable, and Sullivan, always looking for an excuse to stop working, decided he could do nothing with the temperature in the nineties. So he spent most of the time boating. A rainy spell finally drove him indoors and, at two-thirty in the gray pre-dawn of September 29, 1893, his task was finished.

In nine days the operetta was due to open. The time was spent in drilling the orchestra and company in one rehearsal after another. The day before the opening night, the full-dress rehearsal was held, to which the dramatic critics, theatrical folk, and others interested in the theater were invited. This arrangement was Gilbert's idea. "The reason why my work has not met with greater approval is due to the fact that the critics don't understand it. So we'll invite them to the final run-through. That will give them a chance to see the piece twice, once in rehearsal and once on the opening night. Even a dramatic critic should be able to understand something he has seen two times!" This special audience which saw the dress rehearsal was enthusiastic about the new work. The partners and their manager shook hands when the final run-through was over and went home tired—with nothing to do until the following evening. On October 8, 1893, the first performance of Gilbert and Sullivan's *Utopia, Limited* was presented.

Long before the amateur choristers in the balcony of the Savoy had finished their usual concert of old favorites from previous operettas, the theater was filled to capacity. Theater-going London was delighted that Gilbert and Sullivan had joined forces once more and impatiently waited for the rise of the curtain. When Sir Arthur entered the pit, the crowded house gave him an ovation. For over a minute the composer was forced to wait until the applause died down. Then, raising his baton, he began the overture. The last bar of music died away; more applause, and the curtain rose on the first act.

The lush gardens of King Paramount, ruler of the island of Utopia, are seen when the opera begins. Sitting under beautiful bushes is a group of maidens who are admiring the flowers and singing about their enjoyment in "the life of Lazyland." For Utopia is one of those Pacific isles where no one works, or ever has. His Majesty, King Paramount, a most aggressive man, has decided that the old custom of "lying motionless and dreaming of nothingness" must stop. Utopia, Paramount has ruled, must become modernized. There is only one country in the world that Utopia should copy in order to achieve this goal. That nation is, of course, Great Britain. So King Paramount, a widower, has sent his eldest daughter (he has three), to be educated at Griton, a famous British college for women. Princess Zara's main purpose is to acquire "a complete mastery over all the elements that have tended to raise that glorious country to her present pre-eminent position." Meanwhile, the younger twin princesses are learning to be modern Victorian young ladies, through the instruction of Lady Sophy, an English governess.

While waiting for the return of Princess Zara from "the greatest, the most powerful, the wisest country in the world," King Paramount is having trouble with his advisers, the Two Wise Men, Phantis and Scaphio. Their suggestions about government are most annoying, and His Majesty has to follow their advice. If Paramount refuses, Tarara, the Public Exploder, will perform his duty! Among the chores the Wise Men have forced upon the King is the writing, editing and publishing of *The Palace Peeper,* a newspaper which consists of nothing but scandalous stories about Paramount! The Wise Men insist upon this journal as a means of letting the citizens know that their ruler is one of the worst men "that ever disgraced an autocratic throne." Of course, no one buys the paper, for the King purchases every copy— but, unfortunately, Lady Sophy has seen one of the most colorful issues and believes everything printed in it. This is a most difficult situation, for His Majesty has asked Lady Sophy to marry him. Being a most respectable English-woman, she refuses and demands that he "slay the scribbler" responsible. Paramount, unable to tell the governess that he is the author of the articles, admits that he is in touch with the Mikado of Japan, who is an expert on punishments, and that he will soon take care of the matter.

Meanwhile, Princess Zara arrives with six Englishmen,

representative of England's greatness. They are: Captain Fitzbattleaxe, of the First Life Guards, who takes over the Utopian army; Captain Corcoran, K.C.B., who becomes head of the navy; Sir Bailey Barre, Q.C., M.P., who assumes the task of reforming the law courts; Lord Dramaleigh, who becomes Lord Chamberlain; Mr. Blushington, who is put in charge of sanitation and health; and Mr. Goldbury, a stockbroker.

Phantis and Scaphio, both in love with Zara, explain to the Princess that they have not settled which one of them is going to marry her. Alarmed, she asks Captain Fitzbattleaxe what to do. The hearty soldier suggests that the matter be settled in the English fashion. *The Rival Admirers Act,* he explains, covers such situations. All that has to be done is to leave the lady in the care of a cavalry officer until one claimant for the lady's hand blows out the brains of the other:

> *"It's understood, I think all round*
> *That, by the English custom bound*
> *I hold the lady safe and sound*
>   *In trust for either rival.*
> *Until you clearly testify*
> *By sword or pistol, by and by,*
> *Which gentleman prefers to die,*
>   *And which prefers survival."*

Free of Phantis and Scaphio for the time being, Zara discusses with her father, the King, the best methods of raising Utopia to the level of England. The pair are making their plans as the curtain falls on act one.

The second act shows us the throne room in Paramount's palace. The first Drawing Room (a ceremony in which a monarch receives his subjects) in Utopian history is about to take place. During the Drawing Room, "The Flowers of Progress," as the English experts are called, report on the results of their activity. The Utopian army and navy have become so powerful that no nation dares wage war on the island kingdom; sanitary and health regulations have abolished all disease; the new laws have done away with crime, including the publication of such papers as *The Palace Peeper;* and trade is booming, thanks to Mr. Goldbury's promotional schemes. There is only one trouble. The prosperity that has come to Utopia has thrown everyone out of work! Phantis and Scaphio, furious at the change in Utopian life, lead a revolutionary army composed of lawyers who have no cases to try, doctors who have no sick people to treat, and others who have suffered, thanks to "The Flowers of Progress." In alarm, the King turns to Zara and asks what has happened, a revolution is so un-English! Did she, His Majesty demands, through error, omit something in setting up the new government?

"Of course!" cries the Princess. "I forgot the most essential element of all! Government by party. Introduce that, then there will be sickness in plenty, endless lawsuits, crowded jails, interminable confusion in the army and navy, and, in short, general and unexampled prosperity."

Everyone is delighted at this suggestion, except Phantis and Scaphio, who are led off to jail. The two young princesses, Nekaya and Kalyba, announce their engagements to Lord Dramaleigh and Mr. Goldbury respectively. Princess Zara promises to marry Captain Fitzbattleaxe, and Lady Sophy, convinced that the articles in *The Palace Peeper* were untrue, promises her undying love to King Paramount, as the curtain falls.

A wildly cheering audience called Gilbert and Sullivan when the opera ended. The piece had gone excellently and there hadn't been a single flaw in the performance. When the author and composer came before the curtain, they turned, faced each other, and shook hands. How the audience cheered then! Here was public proof that all hard feeling between the two men had vanished. Now there would be more Gilbert and Sullivan operettas, and the Savoy would never have to close again!

Overjoyed, Gilbert, Sullivan and Carte, with a party of friends, went to a midnight supper. The guest of honor was Nancy McIntosh, an American soprano who had made her London debut in the role of Zara. Gilbert had discovered the singer, introduced her to Sir Arthur and Carte, and had written the leading feminine part in *Utopia, Limited* with the abilities of his "find" in mind. By the time the celebration was over, the morning papers were being sold. With very few exceptions, the dramatic critics were loud in their praise of the new piece. It seemed as if the author had been right in inviting them to see the dress rehearsal.

Everyone was particularly enthusiastic about the costumes and scenery of *Utopia*. It was no wonder. Carte, always willing to spend money for publicity purposes, had been lavish in mounting the piece. Nothing had been too good for the work which reunited Gilbert and Sullivan. Long before the operetta was ready, the estimated expenses totaled $35,000! Now it was Sir Arthur who complained that Carte was spending too much money. Gilbert had insisted that the court costumes used in the drawing room scene be authentic—at a cost of $250 each! On other matters he was willing to economize—the jewels worn by the ladies could be, the author suggested, made of the "merest paste." Carte said nothing to his associates, but continued to spend money freely. The setting of the throne room was one of the most effective and expensive ever seen on a London stage. Despite the reduction of some items, the final cost of the operetta was $36,000—the most expensive in the entire Savoy series.

The morning after *Utopia* opened there was only one person connected with the production who openly expressed dissatisfaction with the piece. This was Sir Arthur, who did not like the finale. So the composer sat down and wrote a new one—he alone had noticed the weakness in his original work and decided it would not do. *Punch,* of course, found fault with the entire work, claiming that Gilbert had stolen his material from other plays.

The scorn of the famous English comic journal was nothing, however, compared to that of the royal family. They were highly incensed. Gilbert had pulled no punches in holding the customs of his native land up to ridicule in *Utopia.* The drawing room scene had included a meeting of the Utopian cabinet where the King, anxious to follow the customs of England, asked Lord Dramaleigh if the chairs were correctly arranged, "in accordance with the practice at the Court of St. James." "Well," replies Dramaleigh, "it is in accordance with the practice at the Court of St. James's Hall." St. James's Hall was the theater where the Christy Minstrels, one of the most famous blackface organizations in theatrical history, was playing to full houses. Gilbert, tongue in cheek, while reproducing a state drawing room to the most minute detail, had arranged the chairs in traditional minstrel show fashion! As if this were not enough, the author had insulted the Prince of Wales by having King Paramount appear in the uniform of a British field marshal, wearing the Order of the Garter. The Prince was the only living man entitled to wear such a combination, and His Royal Highness was furious at the liberty Gilbert had taken. In fact, Gilbert's satire cut so deeply that *Utopia, Limited* became the only Savoy opera that members of the royal family did not visit twice! Not that the author minded!

Gilbert had revenged himself for Sullivan's knighthood and the name of the wigmaker on the program at the command performance at Windsor Castle!

Utopia, Limited seemed destined for a long run. The public was thronging to the Savoy. Yet it soon became clear that the operetta was not fashioned of the same material from which *The Mikado, Pinafore* or *The Gondoliers* had been woven. Truth to tell, Gilbert had been too anxious to ridicule English life and customs to be entirely funny. There isn't a quotable song in the entire piece. Then, too, instead of expanding his humorous *Bab Ballads,* the author had borrowed from earlier Gilbert and Sullivan works. Captain Corcoran, along with his most important song, had been lifted out of *Pinafore;* in order to get a laugh, Gilbert had referred to *The Mikado;* nor were any of the new operetta's characters as real and vivid as in previous productions.

Sir Arthur had not done his usual excellent composition either. Musically, the piece is poor, in comparison with such works as *The Gondoliers.* In fact, judged by any of the other Savoy series, *Utopia, Limited* suffers. The skill of the famous pair had vanished on a carpet, but not a magic one.

It didn't take the Savoy combination long to see that their high hopes for *Utopia, Limited* were not to be realized. The huge sum spent on mounting the piece seemed even larger as the three men counted the weekly returns from the box office. It was a bitter blow—everyone connected with the work thought it would have a run equal to that of *The Mikado.* For 245 performances King Paramount welcomed "The Flowers of Progress" to his tropic isle, and then the opera came to an abrupt end, never to be revived. *Utopia* was produced in New York, opening on Easter Monday, 1894, but was an immediate failure.

Carte was not prepared for the failure of *Utopia.* Like his associates, the manager had figured on a long run, at the end of which Sir Arthur and Gilbert would have another piece prepared. However, neither the composer nor the author had shown any desire to work together on a successor to their latest venture. Sir Arthur had gone to Berlin to oversee the production of *Ivanhoe* at the Opera House there. The leading theatrical attraction in the German capitol was *The Gondoliers,* which was playing at the Unter den Linden Theater. Sullivan did not enjoy the German version, as he felt the orchestra conductor was not paying any attention to the composer's tempo. An announcement in the program upset him still more. The management of the theater advertised that the attraction the following week would be *The Mikado,* with Madame Ilka von Palmy playing the role of Nanki-Poo! A cable to Carte resulted in legal objections to a woman performing as a man in a Gilbert and Sullivan operetta.

Back home in England again, Sir Arthur had no desire to write music. He found it far more interesting to visit the various race tracks where he had entered his horses "Cranmer" and "Blue Mark," and watch them run. Sullivan's jockey, in his cerise blouse with violet sleeves and cap, rarely rode a winner, but Sir Arthur did not mind—he knew from sad experience that no one ever made a fortune betting on horse races. All the time that Sir Arthur was visiting race meetings and attending house parties, he was receiving letters from Carte, begging the composer to begin another opera. There was no six-months' clause in the new agreement, and the manager had no legal claim on Gilbert and Sullivan—the fiery Gilbert had made sure of that! Sir Arthur informed Carte that he could not see his way to writing another comic opera at this time. Therefore the manager was forced to produce *Mirette* by Messager, which barely lasted the summer.

Meanwhile, Gilbert had not been idle. With Dr. Osmond Carr as a collaborator, he had written *His Excellency, a* most delightful comic opera which was offered to the public on October 27, 1894, at the Lyric Theater. The piece contains some of the best verse Gilbert wrote in his older years. One of the mysteries surrounding Gilbert and Sullivan is why the author did not offer the libretto of *His Excellency* to Sir Arthur? The work is far more witty than *Utopia, Limited* and contains much of the sparkling dialogue for which Gilbert is famous. The author had written the piece with his American "find," Nancy McIntosh, in mind. The young woman had become a cherished member of the Gilbert household, and both Mrs. Gilbert and her husband treated her as a daughter. Whenever they left Grim's Dyke, they took the beautiful and charming girl with them, and would not accept an invitation unless she was included. While Miss McIntosh had scored a fair success in *Utopia, Limited* as Princess Zara, Sullivan, rumor had it, did not think much of her voice. Perhaps that is why the author did not offer Sir Arthur the chance to collaborate on the work. Gilbert, who considered the American singer perfect in every respect, would naturally consider Sullivan's opinion of her abilities ridiculous—and therefore would not even dream of asking his Savoy associate to work on an opera in which Miss McIntosh was to star. *His Excellency* received good notices and, despite the fact that Dr. Carr's music was not too well thought of by the critics, the piece did good business.

Just before Christmas, 1894, Sir Arthur and Frank Burnard, who had completely rewritten their *Contrabandista,* first produced in 1867, offered the revamped piece at the Savoy. Renamed *The Chieftain,* the operetta was a dismal failure. Burnard had failed to put flesh on the bones of the early work, and it died almost immediately. Sullivan did not care. He had rewritten the music out of friendship for Carte and Burnard. There was no need for him to worry about money. His songs, oratorios, cantatas and conducting engagements were making his earnings total $100,000 a year! If Sullivan had wanted to increase the amount by writing popular songs, he could have done so easily. However, he was too lazy—it was far more fun to drift from race track to society affair or travel. Sir Arthur did, however, write the incidental music to J. Comyns Carr's *King Arthur* and enjoyed the task. After all, Carr's commission was to write serious music, not tripping themes for a light opera!

Carte, seeking vainly for something that would bring people into the Savoy, decided to revive *The Mikado*. It was a brilliant idea. The faithful Savoyards thronged the theater for 127 performances. When the curtain fell on the final performance of the revival, there were no regrets, for *The Mikado* was finally closed in order to make way for a new opera—one written, rehearsed, and produced by Gilbert and Sullivan.

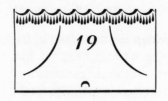

"Your Evil Star's in
the Ascendant"

○

—Trial by Jury

A MOST impatient audience crowded into the Savoy Theater on the evening of March 7, 1896. There wasn't a person who was not anxiously awaiting the rise of the curtain. Despite the fact that the amateur choristers in the balcony gave an exceptionally fine concert composed of selections from the Gilbert and Sullivan operas of the past, their efforts were not too well received. It had been three years since a "new and original" comic opera had been offered by the famous team, and now that one was about to begin, few wanted to listen to old songs—even though they brought back wonderful memories. As a result, time seemed to drag as the audience waited for Sir Arthur to enter the pit. At last the composer made his appearance and everyone wondered why he had delayed the beginning of the overture. As a matter of fact, Sullivan, slightly nervous, had joined his orchestra fifteen minutes earlier than usual! He was greeted by a thunderous ovation. The musicians awaited his signal, and bringing his baton down, he began the overture to *The Grand Duke, or The Statutory Duel*.

As the curtain rises, the audience sees the market place of Speisesall, in the Grand Duchy of Pfennig Halbpfennig. Seated at small tables are the members of Ernest Dummkopf's theatrical company, enjoying the wedding feast of Ludwig, the leading comedian, and Lisa, the soubrette. All are having a gay time; the women particularly as they enjoy themselves making fun of the trousseau of the bride-to-be:

> *"One might say, if one were spiteful*
> *Her bouquet is simply frightful."*

Dummkopf's is no ordinary theatrical troupe. Every member of the company is, in reality, a member of a secret society which has for its aim the deposing of Rudolph, the Grand Duke of Pfennig Halbpfennig, and replacing him with their beloved manager, Ernest Dummkopf! In return for the player's support, Ernest has promised all the ladies and gentlemen of his cast positions at court, assuring them "that all salaries will be paid weekly in advance." The manager is sure he can rule the Grand Duchy, because such a task can't possibly be anywhere as difficult as the chore of managing a theatrical company:

> *"Oh, the man who can rule a theatrical crew,*
> *Each member a genius (and some of them two),*
> *And manage to humor them, little and great,*
> *Can govern this tuppeny State."*

Julia Jellicoe, an English comedienne, draws Ernest aside and reminds him that she has a contract to be the manager's leading lady in all productions. Ernest, who is in love with Julia but has received no encouragement, would rather talk about affairs of the heart than business. He tries to tell her of his love, but the actress wants to talk of nothing but her contract. "Of course," she accuses him, "you, being a man, will insist that I live up to my contract when you assume

the rank of Grand Duke—well, I suppose I'll have to—
very well, there's no help for it—I'll marry you!" Ernest was
overjoyed, and as it looks as if the plot to depose Rudolph
is certain of success, he has absolutely no worries. Just as
the manager is telling everyone how happy he is, Ludwig
rushes in and blurts out news which spoils everything. The
comedian announces that a stranger came up to him and
ate three sausage rolls (the eating of a sausage roll being
the secret sign of the conspirators)—so, naturally enough,
Ludwig ate one too, and discussed the plot to overthrow the
Grand Duke with the maker of the secret sign. Unfortunately the stranger turned out to be Duke Rudolph's private
detective!

What is to be done? Ludwig has revealed the plot! Every
member of the troupe is now sure to be arrested and executed. All turn on Ludwig and berate him:

> *"What folly fell*
> *To go and tell*
> *Our plot to any one's detective!"*

Just when it seems that there is no escape from the Grand
Duke's wrath, the company's notary sees a way to save the
situation. Let Ernest and Ludwig fight a statutory duel, the
winner go to Rudolph, confess the plot and blame the loser
—who, of course, would be dead and therefore safe from
punishment. It is an excellent idea, but has one drawback.
Neither Ernest nor Ludwig wants to be killed. Patiently, the
notary explains that the great advantage of a statutory duel
is that no one gets killed! It is very simple: the duelists draw
cards, the one getting the highest card wins the duel, the
loser is declared legally dead. Moreover, all the dead man's
obligations, privileges, wealth, position and power become
the property of the winner. The law, the notary points out,
is due to expire the next day, so the dead man can come

back to life—and as he has already paid for his crime by dying—would be absolutely free from any danger of punishment for his part in the conspiracy.

Once they learn that no one is really going to be killed, Ernest and Ludwig willingly agree to the duel. They draw cards. The manager turns over a king, the comedian pulls an ace! Ernest Dummkopf is now legally dead! Now matters become complicated. Because the winner of a statutory duel inherits everything belonging to the loser, Ludwig has to take Julia as his bride-to-be. Lisa, of course, is horrified; but there is nothing she can do about it.

Meanwhile, Grand Duke Rudolph is making final arrangements for his own marriage with the wealthy Baroness von Krakenfeldt. The ceremony is going to be a gala affair "at public expense," for if there is anything the Grand Duke dislikes, it is spending his own money. In the midst of preparing for his wedding, Rudolph reads a report outlining the conspiracy, made out by his private detective, and immediately is overcome by fear. In fact, the Grand Duke is so afraid of being assassinated that, in hopes of saving his life, he announces that he will abdicate. Ludwig suggests that Rudolph and he fight a statutory duel to decide which one of them should rule over Pfennig Halbpfennig. The comedian is not being a good sport in making this offer; he takes no chances of losing, keeping an ace up his sleeve. When the duel is over, Grand Duke Rudolph is legally dead. The former ruler is delighted and considers himself the most fortunate of men—for, being dead, he cannot be killed by an assassin! Rudolph knows he will only be dead for a day, for the act allowing statutory duels is due to expire on the morrow. By that time the conspiracy will be over and the ex-Duke need have no fear of coming alive again!

No sooner is the duel over than Ludwig finds that in addition to the ducal crown, he has inherited other belongings of Rudolph, including the Baroness! The actor is now pledged to marry three women: Lisa, Julia and the Baroness! The situation becomes more and more confused, and then, just when everything is so mixed up that it looks as though matters could never be straighted out, the notary discovers that there has been a most serious mistake. In statutory duels, the ace counts the *lowest,* not the highest! Therefore no one has died and all the losers are actually winners. By the time this announcement is made, the statutory duel act has expired and all are restored to their rightful positions, and sing and dance merrily as the curtain falls.

The first-night audience liked *The Grand Duke,* and so did the newspaper critics. Playing in the opera was perhaps the best company ever assembled at the Savoy. Included in the cast was Madame Palmay, whose billing to play Nanki-Poo in the German version of *The Mikado* had so shocked Sir Arthur. Madame Palmay was now a most valuable member of the D'Oyly Carte Company. Carte, as usual, had spared no expense in mounting *The Grand Duke,* and the scenery and costumes were exceptionally well designed. All who saw the opera the opening night were delighted with the production. However, the popularity of the latest Gilbert and Sullivan offering was not to last. For a mere 150 performances—the shortest run of any work the Savoy combination produced—it held the stage. London did not like the opera; the sparkle which theatergoers expected from Gilbert's lines was dim, the usual gay tunes of Sir Arthur were all too few. The public dislike of the piece was made clear by the lack of interest at the box office. What the ticket-buying public wanted was the type of opera written by the partners before their quarrel. This was, unfortunately, something they could not have. Gilbert and Sullivan in *The Grand Duke* proved, all too sadly, that their brilliant collaboration was a thing of the past.

It would have been better, perhaps, if the partners had realized that in the three years since they had worked together, the power to create masterpieces jointly had been lost. No longer were Gilbert and Sullivan in tune, no longer did each bring out the best in the other. Like Rudolph, they were deposed rulers, no longer kings in the land of make-believe. *The Grand Duke* is Gilbert at his worst, while Sir Arthur had little reason to be proud of the music he wrote for the piece. To tell the truth, once in a while there are flashes of the old wit that one expects from Gilbert, and the clever tunesmithing of Sullivan; but they are far too few to make the operetta worth reviving.

From now on until the end, it was Gilbert without Sullivan. The two men continued to share jointly, along with Carte, the profits from the various revivals at the Savoy and from the touring companies in the British Isles and overseas. Following the failure of *The Grand Duke,* however, Gilbert and Sullivan never spoke to each other again. The former partners had definitely drifted apart, and realizing that the famous collaboration was at an end, Carte made no attempt to bring the author and composer together. He turned to the past and revived *The Mikado, Pirates of Penzance, Pinafore, Patience, The Gondoliers* and other old favorites. The evening that *The Mikado* celebrated the anniversary of its thousandth performance, the program was in the shape of a Japanese fan. All of the revived operas played to capacity audiences, and hundreds of would-be ticket buyers were turned away at every performance.

Sir Arthur was not well. Still the desire to write a successful grand opera dominated him. He had always been interested in the legend of King Arthur and his Knights of the Round Table and decided to use it for the plot of his proposed work. Once he had decided to use this theme, though, he promptly discarded the idea. He had neither the will nor the strength to sit at his desk and compose. However, he promised to write ballet music for *Victoria and Merrie England,* which was to be produced in the spring of 1897 as part of the empire-wide celebration of the diamond jubilee of Queen Victoria.

As was his custom when not feeling well, Sir Arthur decided to travel. He set out for Switzerland, met many of his friends there and had a most enjoyable vacation, dining with royalty and playing the piano for his hosts after dinner. When the social season ended in the resort towns of the Alps, Sullivan went on to Germany and Austria. Just as he was about to return to England, he received a telegram from the widowed Empress of Germany—the one-time gay Princess to whom he had given roses on her birthday, while the regimental bands played selections from *The Mikado.* The lonely and homesick daughter of Victoria asked Sullivan to come and visit her at the royal palace. Sir Arthur, always happy when associating with royalty, accepted the invitation.

At last it was time to go home and start work on the proposed ballet music. Originally Sullivan had planned to have his music finished by Christmas, but the holidays of 1896 came and went and he had written only a few bars. He found that he could not work in the damp fog that refused to lift from the streets of London. Depressed by the weather, he went to the Riviera, taking a villa at Beaulieu, and found in that sun-drenched town the inspiration that had eluded him.

Sir Arthur soon was working until five in the morning on his score. Night after night he sat composing and, at last, on March 25, 1897, he had finished his ballet music.

When *Victoria and Merrie England* was produced at the

Alhambra Theater on May 25, 1897, Sir Arthur's composition was one of the greatest successes of the piece. Meanwhile, he had composed a Jubilee Hymn to words written by the Bishop of Wakefield, and a grateful Victoria granted the composer a Jubilee Medal.

Once his part in the Jubilee Celebration was finished, Sir Arthur went to Bayreuth, Germany, for the Wagnerian Festival. He listened critically to *Parsifal, Rheingold, Walkurie, Siegfried* and *Gotterdammerung*—and found fault with them all! While most professional musicians envied the technique of the great German composer, Sullivan scoffed at his work. At last he could not stand any more Wagnerian music and returned to London.

Meanwhile Gilbert was busy supervising revivals of his old plays and writing new ones. The author was an extremely busy man, for in addition to his dramatic work he took a most active part in rehearsing the Savoy revivals. When *The Gondoliers* was revived, Sullivan himself conducted the operetta on the opening night, and at the final curtain both Gilbert and Sullivan were called upon to take bows by the wildly cheering audience. The two men appeared from opposite sides of the stage, responded to the clamor of the crowd, then both turned away without recognizing the presence of the other, a sad climax to one of the most joyful evenings in the history of the Savoy.

In addition to his theatrical activity, Gilbert issued a revised edition of the *Bab Ballads* in 1897. The volume contained many of the old favorites, along with some fresh verses and drawings created especially for the new edition. Lovers of nonsense verse rushed to buy copies and all wished that the author of these ingenious rhymes would write another comic opera with his old partner, Sullivan. It was a vain hope. Gilbert was not thinking of writing comic opera or humorous plays. He was determined to achieve his ambition of becoming known as a serious dramatist. So he worked away—and produced a few plays which are best forgotten, along with *The Grand Duke* and *Utopia, Limited.*

As Gilbert grew older, his gout grew more acute and his temper grew shorter. Members of his clubs, actors in his plays and others suffered in proportion to the twinges of pain that the author suffered. His reputation as a most unpleasant man increased. Few members of the theatrical profession in England were on speaking terms with him during this period, for he lashed everyone and everything with his tongue. Angered at an article in *The Era,* an English theatrical magazine, which made fun of him, Gilbert sued for libel. Before the case was ended, most of the famous actors in England had paraded through the witness box. The lawyer for the defendants tried to get the best of Gilbert, but made little headway. On cross-examination, Mr. Carson, appearing for *The Era,* forced the author to admit that he had spent an evening translating a play from the French and had made $15,000 as a result. "That is better than being a lawyer," remarked Mr. Carson.

"It was better than my experience as one," snapped Gilbert in reply. By the time the acid-tongued author had given his opinion of musical comedy, Shakesperean actors, newspaper reports and the legal profession, the jury was so confused that it brought in the only possible verdict—they were unable to decide either for Gilbert or *The Era.*

Dissatisfied at an interview published in an American newspaper, Gilbert sued for damages. Once again the jury disagreed, and he was furious. For days the author ranted and raved about the injustice he had suffered, and made bitter remarks about the mental qualifications of those who were chosen to serve as judges.

Then something happened that made Gilbert change his mind. He was asked if he would accept an appointment as Justice of the Peace for Middlesex! Secretly overjoyed, he pretended he did not want the position. He wrote the authorities to say it should be borne in mind that he had studied the law—and that would, no doubt, be a handicap to one holding a position on the bench! Once appointed as Justice, however, Gilbert took his duties seriously. Rarely did he miss a day at the Edgware petty sessions. Moreover, he was a keen magistrate, paying close attention to the evidence, taking down notes and making drawings of the persons who appeared before him. It did not take long for him to acquire the reputation of being a most severe judge. In addition to dealing out the maximum sentences, he characteristically punished offenders by telling them just what he thought of them. Indeed, many a prisoner was glad to be escorted to jail in order to escape from the sound of the Justice's voice. Cruelty to animals and children made Gilbert extremely angry, and he would have sentenced the guilty party to death for mistreating a horse, had it been in his power. On the other hand, he would pay a poor man's fine out of his own pocket, or try to find a means of patching up a quarrel between old neighbors. His sentences for motorists found guilty of speeding were famous, yet, being Gilbert, he himself drove his own automobile at an excessively high rate of speed!

When he wasn't sitting on the bench, driving his Rolls-Royce, directing, or writing a play, Gilbert was helping his wife entertain a houseful of guests. The Gilberts' fancy-dress parties were wonderful affairs, and oldsters as well as youngsters were enthralled when the author rolled up his sleeves and began a series of magic tricks. He was an excellent magician, practicing the art and reading books on the subject constantly. The zoo at Grim's Dyke also claimed a great deal of his time and, armed with a camera, Gilbert "shot" his pets over and over again. Accompanied by a dozen or more children, he would tramp about his estate, telling them fantastic stories and listening to their prattle with evident pleasure. Unlike his former partner, Gilbert had learned to enjoy simple things.

Sir Arthur was trying to forget his pain by keeping busy. Dr. Comyns Carr and Arthur Pinero brought the composer the libretto of their romantic musical comedy, *The Beauty Stone*. Sullivan thought the work had merit, but pointed out that some rewriting would not be out of place. Both authors were highly indignant. "Rewrite our work? Why, that's ridiculous! We've slaved over our plot for months—we can't improve it."

The composer was too friendly with Carr and Pinero to argue with them. He took the assignment of writing music for *The Beauty Stone* with misgivings. How he missed Gilbert's pithy lines and extraordinary sense of dramatic construction as he slaved on his music! Long before he had finished his task the composer had developed a strong dislike for the Carr and Pinero work. Always loyal to his friends, he lived up to his agreement to write the music they requested—but his tunes showed that he had not been happy with their libretto.

Sullivan was not the only one who did not like the finished product. The audience which attended the first performance of *The Beauty Stone* at the Savoy on May 28, 1898, was not enthusiastic. The play, for it was not really a musical comedy, lasted only seven weeks. Carte was not caught unawares. He had taken *The Gondoliers* off the Savoy stage to make room for the Carr-Pinero-Sullivan work, and immediately renewed its run. When the box-office receipts started to drop, the manager revived *The*

Sorcerer. As a special attraction, Sir Arthur conducted the opening night and received a reception that was unequaled in his career. At the close of the performance, the audience wildly called for Gilbert and Sullivan. The two men appeared before the curtain in answer to the clapping. They bowed to the audience, but not to each other—nor did they speak. Gilbert and Sullivan turned their backs on each other and left the theater. The two were never to see each other again. Thus ended the collaboration and friendship of the author and composer who had brought about more changes in English stagecraft than anyone since Shakespeare.

On October 8, 1898, Sir Arthur was at Leeds. For twenty years he had conducted the Leeds Festival Orchestra and he looked forward to the assignment. Fortunately, when he raised his baton the composer did not realize that this was the last time he would ever conduct at Leeds. Death, who had looked so often over his shoulder while he composed, sat close beside Sir Arthur on the platform. Despite this grim presence, Sullivan achieved the greatest artistic success of his life. So tremendously did the chorus, orchestra and audience cheer him when the Festival was over that the composer became emotionally upset. He broke into tears and had to be helped off the platform to his dressing room. Finally, he secured control of himself and returned to the podium to express his thanks. Not until the early hours of the morning were the congratulations over.

At last Sullivan fell into bed, weary but happy, and full of plans for the Festival of 1901. This would be the fortieth anniversary of Sir Arthur's professional career, and he thought he would write a composition worthy to rank with *The Golden Legend,* conduct it at Leeds, and then retire. This ambition, like so many others, was never to be achieved.

After Sir Arthur's return to London from Leeds, his secretary, Wilfred Bendall, introduced him to a rising young dramatist named Basil Hood. Sullivan and Hood liked each other at once and decided to collaborate on a comic opera. The pair outlined a piece called *The Rose of Persia,* which was full of Oriental atmosphere and gave the composer ample chance to display his talents. Before Sir Arthur and Hood could get their proposed operetta ready for production, however, Carte offered another work with an Oriental theme at the Savoy. It was, of course, "poor theater" to follow one Eastern piece with another, so the pair laid their work aside. Hood suggested another plot which Sullivan thought had possibilities, and the composer went to the Riviera to work on the score. Once again Sir Arthur was not feeling well and found it impossible to compose. At last he sent for Hood and suggested that they return to their original idea. The young dramatist agreed and began to rewrite his libretto to meet Sullivan's requirements.

Scoring Hood's "book" was a most difficult task for Sir Arthur. He had never been so ill and daily grew more irritable. He went to Switzerland, in hopes that a change of scenery would help, but it made no difference. If the mail were late, he flew into a rage. If the sun shone, it was too hot. If it rained, the weather was unbearable. Nothing seemed to please the man who for years had been known for his pleasant and agreeable personality. There were certain days, though, when he was his normal self and spent hours composing. Slowly the score for *The Rose of Persia* piled up on his desk. Basil Hood had written one of the best librettos Sullivan had ever scored. It was far better than Gilbert's last two efforts and, in some respects, equal to the old master at his best. Sir Arthur, working slowly, rose to the inspiration of his collaborator's creation and composed one of his best scores.

Tired of Switzerland, the composer set off for Monte Carlo. Here the attractions of the gambling casinos, society gatherings and all the other things so dear to him made it impossible for him to stick to his work, so he decided to return to England. By the time he reached Paris on the way home, he was so worn out that he was forced to rest. Once in London, strangely enough, Sir Arthur found that the music came easily, and on November 16, 1899, he finished the orchestration for *The Rose of Persia.* Carte offered the piece at the Savoy eleven days later.

The work was an immediate success. Sullivan was greatly surprised, for he had expected another failure. There were two reasons for this. The first was that he was in a continual state of depression that made him expect the worst of everything. Secondly, London was suffering from the gloom resulting from the South African War. The Boers, led by Kruger, were trying to drive the British from the veldt, and thousands of Englishmen were being killed by sharpshooting, fast-riding men who were proving more than a match for the famous armies of Victoria. Sir Arthur felt that no one would be interested in a musical comedy at such a time.

The composer's reasoning was absolutely incorrect. He and Basil Hood had written an outstanding operetta. London welcomed the chance to forget the war by watching old Savoy favorites play in *The Rose of Persia.* For two hundred performances audiences filled the theater and it looked as if, at last, Sullivan had found someone to take Gilbert's place. However, when the curtain came down on the final performance of *The Rose of Persia,* Hood and Sir Arthur had nothing ready to replace it. Carte immediately revived *The Pirates,* watching with delight the long lines forming outside the box office at every performance.

The Daily Mail, one of London's leading newspapers, asked Sullivan to set Kipling's famous poem *The Absent-*

Minded Beggar, to music. The proceeds of all sales were to go to help the families of service men killed or wounded in South Africa. Sir Arthur, naturally enough, agreed. For days on end, the composer labored with the meter of the poem. But try as he would, he was unable to set Kipling's words. He would walk the streets all night, seeking the tune which would not come.

A friend, meeting him wandering through the foggy London streets, asked, "Sir Arthur, what in the world are you doing roaming about town at this hour of the morning, mumbling to yourself?"

"Please don't stop me, old man," came the reply, "I have, unfortunately, a song to Sing-O."

Nothing ever gave Sullivan the trouble that Kipling's odd meter did, and the composer was five days setting the words to music after deciding on the tune. Immediately upon publication, the song swept the length and breadth of England. It became the rallying cry for a war the man in the street really knew nothing about. Hurdy-gurdies ground out the tune until the din was deafening. Victoria played it on the piano at the palace; troops sang it as a marching song—and the relief fund piled higher and higher. Satisfied that he had done his duty to the war effort, Sir Arthur reluctantly agreed to write a *Te Deum* for the Peace Service to be held in Westminster Abbey when the war was over. He set to work at once, inspired by the good news that was coming from the battlefront—the war in South Africa was soon to be over. It was. So was his work with the *Te Deum,* but Sir Arthur was never to hear it played.

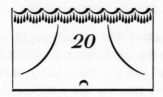

20

"Farewell My Own . . ."

—Pinafore

THEATRICAL London was in an uproar. D'Oyly Carte was planning to revive *Patience!* Opinion was divided. Those who thought the manager-owner of the Savoy Theater was wise argued, "Gilbert and Sullivan will always play to good houses. Carte isn't making any mistake. Look here, there are enough theatergoers around who remember the piece from the old days and will want to see it again to fill the Savoy for several weeks. Then there's a totally new generation who has heard of *Patience* and . . ."

"That's just the point," replied those who thought Carte's venture risky. "It has been nineteen years since the opera was first played. Will these youngsters appreciate Gilbert's jokes on Wilde and his followers? Oh, they know Sullivan's tunes, but will they pay to see something as old as they are? Carte is taking a big risk."

The director of the Savoy paid no attention to the pessimists. Plans were made to produce the piece, with Sir Arthur conducting, on November 7, 1900. It was soon apparent that the composer's strength was not equal to the task—in fact he was never to enter the Savoy again. Despite the disappointment of the opening-night audience that it was not going to see the famous musician in the pit, lines formed in front of the box office early in the afternoon of the opening of the run. By the time the curtain went up, every seat in the theater was filled. When the last note of the finale died away, the cheers were louder than they had been nearly twenty years before. Carte and Gilbert, both hobbling on canes, appeared on the stage to answer the applause. The dramatist was crippled with gout, while his manager was racked with pain arising from the illness which was soon to claim his life. Smiling, the pair bowed, shook hands and waved to the cheering throng. *Patience* was again a smash hit and would, for 150 performances, play to capacity houses—oldsters and youngsters alike willingly standing in line for hours to buy tickets. There was no question about it; there was nothing dated about marching Dragoons, the stout, lovesick Lady Jane, Gilbert's wit or Sullivan's tunes.

Those who had thought Carte was in error in reviving *Patience* were now loudest in their praise of the manager's judgment. The scoffers hastened to cast aside their original convictions, for they now realized that in the light operas of Gilbert and Sullivan there was something audiences of all ages would find enjoyable in any era. In this, they were, as Poo-Bah says in *The Mikado,* "As right as right can be"—for every new generation laughs with delight at Gilbert's humor and applauds Sullivan's music.

Shortly after the opening of *Patience,* Gilbert, always as quick to offer friendship as he was to hurl an insult, wrote Sir Arthur a friendly note from Grim's Dyke. In his letter the dramatist expressed concern at the reports he had heard about his former partner's health. Gilbert, who was planning a trip to the Near East in the hope that the hot tropic sun would bake the gout out of his system, expressed sorrow that he could not come to London to see Sullivan. Sir Arthur's one-time associate explained that he was in no physical condition to make the trip to the city and was saving what strength he had for his voyage. However, he hoped that Sullivan would improve and that when he returned from Egypt, he would find *The Emerald Isle* "running merrily."

Gilbert's gracious note delighted Sir Arthur. The knowledge that the author was still his friend meant much to the man who had seen many of his close friends die during the year just past. Unable to work on the score of Basil Hood's *The Emerald Isle,* Sullivan spent his time inventing a pair of shafts which could be detached if the horse started to run away. The Prince of Wales tried the device on his carriage, but nothing came of the contrivance—any more than of Sir Arthur's automatic window blind, improved pen points and other inventions.

The reason Sullivan never really developed any of his inventions was that once a device had reached the working model stage, the composer found something that interested him to a greater degree. Usually it was music that took him away from his devising, for he was always full of plans for future musical compositions. After the successful test of "Sullivan's Safety Shafts" on the carriage of the Prince of Wales, Sir Arthur returned to his score for Hood's libretto. However, try as he would, he could not force himself to work. Lacking inspiration, he welcomed every excuse to avoid the chore of composition. He took time out to play with Ben, his collie—the lively pup lifted Sullivan out of his depression—but the damage Ben did to slippers and furniture was too great, and the dog was shipped back to the kennel. The composer was lost without the animal, and then came the news of the death of the Duke of Edinburgh. Immediately Sir Arthur went into a fit of deep depression. Early in the year he had lost Sir George Grove, his mentor, and now death had taken his closest friend in the royal family. In desperation, Sullivan thought a change of scenery might do him good and he went to Switzerland. Unfortunately, the Alps failed to give him any inspiration.

While Sir Arthur was trying to settle down to his work, Gilbert, his wife and Nancy McIntosh, who had played Zara in *Utopia, Limited,* set out for Egypt. The author had hopes that the sun and sulphur-baths would cure his gout. No sooner had the party arrived in Cairo than it rained incessantly. All records for rainfall were broken in the land of the Pharoahs! Mrs. Gilbert was quite concerned—the trip to Egypt had been taken with the knowledge that if the sun and baths did not relieve her husband, he would be a cripple for life. Strangely enough, Gilbert did not rant and rave at the rain. He took the weather philosophically, remarking that he hoped the sun would soon shine so he could improve to the extent of being able to wash his own neck!

Finally the weather cleared and Gilbert felt better. The Gilberts and Miss McIntosh decided to take an excursion and were comfortably seated in their train compartment when the engine ran off the rails and fell down a steep bank, dragging several cars with it. The car in which the Gilbert party was seated remained half on and half off the track. Everyone was thrown on the floor and smashed glass was strewn everywhere. Thick clouds of steam from the demolished engine poured into the car through the broken windows and all the passengers fearfully awaited an explosion. Gilbert, crippled as he was, could not get to his feet. Miss McIntosh carried Mrs. Gilbert to safety and then returned for the author. The plucky girl dragged him some distance from the track and then collapsed, exhausted. The trio were severely cut and bruised, but they were extremely lucky. Seven of their fellow passengers lay dead and twenty more had suffered serious injuries. Once Mr. and Mrs. Gilbert were resting as comfortably as possible, their traveling companion set out on foot for Cairo, three miles away, to get a carriage. While the Gilberts awaited her return, they were forced to listen to the screams of the injured and the dying. It was a harrowing experience but, strangely enough, Gilbert's legs were not the least bit hurt.

Fortunately, the doctor who had told the author that he was in danger of being crippled for life was wrong. The sage of the Savoy was soon walking without the aid of a cane and was never severely crippled by gout again. He did not, however, recommend a railway accident as a cure for the disease!

While Gilbert was in Egypt, Sullivan was seeking in Switzerland the tunes which eluded him. The composer found the task of composition difficult. His kidney bothered him and he suffered neuralgic pains. Caught in a rainstorm, he was chilled through and his throat became infected. He could hardly talk and, fearful of his health, he packed the small amount of music he had written and set out for Paris to take the boat for England. Weary and ill, he arrived in London on September 19, 1900, and immediately went to bed. Once again he became the victim of a black depression. What worried the composer the most was that he could not think of a single musical theme—usually his problem was which one of a dozen to develop. As a result, he brooded and suffered mentally as the days dragged.

Slowly Sullivan began to improve. It was still impossible for him to do any composition, but with the exception of the pain in his throat, he seemed physically fit. On October 29th, he and the rest of London turned out in a bitter cold wind to see the triumphal march of the City Imperial Volunteers, just returned from the South African War. The cold breezes were too much for a throat already inflamed with bronchitis, and Sir Arthur's pain became acute. In agony, he returned to his rooms. For days he was unable to speak, but by degrees seemed to improve, and with the exception of being able to speak only in a whisper, it looked as if he would fully recover. It was a comfort to him at this time that Herbert Sullivan, his nephew, was sharing the apartment.

Then, on the morning of November 21, 1900, Sir Arthur violently rang his bedside bell. Louis, his valet, rushed to his master. Before the faithful servant could ask what was the matter, Sullivan cried out, "I cannot stand the pain in my heart!" Louis sent Clothilde, the housekeeper, to wake Herbert, and tell him to come to his uncle's bedroom at once. She was also told to telephone Mrs. Ronalds. By the time Louis had finished giving these instructions and had knelt beside Sir Arthur's bed, the composer was delirious. From time to time, he would seem himself again and, perfectly composed, ask why the servants and his nephew were crying. But as time passed, breathing became difficult for the great composer—and at last it ceased. Sir Arthur Seymour Sullivan, pride of English music, had passed away.

A few minutes after life had left Sullivan's body, Mrs. Ronalds arrived. She had tried in vain to reach Queen's Mansions before Sir Arthur's death, but had been unable to secure a carriage. As she stood in the death chamber, Sir Thomas Barlow, the Physician Royal, arrived to pay a professional visit—like Arthur Sullivan's closest woman friend, the doctor was too late.

All of England was shocked at the news of Arthur Sullivan's death. Queen Victoria was among the first to send condolences, and royalty from all over Europe sent tributes. Theatrical London, as well as the folk who had whistled and sung Sir Arthur's tunes for years, was stunned. It did not seem possible that the great creator of songs was stilled forever.

It had been Sir Arthur's wish (set down in his will, drawn up nearly twenty years previously), that he be buried with his parents. This was not to be. The Dean and Chapter of St. Paul's, agreeing with public opinion that the master musician should be honored by burial in the Cathedral, voted to bury Sullivan in the crypt.

It was eleven o'clock sharp on the morning of November 27, 1900, when the funeral procession began. Slowly the cortege wound its way to the Chapel Royal, St. James, where, by order of Her Imperial Majesty, a portion of the service was to take place. Victoria thought this gesture was fitting, as Arthur Sullivan had begun his musical career at the Chapel Royal. The procession passed through streets lined with thousands of people who stood bareheaded in silent honor to the man who had given them so much pleasure. When the Chapel Royal was reached, the casket was carried inside. Representatives of royalty, society, art, science, sport, drama, music and government mournfully bowed their heads as the service began. The anthems sung had been written by Sir Arthur and many a person present must have thought of the days when Sullivan, himself a chorister in scarlet and gold coat, had sung anthems inside these sacred walls.

Once the service at the Chapel Royal was ended, the cortege continued on to St. Paul's. At the Cathedral, in addition to the famous persons who had come to pay their final respects to Sullivan, were members of the Savoy Opera Company. The last act of the service was theirs. When the body had been lowered into the crypt, the Savoyards, voices breaking through grief, sang one of Sir Arthur's most touching compositions, "Brother, thou are gone before us" from *The Martyr of Antioch.*

Two men were missing among the unnumbered thousands who turned out to honor Sullivan. Gilbert and Carte
were not at the services. The author was still abroad, trying
to cure his gout completely. Carte was ill—too ill, in fact,
to be told of Sir Arthur's death. Lying in his bedroom, the
manager who had created the team of Gilbert and Sullivan
was awaiting death. By some sheer chance, Carte's room
faced one of the streets along which Sullivan's funeral
passed. Some time after the procession had reached St.
Paul's Cathedral, a visitor went into Carte's room and
found him unconscious on the floor in front of the window.
Revived, Carte gasped, "I have just seen the last of my old
friend, Arthur Sullivan!" The manager's visitor stared at
him in amazement. How did Carte know Sullivan was dead?
He had not even been told that Sir Arthur was seriously
ill. The mystery was never solved. . . . In less than six
months, Carte too had passed away.

Despite occasional twinges of gout, Gilbert remained as
active as ever. The author came up to London regularly
from Grim's Dyke to see the latest plays and visit his clubs.
His general health was excellent and when, in 1906, Mrs.
D'Oyly Carte (who had learned all about the theatrical
business as Carte's secretary), revived most of the Savoy
series, Gilbert took complete charge of rehearsals. Mrs.
Carte's revivals were a tremendous success, both artistically
and financially. Even *Punch* was convinced that Gilbert
and Sullivan's popularity was everlasting.

In his later years, honors were heaped upon Gilbert. As
a token of appreciation for the contributions the author had
made to the English stage, the O.P. Club, a theatrical organization, gave him a dinner at the Hotel Cecil. Gilbert,
to be sure, made fun of the entire affair. "I don't," he confided to a friend sitting beside him at the head table, "be-

lieve all the good things said about me." The crowd of nearly five hundred diners applauded Gilbert when he reviewed the history of the Savoy operas, praised Carte's skill as a manager and stated that despite the fact that he felt the loss of Sir Arthur greatly, he was happy knowing that cordial relations existed between himself and Sullivan when the composer died. No one laughed when he told of the supposed failure of *Ruddigore*—a failure, Gilbert took pains to point out, that brought $35,000 into his pockets! Everyone did roar with laughter when the author ended his talk by saying, "While I am dealing with Savoy Opera, I am anxious to avow my indebtedness to the author of the *Bab Ballads,* from whom I have so unblushingly cribbed. I can only hope that, like Shakespeare, I may be held to have so far improved upon the original stories as to have justified the thefts I have committed."

The O.P. dinner was a gay affair and Gilbert smiled broadly most of the evening. During the entertainment which followed the speaking, the guest of honor was observed to be wearing a more characteristic look—a frightful scowl. Those who knew Gilbert well realized the reason for the change. The orchestra was playing selections from the Gilbert and Sullivan operas, but the author was annoyed —Sullivan's music was being heard, but not Gilbert's words! However, the hotheaded Gilbert managed to control himself and walked out of the banquet hall still speaking to all who had attended the testimonial given in his honor.

Busy with his duties on the bench, playing with his pets and doing magic tricks for his young friends, Gilbert had little time or desire to write. In the early months of 1907, Lord Knollys, acting on orders from King Edward VII, approached the author and asked if he would be willing to accept a knighthood. At first Gilbert was not keen about the honor. If it had come years before, when Sullivan was

knighted, he would gladly have accepted the royal gift.
Such a happening was, of course, impossible. As long as
Victoria ruled the British Empire, Gilbert could receive no
honor from the royal family. Now that the staid Empress
was no longer on the throne, belated credit could be given
to Gilbert. For weeks he joked about becoming a knight and
made it clear that he didn't care if he were knighted or not.
Then he suddenly remembered that no dramatic author had
ever been so honored, and hastened to accept.

On June 30, 1907, Gilbert went to Buckingham Palace,
knelt, was tapped on both shoulders by King Edward and
rose Sir William Gilbert. What pleasure the ceremony gave
him was lessened when he read the official honors list, for he
found himself described as "Mr. William Gilbert, playwright." He flew into a rage. "What do they think I am,"
he roared, "something like a shipwright or a wheelwright
or some other kind of a mechanic? Didn't they ever hear of
the word dramatist, or does the author of plays have to be
dead to receive that title? Tell me, did you ever hear of a
novelwright or a poemwright? Of course not!"

Yet, despite the grumbling, Sir William was happy and
proud that he had been knighted. At long last he was revenged on Victoria and that performance of *The Gondoliers*
at Windsor. Moreover, notwithstanding the lack of the
word dramatist in his citation, Gilbert knew that the honor
had been given him as an author of theatrical works. Congratulations poured in from all sides, and he genially accepted them. When Mrs. Alec-Tweedle said, "Really, old
friend, I don't know what to call you, now that you have
been knighted. It sounds so formal to say Sir William—and
Sir Bill sounds silly after all these years of just saying Bill."

Gilbert quickly replied, "You keep on with the billing—
I'll take care of the cooing."

Older, not so quick to anger and feeling fit, Gilbert began to take a greater interest in social affairs than ever before. His favorite spot for visiting with his friends when in London was the Garrick Club. He had only recently joined—for when he had applied for admittance as a young man, he had been blackballed. It was discovered that the members of the Garrick thought they were voting against another man of the same name, and Gilbert was asked to submit his name a second time. Haughty and hot-tempered, he had insisted that as the mistake had been made by the club, he should not be required to re-apply for admission. The club refused to listen to his argument, and there the matter rested. Then, thirty-seven years after this clash, the membership committee of the Garrick Club invited Sir William to enroll, and he, satisfied that the club had finally done the proper thing, willingly accepted the offer.

Sir William wasn't always agreeable. Whenever an issue on which he had strong personal feelings arose, his traditional temper would show itself. Always against unjustified censorship of plays, he welcomed the chance to appear before a Joint Committee of the Lords and Commons who were investigating the subject of stage censorship. His testimony was excellent, but he seized the opportunity to complain about the banning of *The Mikado* on the grounds that it might cause war with Japan. It was absurd, snarled Gilbert, "to bar a play, the music of which was being played on the warships of the very nation the piece was supposed to offend!" The gentlemen of the committee tried to confuse Sir William but failed. "Men of the highest order of intelligence," the dramatist pointed out, were opposed to the traditional method of censoring plays presented on the English stage—those who were not opposed to the system were persons of little ability and talent. Gilbert left no doubt in his listeners' minds into which classification he fell!

Although Sir William was not engaged in writing for the

stage, he still took a great interest in the theater. From time to time this amazing man would take part in amateur shows and, on several occasions, appeared in benefit performances with well-known figures in the dramatic world. When the famous benefit for Ellen Terry, the brilliant British actress, was held in June 1906, dressed in wig and gown, Sir William took a prominent part in *Trial by Jury*. The seventy-year-old Gilbert was not spry enough to play Harlequin as he had years before, but he made a most grave and distinguished member of the bar, while Angelina sued Edward for breach of promise.

In 1911 Sir William asked permission to visit Pentonville, a British penitentiary, and received a pass to spend an hour in the death cell. From this experience came his short play, *The Hooligan*, a one-scene sketch. It was a gruesome work, telling of a young lad who is about to be executed for the murder of his future bride. The boy suffers from a bad heart, and when the word reaches him that he has been reprieved and, instead of being hanged, is to serve twenty years, he drops dead. Produced at the Coliseum Theater with James Welch, a famous comic actor (a typical Gilbertian touch), in the tragic role of the condemned man, the play was a great success. *The Hooligan* was the last thing Sir William was to write. He had begun his career with a legal piece called *Trial by Jury* and ended it with *The Hooligan*, another legal work. So it is that these two, like bookends, enclose the scope of his sixty-three plays, comedy and tragedy.

The 29th of May, 1911 was a glorious spring day. Sir William awoke early, fed his pets, wrote a few letters and then walked through the garden, enjoying the fragrance of the flowers and the full bloom of the rhododendrons. Then he set out for the Royal Hospital at Chelsea, to see the Annual Parade and Inspection. Gilbert never missed this event, for he was most friendly with Sir Charles Crutchley, who was Lieutenant-Governor at the institution, founded in 1692 to care for needy soldiers and to administer various pensions. Lady Crutchley expected Gilbert to stay for lunch, but Sir William excused himself, explaining that May Fortescue (an actress who had appeared in many of his plays and who had, as manager, produced several others), was ill and that he wanted to visit her. After that, confided the spry oldster, he had an engagement with *two* young ladies. "I am," he announced, "going swimming with them in the artificial lake I helped construct at Grim's Dyke!"

So, saying good-by to Sir Charles and his wife, Gilbert left to pay his call on May Fortescue. Finding himself near the Junior Carlton Club, of which he was a member, he decided to lunch there first. Entering the dining room, he saw W. H. Kendal, a leading English actor who had starred in some of Gilbert's early plays—a man who had fought so vehemently with Sir William over questions of stagecraft that the two had not spoken to each other for years. Gilbert walked directly to Kendal's table. "May I join you at lunch?" he asked. Surprised, the actor looked up and replied, "It is a rule of this club that members may sit at any table they please." Sir William smiled, sat down, and in a few moments the two were recalling old days in the theater when Gilbert was turning out such plays as *Broken Hearts* and *Charity* and was yet to meet Sullivan.

By the time the luncheon was over, the two men were completely reconciled. Sir William excused himself and went on to visit Miss Fortescue, who had been thrown from the back of her horse, injuring her optic nerves so that she had to remain in total darkness. Famed for her beauty, the actress was wan and weak when Gilbert arrived. "I wonder what you think of my appearance?" asked the author's old friend.

"I'm not thinking of your appearance at all," retorted her caller. "It's your disappearance I'm concerned about."

Fearing he was tiring the invalid, Sir William left and took the train to Harrow-on-the-Hill, the nearest station to Grim's Dyke, where he met Winifred Emery, niece of Cyril Maude, an actor-friend of Gilbert's, and her pupil, Miss Preece. The two women went into the water almost immediately on arriving at the house. Gilbert who had been delayed was just about to enter the pool when Miss Preece cried out, "Help! I'm drowning!"

Sir William rushed to the water's edge shouting, "Don't worry, I'm coming! You'll be perfectly all right in a minute!" In a matter of seconds he reached the frightened girl and in a calm tone commanded, "Now, my dear, don't struggle! Put your hands on my shoulders! Here we go! We'll be safe on dry land in no time!"

No sooner were the words out of his mouth than he sank out of sight. Both women screamed and Gilbert's gardener came running to see what was the matter. Once the two women were safe, Gilbert's body was pulled from the bottom of the lake. Medical assistance was rushed to the scene, but it was too late. William Gilbert was dead. There was no water in his lungs; death was due to a heart attack. Rushing to rescue a drowning girl was too much exertion for a man of seventy-four. Sir William's death, like his life, was Gilbertian—for the last lines he had written had been the words of the doctor who had examined "The Hooligan" in his cell—"Dead, Heart Failure."

In accordance with Gilbert's wishes, he was cremated. Sir William's burial took place in the churchyard at Stanmore Church, Middlesex. The service was a far simpler ceremony than Sir Arthur's, but most of theatrical London attended. In a few minutes the funeral of William Schwenck Gilbert was over—for the author had left definite instructions that there was to be as little pomp connected with his burial as possible.

If you are ever in London, walk along the Thames Embankment and you will see two memorials. One is to Sir Arthur Seymour Sullivan, the other to Sir William Schwenck Gilbert. Sullivan's memorial, created by Sir W. Goscombe John, consists of the composer's bust, with "Grief," molded in bronze, sobbing against the pedestal. On the tablet is a quotation from one of the Savoy Operas, which was Gilbert's choice when he was requested to supply one by Herbert Sullivan, Sir Arthur's nephew. It is from *The Yeomen of Guard:*

> *"Is life a boon?*
> *If so, it must befall*
> *That Death, when'er he call,*
> *Must call too soon!"*

Sir George Frampton did the bronze medallion of Sir William, featuring the figures of Comedy and Tragedy paying tribute to Gilbert. The Authors' Society appointed a committee to choose an appropriate inscription, and Sir Anthony Hope, author of *The Prisoner of Zenda* and *Rupert of Hentzau,* provided the line: "His Foe Was Folly And His Weapon Wit."

Thus Gilbert and Sullivan are honored in everlasting bronze. Yet the memorials on the Thames Embankment are not the greatest tributes paid them. Tonight, as on every night for the past eighty years, somewhere a curtain will rise—and an audience will laugh at Sir William's jests and delight in Sir Arthur's music. There lies their greatest honor.

Sigmund A. Lavine

just missed being cradled in a theatrical trunk. His parents were permanent members of John Craig's famous stock company, and his arrival made it unnecessary for the stage-manager to provide a doll whenever the play called for a baby!

Highly active while in college, he wrote features for the Boston *Sunday Post,* covered Boston University sports for two wire services, occasionally sold two-line jokes to *College Humor,* played leads in Shakespeare productions and stage-managed five annual productions of the Gilbert and Sullivan Association. "This last experience," Sigmund Lavine maintains, "was the beginning of a search for anything by or about Gilbert and Sullivan—with the result that my wife has had to give up our Dorchester, Massachusetts, dining room in order to house my Gilbert and Sullivan collection."

After receiving his M.A., he taught in an United States Government Indian School at Belcourt, North Dakota, for two years, learned to speak both the Sioux and Cree languages, talk in sign language, had long conversations with old-timers who could remember the creak of the axles of covered wagons, and was invited to tribal dances, ceremonies, and Indian Court in reservations throughout Canada and the Northwest.

Sigmund Lavine has taught in the Boston Schools for over twenty years, lectures and writes literary criticism.

With his wife, their two children (Maxine and Jerrold) and Carrie, their whippet, he lives in a house filled with books, fish-tanks and historical china. His family enjoys cruises to South America, cross-country motor trips and truck gardening on a piece of New Hampshire land "containing all the rocks the glacier had and didn't know what to do with—however, we always have a pumpkin for jack-o-lanterns."